Best resumes
for College Students and New grads

SECOND EDITION

Louise M. Kursmark

JiST Works
America's Career Publisher

Best Resumes for College Students and New Grads, Second Edition

© 2006 by Louise M. Kursmark

Published by JIST Works, an imprint of JIST Publishing, Inc.
8902 Otis Avenue
Indianapolis, IN 46216-1033
Phone: 1-800-648-JIST   Fax: 1-800-JIST-FAX   E-mail: info@jist.com

Other JIST Books by Louise Kursmark:

Sales and Marketing Resumes for $100,000 Careers, Second Edition
Sales Careers (with Ted Newell)
15-Minute Cover Letter (with Michael Farr)
Expert Resumes for Computer and Web Jobs, Second Edition (with Wendy Enelow)
Expert Resumes for Teachers and Educators, Second Edition (with Wendy Enelow)
Expert Resumes for People Returning to Work (with Wendy Enelow)
Expert Resumes for Health Care Careers (with Wendy Enelow)
Expert Resumes for Managers and Executives (with Wendy Enelow)
Expert Resumes for Career Changers (with Wendy Enelow)
Expert Resumes for Military-to-Civilian Transitions (with Wendy Enelow)
Cover Letter Magic (with Wendy Enelow)

Visit our Web site at **www.jist.com** for information on JIST, free job search information, book chapters, and ordering information on our many products! For free information on 14,000 job titles, visit **www.careeroink.com**.

Quantity discounts are available for JIST books. Have future editions of JIST books automatically delivered to you on publication through our convenient standing order program. Please call our Sales Department at 1-800-648-5478 for a free catalog and more information.

Acquisitions and Development Editor: Lori Cates Hand
Interior Designer: Aleata Howard
Cover Designer: designLab
Page Layout: Marie Kristine Parial-Leonardo
Proofreader: Jeanne Clark
Indexer: Tina Trettin

Printed in the United States of America
10 09 08 07 06   9 8 7 6 5 4 3 2

Library of Congress Cataloging-in-Publication Data

Kursmark, Louise.
  Best resumes for college students and new grads : jump-start your career! / Louise M. Kursmark.--
    2nd ed.
      p. cm.
  Includes index.
  ISBN 1-59357-238-7 (alk. paper)
  1. Résumés (Employment) 2. College students--Employment. 3. College graduates--
    Employment. I. Title.
  HF5383.K867 2005
  650.14'2--dc22
                                                                    2005021335

We have been careful to provide accurate information in this book, but it is possible that errors and omissions have been introduced. Please consider this in making any career plans or other important decisions. Trust your own judgment above all else and in all things.

Trademarks: All brand names and product names used in this book are trade names, service marks, trademarks, or registered trademarks of their respective owners.

ISBN-13: 978-1-59357-238-9
ISBN-10: 1-59357-238-7

About This Book

You're a soon-to-be college graduate. Or maybe you're still in college, looking for a co-op job or internship. Perhaps you're a nontraditional student, with years of work experience that's only marginally related to your degree. Even if you're finishing up an advanced degree, you're probably a beginner in your career.

Best Resumes for College Students and New Grads will help you make a successful move from college to the world of work. It's a step-by-step guide to writing an effective resume, starting with some prep work (chapter 1, "Proving Your Value to Employers") that will help you pinpoint what it is about you that is interesting and valuable to employers. Chapter 2, "Writing Your Resume," provides easy-to-follow guidelines, worksheets, and examples to draft your own unique resume. Once you've learned how to write your resume, use chapter 3, "Managing Your Job Search—Online and Off," to gather the latest techniques for an electronic job search as well as strategies for traditional networking activities. Because you'll need a variety of job search letters to go along with your resume, I've included an overview of the types of letters you'll need and some good examples of each type (chapter 4, "Writing Effective Job Search Letters"). Throughout these "how-to" chapters, I answer the questions and address the issues new grads raise most often.

In chapters 5 through 10, you can browse through nearly 150 resumes to get ideas for strategy, organization, language, and formatting. All of the resumes are authentic; they were written by professional resume writers for real people with newly earned degrees from associate to doctoral level. Each student had unique circumstances, educational and work experiences, career goals, and areas of strength and weakness. I've provided comments that will tell you such things as how the strengths were emphasized, how shortcomings were downplayed, or why a particular approach was taken for this resume—information that can help you strategize, write, organize, design, and format your own resume.

New in this second edition is chapter 10, "Resumes for Average Students." We wanted to demonstrate clear, strong, and effective resumes for people who aren't the class valedictorian, fraternity president, or dean's scholar; for students who haven't participated in campus activities or held meaningful internship or co-op jobs. If this is your situation, and you're worried that this book won't help you, relax! Not only do all of the strategies discussed in chapters 1 through 4 apply to you, but the resumes in chapter 10 were written for students exactly like you.

But You Need More Than Just a Resume

As a professional resume writer, I believe wholeheartedly in the value of a good resume. But I'm well aware that the resume is only one piece of the puzzle—and maybe not even the most important piece. **Learning how to look for a job is probably the most valuable skill you can acquire as you start your professional career.** In addition to serving as a comprehensive guide to writing your resume, this book is will also cover some job search essentials:

- How and why to look at the job search from the employer's perspective
- How to extract meaningful information from education and experiences that seem unrelated to your career goals
- How to make your resume and cover letters appealing to the "what's in it for me" mentality of hiring authorities
- Why networking is so important and how you can do it effectively

This book is an early step in what will be a lifelong journey. Just as you pursued your major field of study in college, you should devote the time and energy to build a solid base of knowledge in the field of job search and career self-management. The knowledge and skill you develop will make it easier for you to land jobs that will provide intellectual challenge, professional growth, financial reward, and personal satisfaction.

Contents

INTRODUCTION

Thirteen Steps to an Effective Resume

This book is built on the framework of 13 steps to writing an effective resume that will get you interviews for the jobs you want:

1. Identify Your Job Target and Write Job Target Statements (see chapter 1)
2. Identify Your Core Job Qualifications (see chapter 1)
3. Compile Evidence of Your Hard and Soft Skills (see chapter 1)
4. Start Strongly with Well-Organized Contact Information (see chapter 2)
5. Sell Your Strongest Qualifications in a Powerful Skills Summary (see chapter 2)
6. Emphasize Education as a Key Credential (see chapter 2)
7. Describe Your Work Experience with a Focus on Skills and Achievements (see chapter 2)
8. Add the Extras to Give You a Competitive Advantage (see chapter 2)
9. Format, Edit, and Polish Your Draft (see chapter 2)
10. Cross-Check Your Evidence Against Core Job Qualifications (see chapter 2)
11. Proofread Your Final Resume (see chapter 2)
12. Convert Your Resume for an Online Job Search (see chapter 3)
13. Make Networking Work for You (see chapter 3)

PART 1

Working Toward Your New Career

CHAPTER 1

Proving Your Value to Employers

Why would a company want to hire you?

Looking at hiring from an employer's perspective is an essential first step in preparing your resume and launching your job search. Generally speaking, companies hire people who have the skills needed to do a particular job and the attributes that will make them a good employee, one who will contribute to the mission and goals of the organization.

Please don't assume that your new college degree automatically qualifies you for a great job. Yes, you've worked hard, learned a lot, and feel prepared to launch your career. Now it's essential that you show employers that you have skills, attributes, and abilities that will help them be more successful.

Your resume is the tool that you will use to show employers that you have those skills, attributes, and abilities. The result—you hope—is that they will be motivated to call you for an interview to better determine whether you are, in fact, a good fit for their needs. Your resume must clearly relate your education, activities, and work experiences to specific job qualifications—both the "hard" and "soft" skills that together paint the picture of the ideal candidate.

STEP 1: Identify Your Job Target and Write Job Target Statements

Before you can create a resume that is effective—that presents your skills, abilities, and potential that will interest employers—you must know what kind of job you want.

FAQ

I'm not sure exactly what I want to do. I'm open to a lot of different jobs, and I'm afraid that if I pin down a position, I won't be considered for others. Won't that hurt my job search?

Keep in mind, companies aren't in business to help you figure out your career path. It's not enough to present yourself and your spanking-new degree to a company and expect the employer to determine where (or if) you fit in. Businesses have specific hiring needs. If your resume shows skills and attributes that fit those needs, you're likely to get an interview. But if your resume is vague and unfocused, the employer won't make the connection (and doesn't have time to try). Instead of being an attractive candidate for *many* opportunities, chances are you'll be attractive for *none*. As you continue in this chapter, you'll learn how to research job descriptions to find those that match your skills and education. And you'll see that you don't have to tailor your resume for a very narrow target, but can instead show yourself as a good candidate for a number of different jobs that call for similar skills.

Don't worry that by writing your resume for a specific job you'll be aiming for a target that's too narrow. The skills and accomplishments approach I recommend—which you'll be learning as you work your way through the exercises in this chapter and the next—will result in a versatile resume that you can use when applying for a variety of related jobs, or one that you can change quickly and easily to steer toward a slightly different target.

But if you're interested in several jobs that are quite diverse—say you're a business major torn between a job in human resources and one in retail sales management—you'll want to develop two different resumes so that you are a credible candidate for each position. Start by choosing one target and completing your resume. Then repeat the process for the second target. (It will be much quicker and easier the second time, and you will be able to use much of the same information.) You'll end up with a focused and effective resume for each target.

You can see how this works by looking at the first four resumes in chapter 7. Each pair represents two different, focused resumes for one individual seeking two different positions.

Write Your Job Target Statements

Use the following form or open a new document in your word-processing program and label it "Job Targets." Write the specific jobs you're interested in. You might be definite about one particular goal ("design engineering position with a robotics manufacturer" or "med-surg nursing position in a teaching hospital"), or you might want to list three or four jobs that use similar skills; for example:

1. Public relations position with a large corporation, ideally involved in writing press releases and newsletter articles
2. Marketing communications position (agency or corporate) with primary focus on marketing writing
3. Reporting and copyediting job with a major metropolitan newspaper

Beware of confusing an industry or general profession with a job target! "Advertising" is an industry. "Accounting" is a profession. Neither is a specific job target. Do some research to find out what jobs are available in your chosen industry or profession, and work to refine those broad targets into something more specific, such as "account executive in an advertising agency" or "entry-level auditor for a Big 5 accounting firm." If you need help developing your specific job targets, the resources described on pages 7–8 will help you understand what different job titles mean and how specific jobs are defined. And don't forget about your college or university career center. There you'll find all of these resources and more—plus the expert advice of career professionals—to help you define your job targets, identify your skills, prepare your resume, and perform all of the other activities involved in a job search campaign.

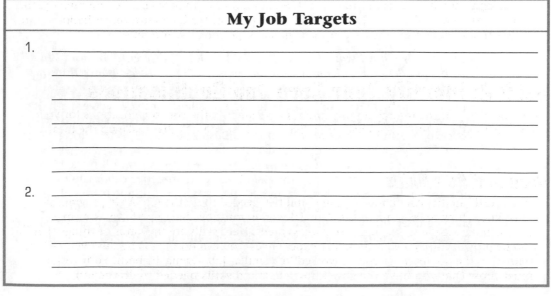

My Job Targets

1. _____

_____

_____

_____

_____

_____

2. _____

_____

_____

_____

3. _____

4. _____

STOP!

If you can't write a specific position for your job target, or if your desired positions are wildly different from one another, take a step back before moving forward with your resume.

Start by talking with the people in your college's career center. They have resources and knowledge that can help you figure out a variety of potential jobs that might fit your skills and interests. Next, meet with people who are actually working at the jobs you're considering. Find out what they do all day, what they like about the job, what frustrates them, and what the opportunities for career advancement are. (Your career-center advisor can guide you in finding people to talk to and approaching them for advice.) If you're really stuck, consider hiring a career coach or counselor, someone who's an expert at helping people determine the best career fit for their talents.

If finding a job immediately is your first priority—if you don't have the time or money to invest in the career-planning process—pick one job that you can "live with" while you're figuring things out. Keep in mind that you'll be making several job and career changes during your working life, so this first step does not have to be your ultimate career path. But please don't abandon the career-planning process. For long-term career happiness, it's essential to determine the best fit for your skills, personality, and interests.

STEP 2: Identify Your Core Job Qualifications

The next step in the resume writing process is to identify the core qualifications for your specific job target—the combination of "hard" and "soft" skills that make up the ideal candidate.

Hard and Soft Skills

Hard skills are the core knowledge and abilities needed to do the job. A C# programmer must know how to program in C#. A social worker must be able to perform assessments, counseling, case planning, and case management. Hard skills are the kinds of things that can be proven through education and experience—you can do the job because you've been trained in the discipline or you've worked in a similar job. Or maybe both. **Your resume must show that you have the core knowledge and skills needed to do the job.**

skills describe personal attributes—how you get things done. Soft skills are more diffi-
to measure and quantify. They include things such as teamwork, drive, leadership, a
ve attitude, a good work ethic, attention to detail, or a customer-first attitude. **To be**
able, your resume must *prove* your soft skills—not just list them.

> ## FAQ
>
> *Aren't companies always looking for good employees? I know lots of people who have*
> *landed jobs when all they had going for them were good grades. They had no clue what*
> *jobs they were applying for when they met with potential employers.*
>
> There's always a chance that you'll get a job offer because your mother's college room-
> mate is the CEO, or the hiring manager likes your positive attitude, or someone they
> hired last year with a background just like yours has turned out to be one of their bright-
> est and best employees. (This illustrates the power of networking! Learn more about it in
> chapter 2.) But don't let your job search depend on happenstance or luck. Instead, use
> your resume to tell employers what you can do for them. Show that you understand their
> priorities. Let them know how what you've studied relates to their needs. That way, even
> when you don't have a heavyweight in your corner, you'll still capture their interest.

Finding Job Qualifications

One of the easiest ways to unearth job qualifications is to look at want ads or online postings. Most ads specify a variety of required hard and soft skills. Let's take a look at some
examples.

This listing for a Telesales Account Executive calls for specific hard skills and experience:

TELESALES ACCOUNT EXECUTIVE
The ideal candidate will have a Bachelor's degree and 3+ years of experience in outbound telesales.
PC literacy including Windows, Microsoft Office, and contact-management software needed.
Familiarity with the World Wide Web is also required, and prior recruiting experience is a PLUS.

This next ad, for an Executive Assistant, is much less explicit—it doesn't even specify what
kind of computer skills are needed, nor does it demand a degree. But it clearly communicates the kind of attitude the company is looking for, along with some basic competencies
(organization and follow through; and administrative, clerical, and computer skills).

EXECUTIVE ASSISTANT
We are looking to hire a person who has not only the right basic skills but also the attitude we
need. Are you a person with a "roll your sleeves up, happy to pitch in and help" attitude? If you
answered YES, then this job is for you!

You are a highly organized person with the confidence to see tasks through to completion with
minimal supervision. You possess administrative, clerical, and computer skills.

Most postings specify a combination of hard and soft skills, as in these next examples. By
communicating information about attitude, atmosphere, and expectations along with the
specific competencies required for the job, employers are hoping to find the best match for
their needs and the best fit for their culture and environment.

ENTRY-LEVEL APPLICATIONS DEVELOPER

The candidate should have knowledge of Visual Basic, HTML ASP, C#, and database design. Strong communications skills are important to work in a highly interactive team environment. Candidate should be a self-starter who can work under a project manager. The candidate should understand and have practical software development knowledge of Object-Oriented environments, client/server environments, and a broad range of operating system platforms. Experience with SQL Server, Crystal Reports, and/or Microsoft FoxPro a plus.

SOCIAL WORKER

Under general supervision, a Social Worker IV provides social services requiring a high level of expertise and the application of advanced techniques related to the provision of protective services for children and adults. This position utilizes assessment, counseling, interviewing, case planning, and writing skills.

Minimum qualifications include the possession of an MSW or a Master's Degree from a two-year counseling program if the program's course of study emphasized vocational rehabilitation, family or marriage counseling, gerontology, or a closely related field.

PACKAGE DESIGNER

This position is with the department of Creative Services/Marketing. Our client operates on the idea that teamwork overrides ego—they seek designers who want to create, but who do not believe that artistic prima donnas rule.

Qualifications: Adept with QuarkXPress, Adobe Illustrator, Photoshop, multimedia, and 3D.

3+ years of applicable experience as a package designer, ideally with consumer products, but also will consider graphic designers with strong portfolios.

QUALITY ENGINEER

Qualifications: Bachelor's degree; 1–2 years of experience in Quality in a QS-9000 environment; exposure to machining, casting, and assembly a plus. Must be hands-on and have a real desire to grow in the Quality field. Must have good interpersonal skills and be a team player.

Beyond job postings, there are other sources you can use to identify the hard and soft skills your target positions require:

- *Occupational Outlook Handbook (OOH).* This guide produced by the U.S. Department of Labor describes job duties, working conditions, required training and education, job prospects, and typical earnings for a wide range of occupations. The *OOH* is revised every two years and can be found online at www.bls.gov/oco/, in your college or public library's reference section, or in bookstores.

- **Company job descriptions.** More complete than a want-ad posting, job descriptions are a comprehensive account of the activities and expectations for a specific job within a particular company. When you interview for a job, you can ask to see the job description. You can approach a company's human resources department and ask whether you can view a description. You can also request a copy from your employed friends and relatives, especially those whose jobs are related to your target position. Be aware that not all companies have formal job descriptions, and not all descriptions are up-to-date or an accurate reflection of the job as it really is.

- **Interviews with people who do that kind of job (also known as "informational interviewing" or "field research").** The information you get "from the horse's mouth" is probably the most valuable of all. People who are actually doing the work can tell you the ups and downs of the job, the level of knowledge and experience required, and the soft skills that they have found to be most valuable. How can you find people to talk to? Start by asking your friends and their parents, your parents and their friends, neighbors, and relatives. Your college career center can help you find the names of college alumni who are working in your target field. Most people love to talk about their work and will be more than happy to spend a little time helping you define your career goal.

- **Resume sample books (like this one).** Look at resumes in the field you're interested in. Don't limit yourself to entry-level jobs or new-grad resumes. Take a look at the resumes of successful people who have advanced their careers. Their resumes should be chock-full of specific skills and traits that paved the way for their success.

- **"How to get a job in..." books.** Check your local library, bookstore, or college career center for guidebooks that are specific to the field you're interested in. Publications of this kind may also be available for free from the appropriate professional association (see the next item).

- **Professional associations.** Most fields have a professional association that provides such services as a newsletter, annual professional conference, and continuing-education opportunities. Associations also serve as the public "voice" of the profession and are often involved in publicity and lobbying for the benefit of members. Associations can be a great source of career information. At the Web site of the American Society of Association Executives (www.asaenet.org/cda/asae/associations_search/), you can search for an association in your field. For instance, if you enter the keyword "accounting," you will get 19 association names and links to their Web sites. In print, the *Encyclopedia of Associations* is the definitive source.

- **College career center resources.** In addition to giving you access to the resources mentioned previously, your college career center will provide one-on-one assistance if you're having difficulty getting the information you need. Don't expect the counselors to figure out your career path, write your resume, or find you a job; but do call on them for advice, guidance, and expertise.

Some Skills Are Always Valuable

There are some skills and attributes that employers always value no matter what job they are trying to fill. These skills are found in the best employees, those who can handle a variety of challenges and succeed in just about any environment.

What are these important attributes? A 2003 survey by the National Association of Colleges and Employers (NACE) tells us what employers value most. More than 300 employers responded to the survey, rating the importance of candidate qualities and skills on a five-point scale, with 5 being "extremely important" and 1 being "not important." Here are their top responses and the ratings each received:

- Communication skills (4.7)
- Honesty/integrity (4.7)
- Teamwork skills (4.6)
- Interpersonal skills (4.5)
- Motivation/initiative (4.5)
- Strong work ethic (4.5)

It's difficult to showcase honesty and integrity in a resume, but using these findings and adding two more key items, we can develop a list of core attributes that are valuable for every type of job in every organization.

- Communication skills
- Leadership and initiative

- Interpersonal skills ("people" skills)
- Organization, time management, planning, follow-through
- Reliability and work ethic
- Problem-solving skills

These skills are included on the Core Knowledge and Skills worksheets in this book because they're so important. You should try to communicate these skills in your resume even if a job description doesn't call for them specifically.

Put Together Your Skills List

Now that you've reviewed a variety of resources, it's time to put together your own skills list. Here are two samples.

Core Knowledge and Skills for My Target Position: <u>Pharmaceutical Sales Representative</u>

Hard Skills and Requirements

- Bachelor's degree (preferably BS), minimum GPA 3.0 ☐
- Proficiency in Microsoft Word, Excel, and PowerPoint ☐
- Driver's license and ability to travel throughout territory ☐

Soft Skills

- Presentation skills ☐
- Outgoing personality ☐
- Ability to work with limited supervision ☐
- Ambition and drive to succeed ☐

Added Value

- Sales experience ☐
- Master's degree in science-related field ☐
- Knowledge/experience in medical-related field (such as nursing or physical therapy) ☐
- Willingness to relocate ☐

Always Valuable

- Communication skills ☐
- Leadership and initiative ☐
- Interpersonal skills ("people" skills) ☐
- Organization, time management, planning, follow-through ☐
- Reliability and work ethic ☐
- Problem-solving skills ☐

Core Knowledge and Skills for My Target Position:
<u>Mechanical Design Engineer, Aerospace</u>

Hard Skills and Requirements

- Bachelor's degree in mechanical engineering or aeronautical engineering ☐
- PC skills ☐
- Experience with CAD (computer-aided design) software ☐
- Analytical and problem-solving skills ☐

Soft Skills

- Ability to work in a cross-functional team environment ☐
- Self-starter ☐
- Creativity ☐
- Ability to use technical data to sell your ideas ☐

Added Value

- Design experience ☐
- Master's degree in engineering ☐

Always Valuable

- Communication skills ☐
- Leadership and initiative ☐
- Interpersonal skills ("people" skills) ☐
- Organization, time management, planning, follow-through ☐
- Reliability and work ethic ☐
- Problem-solving skills ☐

Now it's your turn. Use this form, or you can create a new word-processing file.

Core Knowledge and Skills for My Target Position:

Hard Skills and Requirements

- _____ ❑
- _____ ❑
- _____ ❑
- _____ ❑
- _____ ❑
- _____ ❑

Soft Skills

- _____ ❑
- _____ ❑
- _____ ❑
- _____ ❑
- _____ ❑
- _____ ❑

Added Value

- _____ ❑
- _____ ❑
- _____ ❑
- _____ ❑
- _____ ❑
- _____ ❑

Always Valuable

- Communication skills ❑
- Leadership and initiative ❑
- Interpersonal skills ("people" skills) ❑
- Organization, time management, planning, follow-through ❑
- Reliability and work ethic ❑
- Problem-solving skills ❑

STEP 3: Compile Evidence of Your Hard and Soft Skills

You've clarified your job target and defined the hard and soft skills needed to be considered a great candidate for that job. Now your resume needs to prove that you have those skills. In this step, you'll dig through your various experiences to find that proof—specific examples of when you used or demonstrated those skills and attributes.

At this point, don't worry about how to word your experiences or how they will fit into your resume. The notes you'll make in this section are the raw material that you'll mold into the polished resume in the next chapter.

Start by reviewing the list of core job qualifications that you created in Step 2. Use the box at the right of the form to check off the qualifications that you possess.

STOP!

It's time for a reality check. Have you checked off all or most of the "hard skills" and "soft skills" required for the job you'll be seeking? Remember, these represent the core knowledge required for the position. You won't be able to write an effective resume for this job if you don't meet the basic requirements. Even more important, this might not be a good career choice for you. Your job target should not be a "pie in the sky" wish, but rather an appropriate, achievable goal that fits your education and personality.

If your skills don't match your job target, take a break from resume writing and do some career planning, as advised earlier in this chapter.

But don't worry if you can't check off every single skill on your list. With a resume that highlights your strengths and shows employers your potential, you'll be a viable candidate for your target position and other, related roles in the company, as long as you clearly communicate *most* of the core skills and other positive employee attributes that the job requires.

You can now start to put together your "evidence" information that shows you have what it takes to be successful for the jobs you're seeking.

Consider All Sources for Evidence of Your Abilities

Before starting to write, think about the sources you might consider in searching for this evidence. Your recent educational experience, of course, is a prime source for relevant material. But don't stop there! You've had many opportunities to develop and demonstrate specific skills, and you'll want to consider a wide variety of sources when compiling your proof.

Keep this list handy as you start the next section. It will help jog your memory and give greater depth to your resume than if you concentrated only on your most recent college experience.

Education
Degree
Major studies
Class/team projects
Theses
Case studies
Areas of concentration
Research

Academic honors and awards

Other honors and awards
Leadership
Contribution
Peer recognition

Extracurricular activities
Clubs and organizations
Varsity and intramural sports
Fraternities and sororities

Internship or co-op experience

Employment
During the school year
Summer jobs
Prior professional experience if you're a nontraditional student

Volunteer activities
High school
College
Community

High school
Academic honors
Significant activities

Travel

Family background

Special skills and interests

In addition to searching your memory, you might find evidence of your abilities in any of the following:

- Performance reviews from your various jobs
- Letters of recommendation from teachers, friends, and employers
- Your college application materials and application essay

Draft Your Skills Evidence

Open a new word-processing document or use the following form (make several copies so that you can write a proof for each of your skills).

Consider each important skill and attribute for your job target and come up with specific examples of how you have demonstrated that skill. Review the "source" list in the preceding section to be sure that you're not overlooking any important areas of your background.

Be specific! Vague generalities are not credible proof of your abilities. Don't worry that you're getting too detailed or including information that you won't use on your resume. Remember, this is your raw material. It's better to select from a large number of "possible" items instead of having to scrounge around to find evidence that supports a key skill area. As long as your examples are specific and credible, employers will be happy to consider them as proof of your qualifications.

In the examples that follow this blank form, you'll see how a co-op student and three new graduates compiled their proof lists.

"Proof" for My Skills Summary

Core Skill or Requirement	Evidence
_____	_____
	_____
	_____
	_____
_____	_____
	_____
	_____
	_____
_____	_____
	_____
	_____
	_____
_____	_____
	_____
	_____
	_____
_____	_____
	_____
	_____
	_____

Sample Skills Summary Proof Worksheets

Here's an example of a skills list with supporting proof, compiled by a college sophomore looking for a co-op position in a medical research environment.

Target Position:
Medical Research Assistant (Co-op)

Core Knowledge and Skills	Proof
Hard Skills and Requirements	
Two years of undergraduate studies in biology or psychology	Completed two years, psychology major, Northeastern University—3.9 GPA.
Research experience/ability to conduct research-quality phone interviews	Performed extensive research for National History Day project, 11th grade—won regional competition and advanced to state.
	Did biology, chemistry, physics, statistics, and behavioral research and lab projects as part of first- and second-year coursework.
Administrative abilities to manage follow-up mailings	Part-time work experience includes office assistant position. Filed papers, handled large mailings, and sorted and organized material for two books.
Soft Skills	
Teamwork skills	In ER volunteer position, work as part of the emergency team doing whatever is needed for doctors, nurses, and patients.
	Worked as part of sales/customer service team for Organized Living.
	Worked with teams on community clean-up projects with Circle K and President's Leadership Institute.
Added Value	
Experience in a health-care environment	Volunteer: N.E. Medical Center, Emergency Department 2006, Pediatric Department 2005.
	Volunteer: Children's Hospital, summers 2004 and 2005.
Always Valuable	
Communication skills	Gave winning oral presentation for National History Day project.
	Speak conversational Spanish.
Leadership and initiative	Selected for President's Leadership Institute at NU.
	Sought volunteer experience at NE Medical Center and initiated transfer to ER in second year.
Interpersonal skills ("people" skills)	Worked in retail/customer service job during high school. Interacted with many different kinds of customers.
	Interacted with sick children and adult patients as hospital volunteer for last three years.

(continued)

(continued)

Core Knowledge and Skills	Proof
Always Valuable (continued)	
Organization, time management, planning, follow-through	Planned and coordinated trips to New York City, Boston, Chicago, and Asheville involving plane, train, and auto transportation; hotel selection; activity scheduling; and syncing the schedules of people coming from different places.
	As high school senior, balanced heavy course load (all AP-level courses) with work and volunteer activities. Completed all assignments, papers, and projects on time.
Reliability and work ethic	Never missed work or was late in two and a half years at Organized Living.
	Worked part-time in high school, full-time summers, and part-time in college, as well as volunteering. Never missed scheduled volunteer dates.
	Mrs. Ellis' recommendation: "the most organized, observant, conscientious, and reliable person we have ever hired to care for our children."
Problem-solving skills	Working with children for more than five years (baby-sitting and hospital volunteering), used creativity and problem-solving skills to keep kids interested and active.
	In team project for Bio II, came up with creative solution that enabled us to identify results more quickly and gave us extra time to work on the report (earned an *A*).

This example is a good illustration of how varying areas of life—school classes and projects, part-time work experience, extracurricular activities, volunteer pursuits, and personal activities—can provide material for your resume.

Following are additional examples of proof statements for

- A new Business Administration graduate seeking an entry-level human resources position.
- A recent MSME graduate looking for a design engineering role with a major industrial manufacturer.
- A nontraditional student who recently completed a Bachelor of Liberal Arts degree, is planning to relocate, and wants to find a customer-service or account-management job in the health-care industry.

Target Position:
Human Resources Generalist

Core Knowledge and Skills	Proof
Hard Skills and Requirements	
Bachelor's degree in HR or related field	Bachelor of Arts in Business Administration, concentration in Management.
Ability to handle confidential material	As Assistant Manager at Blockbuster, have access to confidential employee information and the store's financial information.
Computer proficiency (MS Word, Excel, e-mail, Internet, database)	Used computers since grade school. In high school and college, prepared all reports and projects using MS Word, Excel, and PowerPoint.
	Trained new employees on computerized cash-register system.
Attention to detail and accuracy	At Blockbuster, manage details of keeping inventory sorted, shelved, and tracked.
	Prepared financial reports of daily activity.
Business writing ability	Wrote college papers and reports.
Soft Skills	
Ability to work with diverse personalities	Had excellent relationships with all staff, whether subordinates, peers, or managers.
Added Value	
General office/administrative experience	Managed reports and paperwork in Assistant Manager role with Blockbuster.
Always Valuable	
Communication skills	Extensive training experience. Able to adapt training methods to meet needs of staff. Take responsibility if they don't learn something—I need to find a more effective way to teach them.
	Able to solve customer problems.
Leadership and initiative	Promoted five times at Blockbuster.
	Helped make hiring decisions.
	Chosen as part of regional training team for a new corporate training program.
	Selected to train new managers as well as new clerks.
Interpersonal skills ("people" skills)	Worked successfully in customer-service positions for five years.
	Able to get the most out of staff by finding what motivates them and creating rewards and incentives that fit their motivations.

(continued)

(continued)

Core Knowledge and Skills	Proof
Always Valuable (continued)	
Organization, time management, planning, follow-through	Worked full-time while in school and still managed to finish in only four-and-a-half years.
	Set training schedules for entire region and followed through to be sure all training was complete.
Reliability and work ethic	Worked full-time while going to school almost full-time.
Problem-solving skills	Came up with a new way to organize returned videos to get them back on the shelves more quickly.
	When employees weren't working hard, took a look at what motivated them and came up with new rewards and incentives.
	Can adapt management and communication style to very different people.

Target Position:
Mechanical Design Engineer

Core Knowledge and Skills	Proof
Hard Skills and Requirements	
Bachelor's degree in mechanical or aeronautical engineering	BSME, 3.8 GPA; MSME, 3.9 GPA.
PC skills	Fully proficient in MS Word, PowerPoint, Outlook; some experience with Access; extremely strong Excel skills.
Experience with CAD (computer-aided design) software	Used CAD for numerous design courses and projects, both undergraduate and graduate.
	In two six-month co-op jobs, used CAD daily for engineering projects related to industrial machinery design and power systems design.
	Professor Burke's comments on senior design project: "You have a talent for conveying both the art and the precision of your designs—excellent CAD skills."
Analytical and problem-solving skills	Analytical skills essential to successful completion of master's degree project.

	Brainstormed and problem-solved with design team at Apex Power Systems and came up with more than a dozen ways to trim cost from our "legacy" system. This will save the company $12 million per year and also make the product more efficient for customers to use.
Soft Skills	
Ability to work in a cross-functional team environment	Assigned to new product development team at Acme Industrial Systems. Worked with people from marketing, sales, manufacturing, and engineering to develop new FS-17 industrial motor.
	As part of campus program-planning committee, worked with diverse students and administrators to develop and carry out entertaining and educational programs for the entire student population.
Self-starting	At first co-op job (Travant Consulting), came up with new scope of responsibility for co-op assignment; developed overall plan and prioritized action-item lists; completed scope with minimal supervision.
Creative	Earned *As* in all design classes.
	Compiled portfolio of original designs and class projects.
Ability to use technical data to sell your ideas	Supported master's thesis in oral and written presentation.
	Proved value and cost benefit of using titanium in FS-17 motor; convinced design team to adopt that material.
Added Value	
Design experience	Two six-month co-op assignments in design engineering role.
Master's degree in engineering	MSME
Always Valuable	
Communication skills	With Apex Power Systems, drafted all initial reports for the new product design team. Most were approved with only minor changes.
	Columnist for *Campus Chronicle*—"Geek Speak," commentary from engineering/science viewpoint to balance liberal arts focus of newspaper.
Leadership and initiative	See notation re: designing co-op job.
	Elected to leadership positions

	(campus program-planning committee, finance committee for frat house).
Interpersonal skills ("people" skills)	See "leadership positions," above; worked with diverse teams and people in a variety of jobs and activities.
	As part of fraternity outreach, mentored high-school students considering engineering careers.
Organization, time management, planning, follow-through	Fulfilled all expectations for co-op assignments, "going the extra mile" when needed to get the job done.
Reliability and work ethic	Worked part-time through high school and full-time summers until beginning co-op.
	Asked to return to Acme based on excellent performance, reliability, and work ethic.
Problem-solving skills	(Covered in "Hard Skills and Requirements," above.)

Target Position:
Health-Care Account Manager

Core Knowledge and Skills	Proof
Hard Skills and Requirements	
Bachelor's degree in business, allied health, or a related field	Bachelor of Liberal Arts degree.
PC skills	Daily use of MS Office products and proprietary CRM system.
Knowledge of medical terminology	Daily use of medical coding and medical terminology in resolving claims with health-care providers.
Experience in account management or customer service within health-care environment	15 years of experience in health-care claims, billing, and account management (managed care).
Soft Skills	
Planning work and carrying it out with minimal supervision	Have decision-making authority for a wide variety of customer issues and problems. When back-up is needed, manager always approves of my decision to call her in.
Customer-service skills	Meet or exceed all performance goals for customer satisfaction and call volume while handling heavy call load.
Ability to work in a team environment	Recognized for exceptional teamwork skills in most recent performance evaluation.

Added Value

Team leadership experience	Co-led Policy and Procedure team—administered survey, led team in reviewing results, and presented proposals to management.

Always Valuable

Communication skills	Able to de-escalate issues—often called on by other claims specialists to help with difficult calls.
	My job calls for constant written and verbal communication with health-care providers, other team members, and management.
Leadership and initiative	Policy and Procedure project was my idea.
	Recognized by manager for expertise and ability to complete extra projects while maintaining heavy call volume.
Interpersonal skills ("people" skills)	Frequently complimented by customers on ability to calm them down when they're upset about a claim.
Organization, time management, planning, follow-through	Went back to school and finished degree while working full-time and raising two children as a single mother.
Reliability and work ethic	See above.
Problem-solving skills	When dealing with sticky claim situations, able to keep focus on the issue and what we can do about it. Can come up with "workarounds" when the regular methods won't work.
	Manager received two complimentary letters last year on my ability to help customers with difficult problems.

Spend some time developing your "proof." You'll end up with lots of great material to use as you construct the first draft of your resume in the next chapter.

Chapter 1 Checklist

You're ready to move on to chapter 2, "Writing Your Resume," if you have done all of the following:

❑ Identified one or more specific job targets that are a good fit for your qualifications and your interests.

❑ Made a list of the core qualifications for your target positions and matched these with your education, skills, and experience.

❑ Written "proof" statements that provide evidence that you possess the core qualifications for your target positions.

Writing Your Resume

You've done your background work and now it's time to put together the pieces you've assembled into a resume that "sells" you to an employer.

That's right—resume writing is selling. Your resume is an advertisement for what you can bring to an employer. Similar to newspaper and TV advertising, to be effective your resume must do the following:

- Capture attention in the first few seconds.
- Establish credibility—a reason for the reader to believe that you can do what you say.
- Inspire the reader to want to know more.

When you're making a big purchase, an ad alone will not usually inspire you to act. (Have you ever bought a car or a computer based solely on a magazine or TV ad?) But a good advertisement will create interest in the product and make you want to know more. That's what your resume should do for you. Your goal in sending your resume is to get the employer to become interested enough to pick up the phone and call you for an interview.

But your resume can do more than just get you in the door for an interview! It will also serve as a basis for the questions and discussions you'll have with the hiring authority. So for your interviews, you must be prepared to explain every item on your resume in a way that continues selling the "product"—you!

In this chapter, you'll start by creating a powerful introduction that quickly draws notice to your most important qualifications. You'll move through the other sections of the resume, detailing your credentials, and you'll learn the importance of adding numbers, results, and accomplishments as further support to the "proof" you compiled in the preceding chapter. And finally, you'll proofread and polish your draft to perfection.

Before we launch into writing your resume, let's take a look at a few frequently asked questions and clear up some common misperceptions about resumes.

FAQs

Does my resume have to be just one page?

Whereas most new college graduates can fit their most compelling and relevant information onto one page, some simply cannot... and it would be a mistake to try. There are absolutely no rules about resume length. Most of the samples in this book are one page; some are two pages. In each case, the decision on "how long should it be" was made after the resume was written, based entirely on the amount and type of information to be presented. *Recommendation: Write your resume first, following the guidelines later in this chapter. Organize and format the information, and then see whether you can fit everything comfortably on one page. Use the samples in this book to get some creative inspiration for layout and design that will create maximum impact and readability within a fairly concise format. Strive for one page—edit and condense your first draft—but don't sacrifice information that is truly important.*

I've been told I need a "functional" resume. What is it and how do I get it?

A functional resume groups and emphasizes related skills (functions) instead of presenting every fact within a chronological category on the resume. The functional style is a great way to pull together "proof" from different areas of your background. For instance, you might create a "Leadership Skills" section that includes examples from your college activities, part-time work experience, and volunteer activities—"proof" that might be overlooked if each stood alone in a purely chronological history. For *experienced* employees, a chronological resume usually works best, because employers can see at a glance their career progression and the specific responsibilities and achievements of each position. But if your work experience is not your strongest qualifier (and it usually isn't for new grads), a functional style may work better. Most of the resume samples in this book use a *combination* style that groups strengths into a skills summary at the top and then follows with a roughly chronological listing of education, experience, and activities. *Recommendation: Don't worry whether your resume is strictly "functional" or strictly "chronological." Create a strong summary (as described later in this chapter) and then organize your other information into sections that make it easy for the reader to pick up relevant information.*

I don't have any real work experience. Why would an employer be interested in me?

By now, following the guidelines in chapter 1, you should have compiled plenty of "raw material" to write a resume that will sell you for the job you want. Prior work experience is only one thing employers look for. They realize that most new grads will not have work history that is really relevant to their professional careers. The employer might rely on an employment history to prove work ethic, time-management skills, reliability, interpersonal skills, and other attributes that make a good employee; so if you don't have prior paid work experience, make sure you document these important traits from other areas of your background. Volunteer activities, unpaid work experience, leadership of student organizations, extensive personal travel, and even undocumented work experience such as baby-sitting can all be used to provide evidence of valuable, provable skills. *Recommendation: Use your diverse experiences to "prove" you have the attributes of a good employee. But don't worry too much about what you don't have. Instead, put your best foot forward with what you do have to offer and feel confident about your abilities!*

All of my work experience is from part-time retail sales jobs. Does this really count to an employer?

Yes, indeed! As noted above, employers will look for evidence of your "good employee" traits by looking at your past work experience. If you can prove you were a good employee for someone else, the employer can guess that you're likely to repeat that success in another job. Every job exists for a reason and is very important to the organization. So even though you might not think much of your part-time cashier job at Megastore, you learned some valuable skills (customer service, teamwork, and flexibility, for instance). *Recommendation: When writing about your past positions on your resume, don't inflate your responsibilities or importance (don't make your pizza-delivery job sound like you were the CEO), but do communicate the value you brought to the organization and the kinds of skills you used every day.*

Should I include high school information?

That depends. If it's truly impressive and adds weight to your more recent college information, there is a good argument for including it. But don't overemphasize it—you don't want to appear as if you "peaked" at age 18 and have done nothing memorable since! *Recommendation: Include high school information that's truly relevant, adds to your qualifications, or will give you a competitive advantage. Don't overload your resume with high school activities, and be sure that they are balanced by more recent examples of your success.*

Where do I start?! It all seems overwhelming.

Take a deep breath and relax! If you followed the guidelines in chapter 1, you have already gathered the raw material you'll need for your resume. In this chapter, I'll guide you through the process, step by step, and you'll see how smoothly everything falls into place.

(continued)

(continued)

> **How will I know when it's right?**
>
> Perhaps the number-one misconception is that there is a "right" and a "wrong" way to write your resume. In fact, there are no rules! You can include what you like (as long as it's truthful), emphasize the most important information, and organize and present the material in any way that makes sense to paint the perfect picture of who you are and what you have to offer. ***Recommendation:*** *You'll know your resume is right* for you *when it helps you define and organize your skills and attracts interviews for jobs you're interested in. Your friend's or roommate's or cousin's resume is* not *the right resume for you, no matter how well it worked for them; and yours will not be right for anyone else. It's as unique as you are.*
>
> **When I have my resume done, what do I do next?**
>
> Now it's time to put your resume to work. You'll need to get it out to potential employers and networking contacts (you'll read more on this in chapter 3) and create an action plan that will keep you on track as you move from new grad to newly employed. No one can do it for you, but your college career center, parents, friends, and other advisors can give you a great deal of help and guidance. And the more you learn about the process of looking for a job, the more successful you'll be in every job transition of your working life.

Resumes are incredibly flexible documents. There are no "rules" about what you must or cannot include, how or where to present the information, or any real taboos except that your resume must not contain any spelling, grammatical, or punctuation errors. You can select and present the most positive, impressive things about you—things that relate to the employer's needs, as you've identified them in your Core Qualifications list. But because a good resume is concisely written and tightly formatted, it's important that you start out with a good organizational structure so that you can include just the right information, arranged for maximum impact.

To create that structure, resumes are sectioned into five principal categories:

- **Header/Contact Information:** A well-organized presentation of your name and contact information (one or more mailing addresses, telephone numbers, e-mail addresses, and other ways of reaching you).
- **Objective and/or Skills Summary:** A section at the top of your resume that immediately identifies what you're looking for and highlights your most important qualifications.
- **Education:** Presents all facets of your recent college experience, such as coursework, academic honors, internships, and activities.
- **Work Experience:** Chronicles the details of your employment experience, whether co-op or internship; part-time during school year or summers; or full-time experience before, during, or since you graduated from college.
- **Extras:** In this category go the many bits of information that you'd like to include but that don't fit neatly into any of the prior categories.

You can start with the easy stuff and work your way through the process in the following steps.

STEP 4: Start Strongly with Well-Organized Contact Information

Give potential employers the information they need in a format that makes it easy for them to find what they're looking for. Your name should be prominent. Use bold and/or larger type to catch the reader's attention.

Should you use a nickname? Because a resume is a fairly formal business document, it's traditional to use your full given name (Richard J. Williams, not Ricky Williams). But you might want to consider using a nickname in the following circumstances:

- If no one ever uses your real name (for example, Jay Vasipoli rather than Mortimer J. Vasipoli III).

- Your name appears difficult to pronounce (for example, Shayna O'Riordan, not Séadhna O'Riordan).

- You want to use an Americanized name or nickname in place of or to supplement your traditional name (for example, Manh "Mike" Nguyen).

If you are sending out your resume while you are still living at school, you'll need to include both school and home addresses and telephone numbers. If the best way to reach you is on your mobile phone, be sure to include that number as well. And be certain that you have a reliable answering service for any number you include. Don't include pagers or fax numbers unless there really is no better way to contact you.

You must have an e-mail address that's professional, permanent, and reliable. Consider getting a separate Hotmail or Yahoo! address just for your job search (this is especially important if your everyday e-mail address is something like fratparty@bigu.edu).

Create a new word-processing document or use the resume-development worksheet in the appendix to organize your contact information. Here are a few sample formats to consider:

Meredith Johnson

School Address
780 Columbus Avenue #3-G
Boston, MA 02120
(617) 559-9049

meredithjay@yahoo.com

Permanent Address
4520 Hillsview Circle
Cincinnati, OH 45249
(513) 729-8350

Tyler Van Aark

tylervanaark@hotmail.com

Through 6/15/06: Fellowes Hall #4-G, Loyola College, Baltimore, MD 21210 — 410-349-7009
After 6/15/06: 759 Pfeiffer Rd., Hendersonville, TN 37075 — 615-942-4493

EDWARD J. NILSSON III

ejIII@tampabay.rr.com
257 West Shell Court, Bradenton, FL 34201
941-459-3890 Home — 941-709-3490 Mobile

Dale Okenga, MD

Telephone	781-523-0909
Pager	617-990-4389
Email	daleokenga@worldnet.att.net
Residence	7 Willow Drive
	Winchester, MA 01890

MORGAN VALLENCOURT

Home address......................7409 37th Avenue SW, Seattle, WA 98136 ● 206-923-1761

Contact through June 2006.............................415-552-0983 ● m.vallencourt@ucla.edu

STEP 5: Sell Your Strongest Qualifications in a Powerful Skills Summary

This important introductory section of your resume should present a quick "snapshot" of who you are and what you have to offer. Whether you use a formal Objective statement, use both an Objective and a Skills Summary, or combine the two into some kind of Summary/Profile, be sure you do the following for greatest impact:

- Instantly communicate just what kind of job you're looking for.
- Highlight your strongest qualifications.

This essential information must be crystal-clear in just a quick glance at the top part of your resume. Equally important, you must write this section with the employer's interests in mind. Stating *what you want* is not nearly as effective as telling employers *what you can do for them.*

Write Your Objective/Skills Summary

There are many interesting ways to communicate your objective and key skills. To make it easy for you, first I'll walk you through a step-by-step process. Then, if you're feeling creative or would like to consider a different way of presenting this information, we'll review a variety of options and examples for alternatives to a simple Skills Summary.

Possible Titles for Your Objective/Skills Summary Section

Accomplishment Summary	Job Target	Related Skills and Achievements
Areas of Interest	Key Credentials	Selected Accomplishments
Capabilities	Key Qualifications	Skills and Accomplishments
Career Focus	Objective	
Career Interests	Position Sought	Skills
Competencies	Professional Qualifications	Skills Summary
Core Competencies	Profile	Skills Synopsis
Goal	Proven Capabilities	Summary
Highlights of Skills and Experience	Qualifications Summary	Summary of Qualifications
Immediate and Long-Range Goals	Qualifications	Value Offered

Write an Objective, Goal, or Target Statement

Although it's not strictly necessary to lead off your resume with an objective, I do recommend it for new graduates. It is a quick, easy way to focus the employer's attention on your areas of interest. Otherwise, because you probably don't have a lengthy or relevant employment history, it might be difficult for the employer to understand what jobs you're qualified for.

When writing your objective, be specific, brief, and direct; avoid meaningless statements such as "Seeking a challenging, rewarding position with the opportunity for career advancement."

Here are a few examples:

OBJECTIVE
To be one of the 15 transfer students selected this year for Florida State University's School of Motion Pictures, Television, and Recording Arts.

Seeking an entry-level position in the capacity of

Marketing Associate

OBJECTIVE: Entry-level position utilizing training and skills in financial research, strategic planning, investing, and financial analysis.

Career Focus
Entry-Level, Full-Time Law Associate
• Corporate • Labor • Civil

Goal: Internship—Summer 2006
Public Relations / Marketing / Media Production

Objective
A **Contract Design Internship** utilizing communication and organizational skills in a team-oriented environment. Qualified by a unique blend of design knowledge and a business administration background.

Write your objective statement directly below your contact information on your resume.

List Your Most Important Skills

Next, make a list of the four or five most important skills or credentials you possess that are directly related to your target position. This is easy—you've already identified the core skills as part of your prep work. Because you probably have more than just four or five skills listed, select those that you feel are *most* important for your target job and correlate *most strongly* to your qualifications. Write them here:

- ■ _____
- ■ _____

- _____
- _____
- _____

Summarize Your Evidence

Next to each skill, summarize your "evidence" to show that you possess that requirement. Here's an example:

GOAL: Management Training Opportunity with Emphasis in Human Resources and Operations Management

Core Skill or Requirement	Evidence
Bachelor's degree in business or management	Bachelor's degree in Business Administration, with concentration in management and additional coursework in organizational behavior.
Human resources or training experience	Chosen to train all new employees and new managers for a 12-store retail district.
Leadership skills	Able to effectively supervise and motivate staff to high performance levels.
Management knowledge or experience	Two years of management experience in a fast-paced retail environment.
Reliability and work ethic	Track record of advancement based on proven capabilities, work ethic, and enthusiasm. Promoted five times in seven years with Blockbuster Video.

To see how this summary was finalized and integrated into a completed resume, see page 96.

Here's another example:

GOAL: Position as Counselor, Teacher, or Case Manager for Special-Needs Youth

Core Skill or Requirement	Evidence
B.S. or M.S. in Social Work or Special Education	Master of Arts in Special Education/California Teaching Credential expected in 2006.
Experience diagnosing and treating developmental disabilities	Seven years of case-management experience—specialist in diagnosis and treatment of developmental disabilities.
Communication skills	Bilingual teaching experience: Spanish/English.

You can see the finished resume, including the skills summary, on page 174.

Here's one more:

GOAL: Internship in Public Relations/Marketing/Media Production

Core Skill or Requirement	Evidence
Knowledge of media production	Two hands-on summer internships with a multimedia producer of major corporate programs and events.
Presentation and communication skills	Comfortable speaking before groups and in business settings. Model, spokesperson, guide, and peer advisor. Strong writing and editing skills.
Leadership	Repeatedly took on leadership roles in school and community activities. Demonstrated initiative, drive, and ability to manage multiple priorities.
Teamwork and interaction	At my best when interacting with others and working in a team environment.

The finished resume, with this skills summary, appears on page 76.

Now it's your turn. Use this worksheet or enter this information directly into your resume in the word-processing file.

"Proof" for My Skills Summary

Core Skill or Requirement	Evidence
_____	_____
	_____
	_____
	_____
_____	_____
	_____
	_____
_____	_____
	_____
	_____

(continued)

(continued)

Core Skill or Requirement	Evidence

Now, assemble your proof (the "Evidence" column) into a Skills Summary just below the Objective statement in your resume.

Alternatives to a Simple Skills Summary

A Skills Summary like the one you've just written is a relatively easy and usually effective way to highlight your most important qualifications. But it's not the only way! The sample resumes in this book show dozens of different ways to start off your resume. If you're not fully satisfied with your Skills Summary or want to consider a different approach, consider these ideas or flip through the samples for more inspiration.

- With or without a category title, describe the value you offer in your target position:

> Profit-building capabilities I can bring to Melcor as a Customer Service Representative:
>
> - Ability to find and fix customers' problems
> - Experience to help people want to succeed
> - Confidence to master steep learning curves fast

- Fold your objective into a Summary of Qualifications:

> **SUMMARY OF QUALIFICATIONS**
> Energetic, dedicated **Physician Assistant** with strong interpersonal skills • Emergency Medical Technician background • Proven ability to work effectively with people of various ages, cultural backgrounds, and socioeconomic statuses • Long-time interest in medicine and desire to assist those who are suffering physically or emotionally • Provide high-quality medical care with an emphasis on treating patients as unique and valuable individuals • Well-developed organizational skills • Fluent in Spanish language

■ Combine an objective with a brief summary paragraph and a "keyword" list of core competencies (this complete resume appears on page 104):

Seeking an entry-level position in the capacity of

Marketing Associate

Offer a Bachelor's degree in Marketing, diverse experience, and a solid understanding of marketing strategies illustrated through academic projects and an Internet venture that continues to develop and test theoretical marketing strategies and business management skills in the areas of

Conceptual Planning	Web-based Marketing	Advertising Campaigns
Strategy Development	Marketing Penetration	Media/Client Relations
Project Management	Competitive Analysis	Ad Copy Creation

■ Create a "profile" that describes your strongest capabilities (this complete resume is on page 111):

OBJECTIVE   Sales Associate—Retail Sales

PROFILE

• College student with more than 4 years of retail sales experience.

• Professional and approachable manner. Talent for identifying customers' needs and presenting solutions that drive purchases.

• Highly motivated team player—willing to take on added responsibilities.

• Proven skills in problem solving and customer relations. Fluent Spanish.

★ RECAP

This Objective/Skills Summary section of your resume should provide a quick snapshot of who you are and the best you have to offer as it relates to your target positions. Organize and format your material to create a cohesive introduction and capture immediate attention.

STEP 6: Emphasize Education as a Key Credential

Because you've just completed a degree, the Education section of your resume is quite important. As you mature in your career, this section will become less prominent and will simply take its place, in abbreviated form, toward the end of your resume. But for now, create a section that communicates the value of your education in terms of your career target and a company's desired core qualifications.

Write Your Education Section

Use the resume-development form in the appendix or work directly on your computer draft. Start by listing your degree (you can use abbreviations such as BS, BA, MS, or JD if you like), major, minor if applicable, year of graduation (it's not necessary to list the year you started), and your school's name and location (city and state).

If you've earned a license or credential as a result of your education, be sure to list it. You can also include relevant training that you completed outside the scope of your degree. For instance, you might have taken sales-training courses or earned CPR certification.

Next, review the evidence you compiled in chapter 1 and pull out any education-related information to add to this section. If you find a theme—for instance, three examples that show strong leadership skills—consider creating a subheading to group together these items and call attention to them.

? Education FAQs

Should I include my GPA?

That depends. If it's good (generally speaking, 3.0 or above), include it. Sometimes an effective strategy is to list your "GPA in Major," if it's higher than your overall GPA. If your GPA is unimpressive, omit it; including it on your resume can only harm you. Sure, the first question you're asked in an interview might be, "What was your GPA?" But you might not even be in that interview if you had listed a low GPA on your resume. Don't get yourself screened out of consideration by including a low GPA.

I spent my first two years at a community college and then transferred to State U. Should I list both?

It's not necessary to list any school except the one granting your degree. Include other institutions only if you have a specific reason for doing so—say you're going to network with alumni of your first school, or your first school has higher prestige than your graduating school. Two years at Harvard are valuable even if you finished up at Nondescript U.

How do I indicate my graduation date if I haven't finished my degree yet?

If you're starting your job search within a few months of graduation, it's not necessary to qualify the date—a resume with "Bachelor of Fine Arts, June 2006" that is circulated in March does not need to be explained. But if you're using your resume while still in college (say for an internship, co-op job, or part-time employment), use the word "projected" or "anticipated" along with the graduation date: "BSBA anticipated 2006."

Should I list my courses?

In general, I don't recommend taking up valuable space on your resume with an entire course listing. But consider adding "Relevant Coursework" or "Highlights of Courses" if you took unusual or advanced classes or if your degree or major course of study is not well known. Course listings can also be helpful if you are applying for internships or co-op jobs where employers will not know which of the undergraduate courses in your major you've already completed.

Do I need to include high school information?

In most cases you can omit high school information. But if you have legitimate reasons to include it, do so. Perhaps you went to an out-of-state college but are now back in your hometown hoping to make connections with fellow graduates of Midtown High. Or you might have achieved some very impressive honors and awards during high school; it's okay to include these as long as they don't overshadow your college career. Younger students (those seeking internships or co-op jobs) can usually make a stronger case for including notable high school information.

Possible Subheadings You Can Use Within the Education Section

Academic Honors	Fellowships	Licenses/Credentials
Area of Concentration	High School	Major Projects
Athletics	Honors and Awards	Research
Co-op Experience	International Study	Thesis
Relevant Coursework	Internship Experience	Scholarships
Extracurricular Activities	Leadership Experience	Volunteer Activities

Sample Education Sections

Here are a few sample Education sections taken from the resumes in this book.

EDUCATION

Medical   **Baylor College of Medicine,** Houston, TX, 2006: **M.D.**

Undergraduate   Washington & Jefferson College, Washington, PA, 1994: BA Biology

---

EDUCATION

Bachelor of Arts, English, expected May 2006

Saint Thomas Aquinas College, Spring Valley, NY

Alpha Sigma Lambda Honor Society

■ EDUCATION

Bachelor of Arts, Psychology (Magna Cum Laude)   2006 Graduate

VANDERBILT UNIVERSITY; Nashville, Tennessee

Coursework included: Childhood Psychopathology, Abnormal Psychology, Psychology of Women, Multicultural Communications, Racial and Ethnic Diversity, and numerous other Human Service courses.

Education

B.S., Iowa State University
Ames, IA (May 2006)
AGRICULTURAL STUDIES
    TEAM PROJECTS:
      Nutrient Management
      Fly-Ash Environmental Soil Management
AAS, Des Moines Area Community College
Ankeny, IA 2003
AGRICULTURAL BUSINESS

EDUCATION	Boston College, Chestnut Hill, MA
December 2006	**Bachelor of Arts in Business Administration** Area of Emphasis: Management

Relevant Coursework	Accounting	Organizational Management	Organizational Behavior
	Economics	Small Business Management	Operations Management
	Finance	Administrative Personnel Systems	First-Line Supervisor
	Business Law	Quantitative Methods for Business	Introduction to Computers
	Statistics	High-Performance Teams in Business	

Accomplishments

- Personally financed 100% of college education through full-time employment; completed bachelor's degree in 4½ years.
- Won Coach's Award as member of track team, freshman year.

★ RECAP

Your resume's Education section might be a brief one-liner, or it could take up a large part of the page. Choose information that is relevant to your career goal and paints a picture of you in the way you want to be perceived—perhaps as a leader, a high achiever, an involved citizen, a hard worker, or someone respected by peers and administrators.

STEP 7: Describe Your Work Experience with a Focus on Skills and Achievements

Even if your jobs have been totally unrelated to your current goal, they gave you the chance to learn and practice specific skills. When you describe your work experience, relate what you did to a skill you learned or a contribution you made to the business. Try to phrase your work experience in the form of achievements rather than job duties.

For instance, instead of simply listing your job duties as an Admissions Representative for your college, communicate the achievement and importance of that role in a sentence like this:

Admissions Representative: Chosen through competitive interview process to work with Admissions Office and represent Boston University to prospective students.

Wherever possible, support your achievement statements with specific numbers and results. Numbers add substance and credibility and are ten times more effective at selling your capabilities than words are. (Doesn't that last sentence have greater impact and believability than if I just said "much more effective"?)

Even if you can't add numbers, demonstrate that you contributed to the success of the business where you worked. Did you save money or increase efficiency? Multiply sales? Improve customer service or customer satisfaction? Think of a better way to do things? Help co-workers be more productive? Save a sale or placate an unhappy customer? Come to the rescue when the business was short-handed? Come up with an idea for a partnership with another business that added to the success of both? Your achievement statements don't have to be earthshaking; even small things that you did on the job will demonstrate your value as an employee.

Possible Titles for Your Work Experience Section

Career Highlights

Career History

Co-op Experience

Employment Experience

Employment History

Experience

Experience and Accomplishments

Experience Summary

Highlights of Experience

Internship Experience

Professional Experience

Relevant Experience

Relevant Work History

Work Background

Work Experience

Write Your Experience Section

List your job titles, dates of employment, and the name and location of the company where you worked. Add statements that convey the skills you learned and the ways you contributed to the business. You can use the resume-development form in the appendix or enter this section directly into your draft resume on your computer.

Don't go overboard trying to make your positions sound impressive. Generally, employers know what's involved in the typical retail sales, restaurant service, office administration, and customer-service jobs many students hold during high school and college years. Focus on the things that are unique to you and those that demonstrate skill or achievement.

If you have experience that is related to your career target—perhaps through a co-op job, internship, or position you held between attaining your bachelor's and master's degrees— you can provide more detail of your job duties. These duties relate to your current goal and position you as a person with experience rather than an entry-level employee. In these positions, too, you should focus on skills and achievements instead of simply listing the duties of the job. What did you learn or do that will make you an even more valuable employee? What were your unique contributions?

Sample Job Experience Phrasings

Here are a few examples of how you might phrase your job experiences to add impact and value to your resume. All of these examples were taken from the resumes in this book. Most of the statements refer to part-time employment that is typical of many new college graduates.

- Developed loyal clientele and increased sales through personal attention to customers' needs. Resolved customer complaints diplomatically.
- Supported the pharmacy operations as necessary, fulfilling the role of pharmaceutical technician.
- Generated a list of 160 sales leads and contacts through aggressive cold-calling from a database of 1,100 companies.
- Devised 13 on-site strategies to effectively meet and recruit more than 750 Multi-Campus Hillel members in 18 months.
- Implemented creative learning techniques that resulted in student passing exams.
- Kept events running smoothly through effective problem-solving and good decision-making.
- Successfully completed the project on time to specification with full user interactivity.
- Publicized an urban youth organization to the media, the general community, and potential supporters. Wrote and designed a brochure for the organization.
- Defrayed college expenses and gained problem-solving, decision-making, communication, and leadership skills through diverse customer service, training, and supervisory positions.

Include awards, honors, recognition, and other evidence that you were a standout employee. Here are a few examples:

- Earned perfect job evaluation.
- Won three contests for selling the most dinner specials from among 15 servers.
- Received Outstanding Service Award, 2002–2003.
- Was requested to return for third summer internship.

★ RECAP

Write an Experience section that demonstrates your "employability" skills by sharing your achievements and success as an employee.

STEP 8: Add the Extras to Give You a Competitive Advantage

What makes you special? Each person has unique attributes, knowledge, and experiences that might not fit into the standard resume sections or match a list of job requirements. Perhaps you speak fluent Urdu, backpacked across Europe for a summer, or devoted hours and hours of time to disadvantaged kids. Sometimes these "extras" are related to your job target, even though they might seem to be totally irrelevant. They say something unique about you and can set you apart from other candidates.

Just as you did in the Work Experience section of your resume, try to communicate skills and accomplishments, with results where possible, when detailing these "extras." If you volunteered, what were the benefits of your efforts? If you held a leadership role with an organization, did you introduce new programs that boosted membership or increased member involvement? Did you self-finance a summer of travel through nine months of part-time work experience? Use this section of your resume to continue the message of capability and success you've communicated throughout your resume.

Possible Category Titles for Your Resume "Extras"

Additional Information

Additional Qualifications

Community Involvement/Community Service

Volunteer Experience

Computer Capabilities/Computer Skills/Technical Expertise/Technical Proficiency

Affiliations/Membership/Organizations/Professional Associations

Languages

Military Service

Travel

Personal Information

What Do Others Say About You?

If you have performance evaluations, letters of recommendation, customer letters, or other written commendations that sing your praises, consider incorporating one or a few quotes from these sources into your resume. This kind of third-party endorsement is extremely powerful, adds credibility to your resume, and lets you "boast" about yourself by using the words of others.

Quotes can be inserted on your resume in a number of places with great effect:

- As part of your Skills Summary, add a quote as a separate item or in a box to one side.
- Quotes from professors can be placed under Education; quotes from employers can be placed under Work Experience.
- Quotes can be positioned in a narrow left or right column running the length of the page.
- A quote can be positioned as a final, powerful footnote at the end of the resume.

Write Your Extra Section(s)

List the unique points that make you special. Organize them into separate sections (with their own headings) or combine them under one umbrella heading. If you're using quotes, select one or a few that say the most relevant and positive things about you. Determine where on your resume you'll place them.

★ RECAP

The "extras" will make your resume more memorable, might hit on a helpful but not "required" job attribute, and at the very least can provide interesting material for an interview discussion.

STEP 9: Format, Edit, and Polish Your Draft

Now that you've finished drafting the material for your resume, it's time to wordsmith your draft copy, and then organize and format the material to create an attractive, easily skimmed document.

Use Formatting to Guide the Reader

Use formatting to guide readers through your document and focus attention where you want it. Create a "structural hierarchy"—similar to the outline format you would use when planning a research paper. Use indents, different type styles and enhancements, and different type sizes to create a consistent and logical flow for your resume, while drawing the reader's eye to the information you consider most important.

Here's a structural hierarchy you might use in your resume:

CATEGORY TITLE

Subhead

Paragraph Text

- Bullet Text

And here's how that hierarchy would look with text inserted into it:

WORK EXPERIENCE

Sales Associate: Tower Records, New Haven, CT   **5/04 to 6/05**

Filled custom orders and assisted retail customers of full-service music store. Managed store opening and closing in manager's absence.

- "Sales Associate of the Month" 6 of 13 months—top performer among 12 part-time sales staff.
- Trained all new employees in online research for custom orders.

Keep It Short

Avoid overly long paragraphs—dense text is hard to read and even harder to skim for essential information. To break up text-heavy sections, do the following:

- Write concisely.
- Divide a long paragraph into two or more paragraphs.
- List key points in short bullet-point statements.
- Use subheadings to grab attention and divide long lists into shorter, more manageable groupings.

Use Type Creatively Yet Appropriately

There are dozens of font choices available on most computers. Experiment to find one or two that you like and that contribute to the impact and readability of your resume. But don't go crazy with unusual or ornate fonts. A resume is a business document, and readability is key!

Here are some tips on choosing fonts:

- Both serif (with little decorative lines or "feet" attached to the edge of each letter, such as Times Roman) and sans serif (plain, clean fonts lacking decorative flourishes, such as Arial) fonts can be used effectively and can be highly readable.
- Consider using two different fonts, one for your name, headlines, and other material that needs to stand out, and the other for maximum readability in the text sections.
- Because Times Roman is the font most used in resumes and other business documents, you can make your resume stand out from the others simply by choosing a different typestyle.
- As a general rule, choose a text size between 10 and 12 points.

? **FAQ**

Can I use a resume template in Microsoft Word or another word-processing program? It would make formatting much easier.

The problem with resume templates is that they force you to fit your unique background into a rigid organizational structure. Thumb through the resume samples in chapters 5 through 10 and you'll see that there are countless ways to organize and present your qualifications. When drafting your material, it's more beneficial to do so without a template so that you are not confined to the template's categories and layout. Another point against templates is that they are widely used by do-it-yourself resume writers. The person reading your resume has probably seen dozens if not hundreds of resumes with the identical template format. Why not create something unique for yourself?

Write Using "Resume Language"

Resumes have a style all their own. Here are the most important points to keep in mind as you write:

- Write in the first person, but omit the subject (I).
- Use present tense for current activities, and past tense for past activities and achievements.
- For concise writing, omit articles (such as *a, an, the,* and *my*). Here are some examples:

> - [I] Completed [my] bachelor's degree in 3.5 years while working more than 20 hours weekly.
> - [I was] Elected president of [a] 60-member student organization and created [a] new program that boosted membership 20%.
> - [I] Cultivate cooperative, team-oriented relationships with [my] co-workers and managers.

- Summarize and trim to reduce wordiness and increase impact. For example, change this:

> While I was in college, I took a full course load of Honors-level courses while holding down a part-time job, volunteering 5 hours weekly, and actively participating in several organizations on campus.

To this:

> Combined intensive Honors curriculum with employment, regular volunteer work, and active participation in student organizations.

- Begin sentences with strong action verbs; avoid passive phrases such as "responsible for" or "duties included." For example:

> - Exceeded goals for speed and accuracy of data entered after just two days on the job.
> - Completed bachelor's degree in 3.5 years; earned 3.7 GPA.

- Write using parallel structure for consistency and comprehensibility. For instance, avoid listings like this:

> **SUMMARY OF QUALIFICATIONS**
> - Creative problem-solver
> - Work ethic
> - Earned CPA while still a senior in college
> - Strong analytical skills
> - Energetic, industrious, and ambitious

Instead, make the items parallel

SUMMARY OF QUALIFICATIONS (noun format)

- Creative problem-solving skills
- Work ethic
- CPA designation—earned while still a senior in college
- Strong analytical skills
- High energy, industriousness, and ambition

Or perhaps:

SUMMARY OF QUALIFICATIONS (verb format)

- Solve problems creatively.
- Work hard and industriously.
- Possess CPA (earned while still a senior in college).
- Demonstrate strong analytical skills.
- Display energy and drive in all endeavors.

Format, Edit, and Polish Your Draft

Take some time to edit your draft, and then organize and format your resume. Use the samples in this book for inspiration, if you like, or come up with something uniquely your own.

When you're done, proofread carefully! Errors in your resume are simply unacceptable. Don't rely totally on your computer spell-checker—it won't pick up common errors (for example, "advise" instead of "advice," "lead" instead of "led," and so on), nor will it check for consistency in your formatting and presentation. A careless error can cost you a job interview. Ask others to review your resume, too—friends, parents, career-center advisors, and professors. They might pick up errors or inconsistencies that you overlooked or important items you omitted.

The way you organize and present your resume material will have a big effect on readability and impact. Be consistent and clear, and make sure that the format helps readers understand and absorb your capabilities.

STEP 10: Cross-Check Your Evidence Against Core Job Qualifications

You've finished your resume...almost. Before you start circulating it, review your resume with a critical eye to be sure that it does the following:

- Clearly communicates skills and capabilities that match the core job qualifications.
- Uses accomplishments and results to add credibility.
- Makes it easy for readers by using a clear organizational structure and hierarchy.
- Draws attention to important facts and categories.
- Conveys employability—communicates that you have what it takes to be a good employee.
- Presents information that is meaningful to employers and shows that you understand business priorities (profitability, customer service, and other contributions to business success).

STEP 11: Proofread Your Final Resume

Take the time to proofread your resume one last time before sending it out. Don't let a careless error derail your job search.

Chapter 2 Checklist

You're ready to start your job search by reading chapter 3, "Managing Your Job Search—Online and Off," if you have completed these steps in writing your resume:

❑ Created a resume header that displays your name and all of your pertinent contact information for easy availability to hiring managers

❑ Written a skills summary or other introduction that clearly communicates your job target and emphasizes your strongest qualifications

❑ Created an Education section that tells readers the most important things about your recent educational experiences and credentials

❑ Developed a Work Experience section that is appropriate for your background and emphasizes your accomplishments and contributions, not just your job duties

❑ Edited, formatted, polished, and proofread your draft resume so that it creates a positive first impression

Managing Your Job Search—Online and Off

The Internet has revolutionized job search—hasn't it? After all, with thousands of jobs listed, and the chance to post your resume to sites that are scanned daily by recruiters and employers, isn't the whole thing much simpler than it used to be?

The answer is... yes and no.

Yes, it's simpler to distribute your resume than in the past. Yes, it's easier to make your credentials available to a wider selection of employers. And yes, the process of doing so is faster, easier, and much cheaper than traditional methods.

But in reality, only a small percentage of people find jobs through Internet postings, just as only a small proportion of job seekers find positions through recruiters or want ads. In fact, job search continues to operate most productively when candidates use the centuries-old tradition of personal networking.

But because an Internet job search is fast, inexpensive, and easy, you should go ahead and post your resume at top sites, read and respond to appropriate job listings, and visit company Web sites to learn what jobs are available. This chapter discusses how to do this efficiently and effectively (there are a few tricks to learn) and then delves into the all-important networking activity and how you can make it work for you.

STEP 12: Convert Your Resume for an Online Job Search

You can use the Internet to sift through job postings, apply for jobs, and make your resume available to recruiters and companies. There are thousands of resume-posting sites, job banks, and corporate Web sites with employment information. And you'll use e-mail extensively during your job search—it's a fast, convenient way to send your resume to employers or networking contacts.

Up to this point in this book, you've created a traditional resume—meant to be printed and read on paper. It can also be read onscreen, provided that the person you send it to has compatible word-processing software. But there are a few limitations to your traditional resume:

- It won't flow easily into an online resume bank or job application.
- Depending on format, it might not scan cleanly into a company's resume-scanning system.
- Formatting problems can also occur for any number of reasons when you e-mail your traditional resume.

Clearly, then, you'll need to adapt your resume for an online search. You will need a text (also known as ASCII) version, and you may need a scannable version, PDF version, and possibly a Web resume. Here's when you'll use each of the different resume formats:

- **When e-mailing:** Often you can send the *traditional* or *PDF* version of your resume as a file attachment, particularly if you're e-mailing to someone you know or someone you've already had a conversation with.

- **When a job posting specifies "no attachments":** In these cases, paste the *text* version of your resume into the body of your e-mail message. Put your cover letter first.

- **When filling in online applications or posting your resume to online resume banks:** Use the *text* version of your resume to be certain that there are no formatting glitches.

- **When you are snail-mailing or faxing your resume to a large company:** Send the *scannable* version of your resume. Most large and many smaller companies use scanning software to enter resumes into their applicant-tracking system. But you might never need a scannable resume. Their use has decreased dramatically as electronic transmission has increased, because the electronic version of your resume can be entered into the resume database without having to be physically scanned.

- **When an advertisement specifies "scannable" or gives other formatting details that make it clear they'll be scanning your document:** The ad might specify, "No bold or italics; minimum 12-point type; no rules, lines, or graphics." Send the *scannable* version of your resume.

- **If you're in a design field or have superior computer skills:** You could create a *PDF* version of your resume to be sure that the design and format do not get altered during transmission. And you might want to create a *Web* resume that you can store online as well as on a CD-ROM. You can include color, graphics, animation, and other advanced features. You might expand your resume into an online portfolio, which enables you to include samples of your design work, important projects, or other material to demonstrate your capabilities.

Convert Your Resume to Text Format

A text resume contains all of the content of your traditional resume but none of the formatting or graphics—no font variations, no bold or italic type, and no boxes or rules or bullets. It's text, pure and simple. A text resume is ugly but effective, in that any computer can read it without file-conversion issues or formatting problems that often occur with word-processing (Microsoft Word) files.

Here's how you can convert your resume to this useful version:

1. Using the "Save As" feature in your word processor, choose "Text Only" as the file format and rename your document.

2. Close the file, open the renamed version, and you'll see that an automatic conversion has taken place—your resume now appears in Courier font, with most of the formatting stripped out.

3. Review the resume to fix any odd formatting glitches. If you've used tables, columns, or other unusual formatting, take extra time to be sure that all the text is in the right place.

4. Add extra blank lines before key sections, if necessary, and use lines of the available "typewriter symbols" to create graphic separators. (Typewriter symbols include ~, !, @, #, $, %, ^, &, *, (,), <, >, and /.)

5. Don't worry about how long your resume is or whether it breaks oddly between pages. It's not intended to be printed; rather, you will paste it into online applications or enter it into a resume database.

Figure 3.1 is a resume in the traditional printed format. Figure 3.2 is the converted text version of the traditional resume in figure 3.1.

Gerald T. Clark
geraldclark@yahoo.com

School: 275-A Brentwood Road • Manhattan, KS 66506 • (785) 477-9345
Permanent: 909 Main Street • Reading, MA 01867 • (781) 942-0040

CAREER TARGET   **Human Resources/Employee Assistance Programs (EAP)**

SUMMARY OF QUALIFICATIONS

- **Education:** Earned advanced degree in Industrial and Organizational Psychology and Organizational Development; can diagnose and design remedies for organizational issues that affect productivity, employee retention and satisfaction, and bottom-line results.
- **Multicultural/international background:** From six-plus years living outside the U.S., appreciate diverse cultures and understand the challenges faced by relocating employees.
- **Communication skills:** Can build rapport with people at all levels of the organization, speak confidently before business and academic groups, and train and supervise employees.
- **Organization and leadership:** Can take ideas from concept to reality.
- **Adaptability:** Able to adapt quickly in new and changing business, social, and cultural environments.

EDUCATION

UNIVERSITY OF KANSAS, Manhattan, KS
Master of Science in Industrial/Organizational Psychology, 2005
Concentration: Organizational Development

- GPA 3.98/4.0 — Dean's List all quarters.
- Completed coursework in Organizational Development, Organizational Behavior, Counseling in the Work Environment, and Industrial/Organizational Psychology.
- Student Affiliate, Society for Industrial and Organizational Psychology (SIOP).
- Member, OD Network National Conference Committee: Worked with OD professionals to plan and manage 2004 national conference.

BOSTON UNIVERSITY, Boston, MA
Bachelor of Science in Psychology, 2003
Minor: Spanish

- GPA 3.27/4.0.

UNIVERSITAT DE BARCELONA, Barcelona, Spain
Semester Abroad, 1/02–5/02

- Attended college classes that emphasized European culture and heritage.
- Resided with a European family and traveled extensively throughout Europe.

WORK EXPERIENCE

Defrayed college expenses and gained problem-solving, decision-making, communication, and leadership skills through diverse customer service, training, and supervisory positions.

- **Security Guard,** CLUB MARDI GRAS, Manhattan, KS: 10/04–5/05
- **Crew Trainer and Supervisor,** WENDY'S, Manhattan, KS: 9/03–5/04
- **Ski Technician and Rental Clerk,** CANYONS SKI RESORT, Park City, UT: 11/02–3/03
- **Doorman/Crowd Control,** THE RATHSKELLAR, Boston, MA: 10/01–6/02
- **Doorman,** BOSTON UNIVERSITY CLUB PUB, Boston, MA: 1/01–6/01
- **Sales Associate,** RADIO SHACK, Peabody, MA: Summers 1998, 1999, 2000

ADDITIONAL INFORMATION

- Fluent in Spanish; conversationally proficient in Italian.
- Lived overseas from 1988–1994: Japan (grades 3–4), Peru (grades 5–7), and Canary Islands (grade 8).
- Proficient in using Microsoft Office, SPSS, SAS, and the Internet.
- Available for national or international relocation.

Figure 3.1: A traditional printed resume.

```
GERALD T. CLARK
geraldclark@yahoo.com

(785) 477-9345 (school)
(781) 942-0040 (permanent)


----------------------------------------
CAREER TARGET
Human Resources/Employee Assistance Programs (EAP)


----------------------------------------
SUMMARY OF QUALIFICATIONS
* Education: Earned advanced degree in Industrial and Organizational Psychology and
Organizational Development; can diagnose and design remedies for organizational
issues that affect productivity, employee retention and satisfaction, and bottom-
line results.
* Multicultural/international background: From six-plus years living outside the
U.S., appreciate diverse cultures and understand the challenges faced by relocating
employees.
* Communication skills: Can build rapport with people at all levels of the
organization, speak confidently before business and academic groups, and train and
supervise employees.
* Organization and leadership: Can take ideas from concept to reality.
* Adaptability: Able to adapt quickly in new and changing business, social, and
cultural environments.


----------------------------------------
EDUCATION
UNIVERSITY OF KANSAS, Manhattan, KS
Master of Science in Industrial/Organizational Psychology, 2005
Concentration: Organizational Development
* GPA 3.98/4.0 - Dean's List all quarters.
* Completed coursework in Organizational Development, Organizational Behavior,
Counseling in the Work Environment, and Industrial/Organizational Psychology.
* Student Affiliate, Society for Industrial and Organizational Psychology (SIOP).
* Member, OD Network National Conference Committee: Worked with OD professionals to
plan and manage 2001 national conference.

BOSTON UNIVERSITY, Boston, MA
Bachelor of Science in Psychology, 2002
Minor: Spanish
* GPA 3.27/4.0.

UNIVERSITAT DE BARCELONA, Barcelona, Spain
Semester Abroad, 1/01-5/01
* Attended college classes that emphasized European culture and heritage.
* Resided with a European family and traveled extensively throughout Europe.


----------------------------------------
WORK EXPERIENCE
Defrayed college expenses and gained problem-solving, decision-making,
communication, and leadership skills through diverse customer service, training, and
supervisory positions.
* Security Guard, CLUB MARDI GRAS, Manhattan, KS: 10/04-5/05
* Crew Trainer and Supervisor, WENDY'S, Manhattan, KS: 9/03-5/04
* Ski Technician and Rental Clerk, CANYONS SKI RESORT, Park City, UT: 11/02-3/03
* Doorman/Crowd Control, THE RATHSKELLAR, Boston, MA: 10/01-6/01
* Doorman, BOSTON UNIVERSITY CLUB PUB, Boston, MA: 1/01-6/01
* Sales Associate, RADIO SHACK, Peabody, MA: Summers 1998, 1999, 2000


----------------------------------------
ADDITIONAL INFORMATION
* Fluent in Spanish; conversationally proficient in Italian.
* Lived overseas from 1988-1994: Japan (grades 3-4), Peru (grades 5-7), and Canary
Islands (grade 8).
* Proficient in using Microsoft Office, SPSS, SAS, and the Internet.
* Available for national or international relocation.
```

Figure 3.2: The text version of the resume in figure 3.1.

Convert Your Resume to Scannable Format

A scannable resume is formatted so that electronic scanners can read it. It has minimal formatting (although it's not as stripped down as a text resume) to make it easier for the scanning software to read it.

To convert your resume to a scannable format, follow these steps:

1. Using the "Save As" feature in your word processor, save your resume under a different file name.
2. Select all of the text in the resume and assign a clean, common, non-condensed font such as Arial or Times New Roman. Make all body text 12 points; make headline text 14 points.
3. Make sure your name, and nothing but your name, appears on the first line of the resume. Put your address, phone number, e-mail address, and other bits of contact information each on its own line.
4. Remove any lines, boxes, graphics, or other non-text elements.
5. If your resume uses any funky characters as bullets, change them all to round, solid dots. Hollow shapes, stars, arrows, or other unusual shapes can't be read by the scanner.
6. Don't worry if your resume expands from one page to two, but do make sure that the page breaks appropriately. Create a header with your name, phone number, and e-mail address at the top of page 2.

Figure 3.3 is the converted scannable version of the traditional resume in figure 3.1.

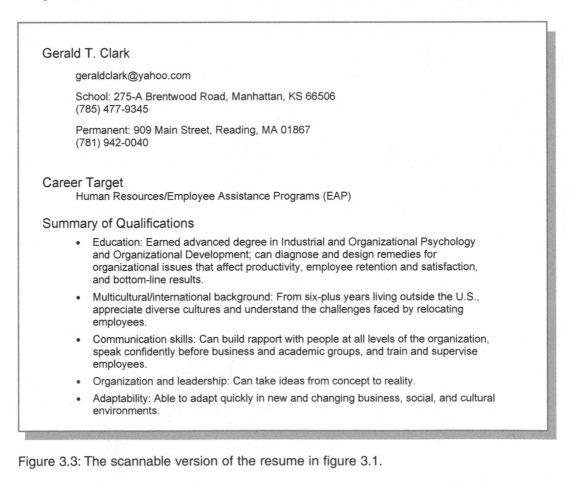

Figure 3.3: The scannable version of the resume in figure 3.1.

Gerald T. Clark

Page 2   geraldclark@yahoo.com
                                                    (785) 477-9345
                                                    (781) 942-0040

Education

UNIVERSITY OF KANSAS, Manhattan, KS
Master of Science in Industrial/Organizational Psychology, 2005
Concentration: Organizational Development

- GPA 3.98/4.0 — Dean's List all quarters.
- Completed coursework in Organizational Development, Organizational Behavior, Counseling in the Work Environment, and Industrial/Organizational Psychology.
- Student Affiliate, Society for Industrial and Organizational Psychology (SIOP).
- Member, OD Network National Conference Committee: Worked with OD professionals to plan and manage 2001 national conference.

BOSTON UNIVERSITY, Boston, MA
Bachelor of Science in Psychology, 2002
Minor: Spanish

- GPA 3.27/4.0.

UNIVERSITAT DE BARCELONA, Barcelona, Spain
Semester Abroad, 1/01–5/01

- Attended college classes that emphasized European culture and heritage.
- Resided with a European family and traveled extensively throughout Europe.

Work Experience

Defrayed college expenses and gained problem-solving, decision-making, communication, and leadership skills through diverse customer service, training, and supervisory positions.

- Security Guard, CLUB MARDI GRAS, Manhattan, KS: 10/04–5/05
- Crew Trainer and Supervisor, WENDY'S, Manhattan, KS: 9/03–5/04
- Ski Technician and Rental Clerk, CANYONS SKI RESORT, Park City, UT: 11/02–3/03
- Doorman/Crowd Control, THE RATHSKELLAR, Boston, MA: 10/01–6/02
- Doorman, BOSTON UNIVERSITY CLUB PUB, Boston, MA: 1/00–6/00
- Sales Associate, RADIO SHACK, Peabody, MA: Summers 1998, 1999, 2000

Additional Information

- Fluent in Spanish; conversationally proficient in Italian.
- Lived overseas from 1988–1994: Japan (grades 3–4), Peru (grades 5–7), and Canary Islands (grade 8).
- Proficient in using Microsoft Office, SPSS, SAS, and the Internet.
- Available for national or international relocation.

Convert Your Resume to PDF Format

A PDF (Portable Document Format) file is practical and easy to create, and will ensure the integrity of your resume design. However, be aware that the PDF format is not readable by most resume-scanning software unless the employer goes to the trouble of physically scanning the PDF file printout. So I recommend that you use this file format only when design is of paramount importance. Along with the PDF, consider sending the text format so that the employer can quickly and easily scan your document and enter it into a resume-tracking system.

Follow these guidelines for creating the PDF version of your resume.

1. PDF files are created using Adobe Acrobat (the full version, not just the Acrobat Reader). If you have this software on your computer, you can use it to create your PDF file.
2. If you don't own Adobe Acrobat, you can easily find a free online service that will convert your Word file to PDF and e-mail the finished version back to you. One that I like is www.gobcl.com. It's fast, easy, and intuitive.

? FAQ

What are keywords and what do they have to do with my resume?

Keywords are exactly what they sound like—important words that relate to your job target. Keywords are the words that a recruiter uses to search online resume banks for good candidates, or the words an employer enters into its applicant-tracking system when looking to fill a position. There is no defined set of keywords for any given position, but it makes sense to include many possible keywords in your resume to maximize your chances of being found in an online search.

Because you've taken the time to match your abilities to the requirements of your target jobs, your resume probably contains just the right keywords. To make sure, go back and review relevant job postings and observe which terms come up over and over, and then make sure that exact terminology appears in your resume. It's not necessary to create a separate section for keywords; you can simply include the words as part of the text of your resume.

Post Your Resume on the Internet

Once your resume is in text format, you can post it to both popular and specialty Web sites where employers go to look for candidates. There are literally thousands of career sites on the Internet, and no matter how specialized your field or narrow your interests, you can probably find a site to meet your needs.

Each site has its own protocol for posting resumes, so just follow the directions on the site. In most cases you'll fill in a few text boxes and then paste your text resume in its entirety into the spot indicated. If asked to provide "keywords," pick out the words and phrases from your resume that exactly match the job descriptions you've been looking at; this will increase the chances of having your resume selected for review.

But a word of caution… simply posting your resume will not guarantee interviews or a job. The respected career site 6figurejobs.com estimates that there are more than *30 million resumes online!* You can certainly add yours to the throng, but it's absolutely essential that you supplement your posting with other job search efforts—such as direct application to companies, response to print and online ads, and active networking to find out about unadvertised jobs or gain an advantage through a personal referral.

To get you started, here are posting sites appropriate for many new grads. You're sure to find dozens more as you negotiate the world of online job searching.

■ **www.monster.com:** This "monster" of a site is one of the oldest and best on the Internet. You can post your resume, search more than one million jobs, research salaries, and read a host of articles on career management.

- **www.monstertrak.monster.com:** This specialty site from the Monster.com company is designed to help college students and alumni find jobs and internships. To use the site, you must be a student or graduate of one of its many participating colleges.

- **www.wetfeet.com:** In addition to resume posting, this site offers information on careers, industries, and specific companies; it also includes a "find an internship" feature.

- **www.collegegrad.com:** Billed as "The #1 Entry-Level Job Site," collegegrad.com is designed specifically for people about to enter the professional workforce.

- **www.campuscareercenter.com:** Join up at this free site and you can apply for jobs, get information on companies, and get job-interview and resume-writing tips.

- **http://college.wsj.com:** This service of the *Wall Street Journal* (which also runs the very successful www.careerjournal.com site) provides comprehensive resources for new-grad job seekers.

- **www.collegerecruiter.com:** CollegeRecruiter.com bills itself as "the highest-traffic, non-password-protected job site used by students, recent graduates, and the employers who want to hire them." Internship listings are included.

- **www.tenstepsforstudents.org:** This is an extremely helpful site for students and new graduates who are considering careers with the federal government.

- **www.careerfair.com:** As we go to press, this resource for campus career fairs is merging with www.hcbu-careers.net, a career site for historically black colleges and universities; you should be able to find the list of career fairs on either of these sites.

- **http://hotjobs.yahoo.com:** Another massive, all-purpose site, Yahoo! HotJobs is a favorite of students.

- **www.thejobresource.com:** The focus of this site is "after college," and it bills itself as "the largest career network specializing in recruiting at the college level."

★ RECAP

You can use the power of the Internet to make some aspects of your job search faster and easier, but don't rely solely on an online career search.

STEP 13: Make Networking Work for You

With the ease of online search strategies, a lot of job seekers reach no further than their computers when starting to look for jobs. Don't make this mistake! Instead, spend most of your time talking to people you know who can give you advice, suggestions, leads, and referrals that will bring you to the notice of people who can hire you.

There's nothing mysterious or frightening about networking. What it means, quite simply, is talking to people. One contact often leads to another, and in this way your web of contacts grows and your visibility expands tremendously beyond your own inner circle.

There are several keys to successful networking:

- **Don't ask for a job.** Most people you talk with will not be able to give you a job, and they'll feel badly if they can't help you. Instead, ask for their advice or suggestions. Tell them you respect their expertise and would appreciate their advice and assistance. And don't worry—if they're looking for someone with your skills, they'll be sure to let you know.

- **Don't assume anyone won't be able to help.** You never know how people are connected, so make a point to mention your job search to everyone you know and everyone you meet. It's surprising how often a casual comment will lead to a solid job lead.

■ **Prepare and practice your introduction.** So that you can approach each phone call or meeting with a feeling of confidence, prepare a 30-second to one-minute introduction that tells your contacts who you are (if they don't already know), why you're contacting them, and what specifically they can do for you. Here are three examples:

"Mr. Smith, this is Patti Dillon. You might remember meeting me at my parents' New Year's Day brunch, when we talked about the advertising business. Well, I'm about to graduate from Wilberforce University with a degree in media communications and I'm looking for my first professional job. Would you have a few minutes to share with me? I'd love to get your advice on my resume and your ideas for people I should contact in the media, advertising, or PR who might know of potential job openings for someone with my qualifications."

"Hello, Ms. Andrews, this is Paul Gonzalez. Sheila Wilkins in the career center at Northeastern gave me your name and said you might be willing to talk with me. I'm just finishing up my degree in physical therapy, and since you've been in the field for a few years, I hope you might be willing to help me pinpoint my career direction. Specifically, I'd love to know more about the differences between hospital-based and outpatient PT from the therapist's viewpoint."

"Sally, this is Rita Hanscomb. I wanted you to know that I took the advice you gave me years ago—I finally went back to school and finished my degree. It's in accounting, and I'm excited about looking for a new job with this new credential. I'm looking for an opportunity with a company that will also value my years of retail sales experience, and I thought you could give me some suggestions. You seem to know everybody in the financial world in Sioux City! Can we get together for a cup of coffee next week?"

■ **Try to set up an in-person meeting, whenever possible.** A personal meeting is more formal, usually lengthier, and more memorable than a phone conversation. If meeting in person is out of the question (your contact is in Detroit and you're in Mobile), set up a time for a formal phone meeting. In either case, e-mail your resume prior to the meeting and reiterate how you think your contact can help you. (Be specific.) Always be on time for your meetings. Dress appropriately in business attire for an in-person meeting.

■ **Don't expect your contacts to run your job search for you.** Your job search might be *your* number-one priority, but it's not that high on the list for most of the people you talk with. Keep the ball in your court and follow up regularly with people you've contacted.

■ **Be clear about your job target and how your contacts can help you.** Asking a contact to "help you find a job" doesn't give them much information to go on. Instead, tell them you're interested in Megacorporation and ask whether they know someone there. Tell them you're thinking about a career in marketing—do they have any suggestions, or can they refer you to someone in that field? Make it easy for them to help you and they'll be delighted to do so.

■ **Follow up on all leads and let your contacts know how helpful they've been.** If your contact gives you a referral, be appreciative, follow up, and then get back to your original contact to let them know how it went. When you've landed your job, send thank-you notes to everyone who helped you in your search. And once you're employed, be ready to help others when you can!

★ RECAP

Networking is a powerful tool in your career-management toolkit. Don't be afraid to ask people for help, but be clear and specific about just what they can do. Don't make the mistake of asking for a job or expecting your contacts to manage your job search. Keep your network alive throughout your working life—you'll benefit immensely.

Chapter 3 Checklist

You're ready to move on to cover letters in chapter 4, "Writing Effective Job Search Letters," if you have mastered these important concepts in chapter 3:

❑ Converted your resume to text format for electronic applications

❑ Carefully reviewed the information on networking and are ready to include this tactic as a critical element of your job search

Writing Effective Job Search Letters

During your job search, you'll be writing lots of letters:

- Cover letters to potential employers when you send your resume for consideration
- Letters to network contacts and the referrals that arise from those contacts
- Thank-you letters as follow-up to networking meetings and interviews
- E-mail letters that might encompass all of the above purposes but often call for a more direct and concise writing style

In this chapter, you'll learn how to quickly and easily write targeted letters to help you find job openings, get interviews, and land the job.

Cover Letters

Cover letters—letters that accompany or "cover" your resume each time you send it out—are essential partners to your resume. Because they can be customized for each person to whom you write, they give you the opportunity to highlight the information that is most relevant for that particular audience. But hiring managers may not read cover letters thoroughly (or at all), so don't count on your cover letter to communicate essential information that's not in your resume. Instead, think of your cover letter as an opportunity to sell yourself in a different way than your resume does.

It's helpful to think of your cover letter as having three parts: a beginning (A), a middle (B), and an end (C). The following sections discuss these cover letter parts in detail.

A: Attention!

Use your opening paragraph to tell readers why you are contacting them. Try to use interesting language to capture attention and make the reader want to know more about you.

Here's an example showing the attention-getting introduction of a letter written to the manager of a retail store where this candidate hopes to become assistant manager:

Mark Strong, Manager
Bethpage Books
255 Seaview Street
Bethpage, NY 11714

Dear Mr. Strong:

If you are looking for a hardworking, dedicated, literate assistant manager, please consider me!

B: Because...

The middle section of your cover letter should answer the question "Why should I hire you?" by communicating your key qualifications for the job you're seeking. You can convey this information in one or two short paragraphs or in three or four bullet-point statements. Be careful not to copy phrases or achievements word-for-word from your resume. Instead, write a summary statement about related achievements or tell a brief story that illustrates your strengths.

Language and Tone

When writing your job search letters, use a natural tone and simple writing style. Avoid stilted, outdated phrases like "per your request" and "enclosed please find." Of course, because these are business letters, they should sound more formal than a quick note or e-mail you'd send to a friend, and they must be absolutely correct in grammar, spelling, and punctuation.

And keep in mind, employers are interested in people who really want to work at their company. Don't be afraid to show interest and enthusiasm about starting your career. These are among the most positive qualities you bring to the workplace.

Here's the middle section of the letter introduced previously:

My education, work history, and personal activities all point to a successful career in retail management—specifically in the book business. I have recently completed my Bachelor of Business Administration (concentration in Marketing) from Hofstra University, and for five years I have worked part-time as a retail sales associate. This experience led to my decision to pursue a career in retail management. I understand retail sales concepts, merchandising, and general business management. Most of all, I am a true book lover and would be able to communicate my knowledge and enthusiasm to your customers.

C: Close

Neatly wrap up your letter with a polite yet assertive closing that asks for an interview; here's an example:

Thank you for your consideration. I am enthusiastic about working at Bethpage Books and will call within a few days to see if we can schedule an appointment to meet.

Sincerely,

When writing your letters, keep in mind the employer's concerns (what you can do for them) and don't overstate your own needs and interests.

Sample Cover Letter

Figure 4.1 is a sample cover letter that demonstrates a good "ABC" format and clearly communicates key selling points. Written by a student seeking a co-op job, the letter is a follow-up to a phone conversation. Note the three "selling points" in the middle section of the resume: a strong academic record, personal attributes shown in prior jobs and volunteer positions, and finally, a hard-to-quantify but very important interest in children that is essential for people who work with sick children.

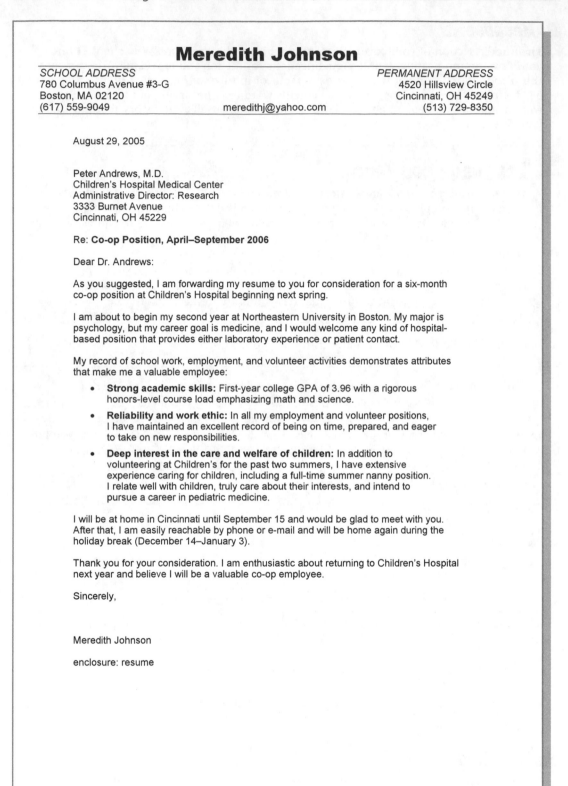

Meredith Johnson

SCHOOL ADDRESS
780 Columbus Avenue #3-G
Boston, MA 02120
(617) 559-9049

meredithj@yahoo.com

PERMANENT ADDRESS
4520 Hillsview Circle
Cincinnati, OH 45249
(513) 729-8350

August 29, 2005

Peter Andrews, M.D.
Children's Hospital Medical Center
Administrative Director: Research
3333 Burnet Avenue
Cincinnati, OH 45229

Re: **Co-op Position, April–September 2006**

Dear Dr. Andrews:

As you suggested, I am forwarding my resume to you for consideration for a six-month co-op position at Children's Hospital beginning next spring.

I am about to begin my second year at Northeastern University in Boston. My major is psychology, but my career goal is medicine, and I would welcome any kind of hospital-based position that provides either laboratory experience or patient contact.

My record of school work, employment, and volunteer activities demonstrates attributes that make me a valuable employee:

- **Strong academic skills:** First-year college GPA of 3.96 with a rigorous honors-level course load emphasizing math and science.

- **Reliability and work ethic:** In all my employment and volunteer positions, I have maintained an excellent record of being on time, prepared, and eager to take on new responsibilities.

- **Deep interest in the care and welfare of children:** In addition to volunteering at Children's for the past two summers, I have extensive experience caring for children, including a full-time summer nanny position. I relate well with children, truly care about their interests, and intend to pursue a career in pediatric medicine.

I will be at home in Cincinnati until September 15 and would be glad to meet with you. After that, I am easily reachable by phone or e-mail and will be home again during the holiday break (December 14–January 3).

Thank you for your consideration. I am enthusiastic about returning to Children's Hospital next year and believe I will be a valuable co-op employee.

Sincerely,

Meredith Johnson

enclosure: resume

Figure 4.1: A sample cover letter.

E-mail Cover Letters

Cover letters that you send by e-mail should be a bit shorter and crisper than mailed letters. An ideal e-mail cover letter is short enough that it is 100 percent visible in the browser window of most e-mail programs.

When e-mailing in response to a job ad or posting, follow these steps:

1. Type your cover letter into the e-mail message area.

2. Copy your text resume from the word-processing file and paste it below the cover letter.

3. Run your e-mail program's spell checker. If your e-mail program does not have a spell-checker, spell check and proofread your resume in the word-processing program before pasting it into the e-mail window. Cover letters (even e-mail cover letters) must be just as perfect as your resume—with no typos, grammatical errors, or careless mistakes.

4. Include a formatted (Microsoft Word) resume as an attachment (unless the ad you're responding to specifies "no attachments"; in that case, simply send the text version without the attachment).

5. Write a descriptive subject line for your e-mail message. To fit many keywords into the subject line, you might want to abbreviate. Here are a few examples of descriptive subject lines:

   PR Assoc (Job #A-924) - BA Northwestern, NBC internship, strong writing skills

   Med Rsrch Co-op - UCLA Bio major, hosp. exp., great work ethic

   App Developer - Visual Basic, C++, database - recent training - team player

   MSW – strong assessment & counseling skills – program mgmt exp

Figure 4.2 is a sample of an e-mail cover letter. Note that it is shorter than the previous sample letters—it gets right to the point and quickly communicates key information.

Subject: Marketing candidate – creative & focused – BSBA

Dear Mr. Andrews:

Are you looking for an enthusiastic, hardworking person for your marketing team?

As a marketing major (graduating with a BSBA in May), I gained a thorough understanding of the concepts of effective marketing, advertising, and merchandising. My activities during college expanded on my classroom learning--I had the chance to take leadership roles that demonstrated my ability to "get things done" while working effectively with both students and administrators.

I have identified your company, its products, and its culture as a good match for my qualifications and interests.

Can we schedule a time to explore your needs and my qualifications? My background, professionalism, and enthusiasm will make me an effective member of your team.

Sincerely,

Tyler Van Aark

Figure 4.2: An e-mail cover letter.

Networking Letters

Networking letters are written to people you know or people you have been referred to. You might be contacting these people about a specific job or simply to ask for their help with your job search.

Most people—as many as 64 percent, according to a 2002 *New York Times* survey—find jobs through someone they know, not through the Internet or print advertisements; these sources, combined, accounted for only about 15 percent of jobs found, according to the survey.

Your network—your friends and relatives, your parents' friends, your friends' parents, and anyone else you can get connected to through anyone you know—is a powerful source of job information, and you should dedicate most of your time during your job search to reaching out to these people. Networking letters are easy to write because you already know the person or have been referred to them, so it's not a "cold call." In general, the tone is more informal and less "hard sell" than other types of cover letters.

Figure 4.3 is an example of a networking contact letter. The writer of this letter doesn't know the person he's writing to, but because he has been referred by a mutual friend, he can assume his letter will get a positive response. You can assume this, too, when you're writing to someone you know or someone you've been referred to.

Subject: Referred to you by Joe Sanders

Dear Ms. Rolfson:

Joe Sanders at All-Sports Marketing suggested that I contact you about my job search.

I am about to graduate from Ohio State with a BS in Athletic Training. When a knee injury ended my competitive baseball career two years ago, I found athletic training to be a good fit for my abilities and my interest in helping athletes achieve top performance.

I was fortunate to land an internship at All-Sports Marketing last year. I couldn't have asked for a better experience! Mr. Sanders offered me a full-time job upon graduation, but I've decided to pursue training rather than marketing, and Mr. Sanders thought your connection with Dr. Samuels and the rest of the Pirates' training team could be helpful to me.

Would you be willing to spend a few minutes giving me your advice and suggestions? I would greatly appreciate it. I'll be in Pittsburgh the first week in April and can meet with you anytime that week, whatever is most convenient for you.

Sincerely,

David McChesney

****
For your convenience, I am including my resume both in text version (below) and as an attached MS Word file.

Figure 4.3: A networking contact letter.

Thank-You Letters

It's common courtesy to thank people who have helped you, so be sure you send a thank-you letter to each networking contact who shares time, advice, or contact names with you. After an interview, use a thank-you letter to reinforce your candidacy, reiterate key points, and make a positive impression on the interviewer. Many job candidates don't take the time to write thank-you letters, so just by doing so you'll give yourself a competitive advantage.

You can send thank-you letters by e-mail as an immediate follow-up, but they make a stronger impression when you send them by postal mail. Don't try to hand-write your thank-you letters unless they are very short (one or two sentences) and you have exceptionally clear handwriting. Instead, use your word processor and compose a neat letter with information that will keep on "selling" you even when you're no longer in front of the interviewer.

Figure 4.4 is a follow-up letter to a networking contact who provided helpful advice and referrals. It demonstrates some "golden rules" of networking. Note that Dale has followed up on referrals that were provided. And, at the end, he offers to be a networking resource for Dr. Grandin's niece.

Dale Okenga, MD

Telephone	781-523-0909
Pager	617-990-4389
Email	dokenga@att.net
Residence	7 Willow Drive
	Winchester, MA 01890

May 27, 2006

Allison Grandin, MD
North Shore Family Practice
275 Edgeware Street
Lynn, MA 01905

Dear Dr. Grandin:

Thank you so much for the advice, suggestions, and referrals you gave me during our meeting on Tuesday. Your perspective is invaluable!

I have followed up with Dr. Collins and will be meeting with her next week. She seemed to be very interested in my Childhood Asthma research study, and I plan to share a copy of my report with her. I have left messages with Dr. Cox and Dr. Saburn, and I'll keep you informed of the results of those calls.

It is exciting to be exploring a permanent practice position after so many years of residency and medical school! Your insights into the benefits and challenges of family practice were extremely helpful. Please be sure to let me know if there is anything that I can do for you (you mentioned your niece, who is considering applying to Tufts... I'd be glad to talk with her about my experiences there).

Again, thank you, and I'll keep in touch.

Best regards,

Dale Okenga

Figure 4.4: A follow-up letter to a networking contact.

Figure 4.5 was written as a follow-up to an interview. It recaps key qualifications and expresses enthusiasm about joining the company. Notice how a timetable for response is set up in the last paragraph. If this candidate doesn't hear back by the time stated, he should give Mr. Lin a call.

EDWARD J. NILSSON III

ejIII@tampabay.rr.com
257 West Shell Court, Bradenton, FL 34201
941-459-3890 Home — 941-709-3490 Mobile

July 27, 2006

Rick Lin
Engineering Manager
Suncoast Systems, Inc.
4527 Monument Street
Bradenton, FL 34201

Dear Mr. Lin:

Thank you for taking so much time on Friday to tell me about the engineering opportunities at Suncoast Systems.

I am excited about working on your leading-edge power systems and believe that my engineering education and co-op experiences have prepared me well to be a productive member of your company.

As we discussed during our meeting, I made significant contributions to several key projects at Simco Systems and Apex Environmental. After a brief orientation, I quickly became a contributing member of the design team and enjoyed adding my abilities to the group projects, while continuously learning from the senior engineers.

I am committed to working hard, working smart, and doing my best in every endeavor, and I would like to help Suncoast Systems become even more successful.

You mentioned that you would get back to me next week about the next step in the interviewing process. I look forward to hearing from you.

Sincerely,

Edward J. Nilsson III

★ RECAP

All of your job search communications should carry the same message as your resume: that you are a skilled, qualified, employable person with lots to offer. Don't be afraid to show the enthusiasm you feel about launching your professional career.

Chapter 4 Checklist

You're ready to launch your job search in earnest if you have completed these essential activities from chapter 4:

❑ Reviewed the "A-B-C" sections of a cover letter and drafted some letters for your job search

❑ Learned the differences between mailed and e-mailed cover letters

❑ Learned what makes an effective thank-you letter and are prepared to write your own letters immediately after any interview or networking meeting

PART 2

Sample Resumes for College Graduates and Students

Resumes for Associate Degree Graduates

Resume Number	Degree	Job Target
1	AA, Recording Techniques	Advanced degree
2	AS, Paralegal Studies	Paralegal
3	AA, Paralegal Studies	Office assistant
4	Associate of Applied Science/ Police Academy Certification	Police officer
5	AS, Nursing	Critical-care nursing position with a major hospital
6	Associate of Applied Science	Occupational therapist assistant
7	Certificate in Dental Hygiene	Dental hygienist
8	AAS, Equine Training and Management	Equine trainer
9	AAS, Hospitality Management	Hotel management position
10	Certificate in Computer Systems Technology	Computer systems technician/field service technician/help desk technician

1

Degree: AA, Recording Techniques.

Target: To pursue an advanced degree.

Strategy: Created an artistic resume that focuses on competencies gained through academic achievement rather than through hands-on professional experience. The resume focuses on two major course projects, emphasizes equipment and gear proficiencies, and includes unrelated work experience to communicate the ability to handle responsibility.

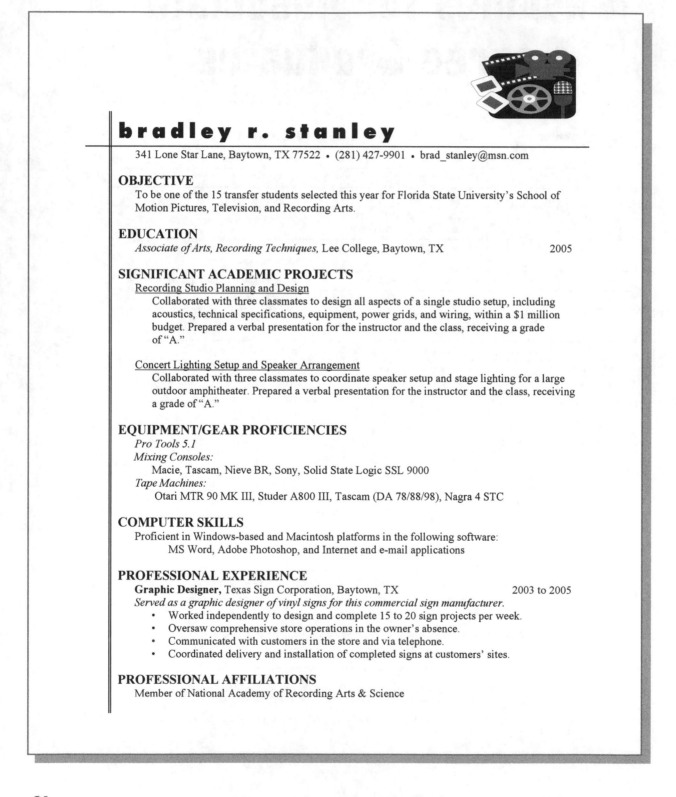

bradley r. stanley

341 Lone Star Lane, Baytown, TX 77522 • (281) 427-9901 • brad_stanley@msn.com

OBJECTIVE

To be one of the 15 transfer students selected this year for Florida State University's School of Motion Pictures, Television, and Recording Arts.

EDUCATION

Associate of Arts, Recording Techniques, Lee College, Baytown, TX   2005

SIGNIFICANT ACADEMIC PROJECTS

Recording Studio Planning and Design

Collaborated with three classmates to design all aspects of a single studio setup, including acoustics, technical specifications, equipment, power grids, and wiring, within a $1 million budget. Prepared a verbal presentation for the instructor and the class, receiving a grade of "A."

Concert Lighting Setup and Speaker Arrangement

Collaborated with three classmates to coordinate speaker setup and stage lighting for a large outdoor amphitheater. Prepared a verbal presentation for the instructor and the class, receiving a grade of "A."

EQUIPMENT/GEAR PROFICIENCIES

Pro Tools 5.1

Mixing Consoles:

Macie, Tascam, Nieve BR, Sony, Solid State Logic SSL 9000

Tape Machines:

Otari MTR 90 MK III, Studer A800 III, Tascam (DA 78/88/98), Nagra 4 STC

COMPUTER SKILLS

Proficient in Windows-based and Macintosh platforms in the following software:

MS Word, Adobe Photoshop, and Internet and e-mail applications

PROFESSIONAL EXPERIENCE

Graphic Designer, Texas Sign Corporation, Baytown, TX   2003 to 2005

Served as a graphic designer of vinyl signs for this commercial sign manufacturer.

- Worked independently to design and complete 15 to 20 sign projects per week.
- Oversaw comprehensive store operations in the owner's absence.
- Communicated with customers in the store and via telephone.
- Coordinated delivery and installation of completed signs at customers' sites.

PROFESSIONAL AFFILIATIONS

Member of National Academy of Recording Arts & Science

2

Degree: AS, Paralegal Studies.
Job Target: Paralegal for SC Bar Association.
Strategy: Positioned this job seeker as "candidate of choice" by highlighting internship experience and *magna cum laude* distinction at graduation.

Lydia C. Hendricks

65 Thorn Hill Court
Greenville, South Carolina 29607
Mobile (828) 516-4548 ▪ Residence (828) 236-9925 ▪ Email lydiac@earthlink.net

PARALEGAL / LEGAL SECRETARY

Dedicated to providing superior, uninterrupted administrative support to legal and non-legal staff.

Confident, articulate, and results-oriented legal-support professional offering a strong foundation of education and experience. Creative and enthusiastic with proven record of success in prioritizing and processing heavy workflow without supervision. Superior organization and communication skills; committed to personal and professional growth. Looking to join an established team that rewards hard work and personal achievement with stability and the opportunity for increased responsibility.

IMMEDIATE VALUES OFFERED

- Highly proficient in word processing, data entry, and Dictaphone transcription using Microsoft application software; noticed for maintaining consistently superior levels of accuracy.
- Organized, efficient, and thorough; maintain flexibility in changing work assignments.
- Perform well under stress, taking pressure off superiors and peers.
- Proficient in the planning and execution of projects in time-critical environments.
- Dependable and successful problem-resolution and time-management solutions.
- Creative and cooperative, working equally well individually or as part of a team.
- Outstanding record of performance, reliability, confidentiality, and ethical business standards.
- Computer skills include Microsoft Word 97/2000 and Windows 95/98, and WordPerfect; familiarity with Microsoft Excel, PowerPoint, and Access. Typing rate approximately 80 WPM.

LEGAL EXPERIENCE

Criminal / Civil	Powers of Attorney	Complaints
Domestic Relations	Divorce	Exhibits / Witness Lists
Affidavits	Adoption	QDRO
Subpoenas	Probate	Personal Injury
Motions	Wills	Client Interviewing
Orders	Estates	Real Estate
Research	Worker's Compensation	Mortgages / Deeds

SUMMER INTERNSHIP EXPERIENCE

Paralegal, **Tranter & Tranter, Attorneys and Counselors At Law** Greenville, SC 2004
(Temporary Replacement) Legal Secretary, **Elmer George, Attorney At Law** Spartanburg, SC 2003–04

EDUCATION AND SPECIAL CERTIFICATIONS

Associate of Science Degree, Paralegal Studies — Sullivan College, Greenville, SC
Magna Cum Laude Distinction
Dean's List
Degree Awarded 6/2005

Attended South Carolina Business College, 19 credit hours accumulated, Legal Writing
Attended Hutchinson Community College, 24 credit hours accumulated, Criminal Justice

Commissioned Notary Public, South Carolina State-at-Large — Status, current

---

3

Degree: AA, Paralegal Studies.
Job Target: Office assistant.
Strategy: Described job activities in some detail because they relate to current job targets. Included an extensive summary detailing both hard skills and personal qualities.

JIM DELANO

845 South Lake
Anaheim, CA 92804

jimdelano@yahoo.com
714-699-4587

EXPERIENCED OFFICE ASSISTANT

PROFILE

Resourceful and dedicated paralegal student offering a combination of education and business support skills and experience. Enthusiastic, efficient, and effective. Proven ability to build and manage relationships with customers, team members, peers, and co-workers. Professional and committed to professional growth.

- Experienced working in fast-paced, deadline-oriented environments
- Proficient in MS Word, Excel, Access, and PowerPoint; WordPerfect; Time Slips; HotDoc
- Accurate keyboarding (65 wpm)
- Adept at handling multiple telephone lines, filing, and performing Internet research
- Tactful, patient, and courteous
- Calm demeanor under stress, yielding a productive, team-oriented environment

EMPLOYMENT HISTORY

Customer Service Representative
Sunshine Instrument Corporation, Buena Park, CA   2003 to Present

Sunshine is a world leader in the design and manufacture of ham, shortwave, and CB radio instruments and accessories.

- Promoted from data entry to customer service rep after only six weeks.
- Act as point of contact for, and respond to, all telephone, e-mailed, and faxed inquiries.
- Serve as direct liaison for customers visiting the Anaheim facility to ensure prompt, courteous, and effective attention to their needs.
- Handle multi-line telephone system.
- Perform other administrative activities as needed, including photocopying, burning software CDs, and filing.

Customer Service Clerk   (part-time)
Kmart, Irvine, CA   2002 to 2006

EDUCATION, HONORS, AND ACHIEVEMENTS

- **Candidate for AA in Paralegal Studies**   2006
  Orange Coast College, Costa Mesa, CA (evening studies)
  4.0 GPA
- Eagle Scout, Boy Scouts of America
- High School Honor Roll and Citizenship Awards

Degree: AAS and Police Academy Certification.

Job Target: Police officer.

Strategy: Focused on related experience as student, intern, and hunting dog trainer. Showed that because he was so interested in being in law enforcement, what he lacked in experience he'd make up for in commitment.

Alex L. McCarthy

9341 Prospect St.   248-555-9240
Romeo, Michigan 48065   alexmcc@hotmail.com

PROFILE
- ◆ Long-standing interest and desire to succeed in law enforcement.
- ◆ Highly self-motivated and eager to meet new challenges; ability to learn quickly.
- ◆ Well developed verbal skills enabling positive communication with diverse populations.

EDUCATION
Southeastern Police Academy—Washtenaw Community College • Ypsilanti, Michigan
Graduate   August 2005

Delta College • University Center, Michigan
Associate Degree in Applied Science   April 2005
- • Earned baseball scholarship.

TRAINING AND CERTIFICATIONS
- ◆ American Red Cross First Aid and CPR
- ◆ Portable breath test (PBT)
- ◆ Pepper gas (OCAT)
- ◆ Chauffeur's license

RELEVANT EXPERIENCE
Village of Otisville Police Department • Otisville, Michigan
Police Officer   2005–Present
- • Perform duties of sworn police officer.

Ingham County Sheriff's Department • Lansing, Michigan
Student Intern   2004
- • Completed five-month internship gaining exposure to patrol, paramedic, detective, and court divisions.
- • Selected from ten students to assist major with special project involving data entry into spreadsheet for budget development.

Michigan State Police Academy • Lansing, Michigan
Student Recruit   1999
- • Received scholarship to attend special academy session for interested students.
- • Completed training designed to challenge participants physically and mentally.

EMPLOYMENT HISTORY
Coca-Cola Bottling Plant • Brighton, Michigan   *Seasonal*
Delivery Driver   2002–2003
- • Delivered beverage products to five-county area, collecting and securing COD payments.
- • Conducted pre- and post-trip inspections of vehicle.

Davison Community Schools • Davison, Michigan   *Seasonal*
Assistant Varsity Football Coach   2002
- • Assisted with training of football team.
- • Acted as liaison between students and coach.

Wildwood Hunt Club • Gaines, Michigan   *Seasonal*
Assistant Dog Trainer/Hunt Guide   2000–2002
- • Collaborated with others to train puppies and adult dogs; conducted daily drills.
- • Performed daily grooming, feeding, and related activities.

References available on request

Degree: AS, Nursing.

Job Target: Critical-care nursing position with a major hospital.

Strategy: Highlighted extensive health-care experience (as a medical assistant, CNA, and EMT) that adds value to recently completed nursing degree. Emphasized work ethic (working full-time while going to school full-time).

Ann-Margaret O'Leary

2479 Oceanview Terrace, Miami, FL 33132   (305) 491-1010 • ann-margaret@hotmail.com

REGISTERED NURSE: Critical Care / Medical / Oncology

Dedicated, hardworking nurse with 7 years of diverse healthcare experience and recent nursing education/RN certification. Recognized by supervisors, peers, and professors for team orientation, high-level critical-thinking skills, and desire for continuous learning. Record of initiative in alerting healthcare team to changing patient status. Exceptional work ethic.

Hospital and clinic experience includes

- Monitoring vital signs
- Administering EKGs and X rays
- Initiating oxygen therapy
- Caring for ventilated patients
- Bathing and tube-feeding
- Administering injections
- Educating patients and families
- Providing compassionate end-of-life care
- Using cardiac monitors/interpreting cardiac rhythms
- Drawing blood and initiating intravenous lines
- Assisting MDs with examinations and sterile procedures
- Operating autoclave/conforming to sterilization protocols
- Training new healthcare and administrative staff
- Communicating patient information to the healthcare team

EDUCATION

Associate Degree in Nursing/RN Certification, May 2005
Miami-Dade Community College (NLN-accredited program), Miami, FL
- Held full-time nursing positions while carrying full course load.

Medical Specialist Course, 2000
Army Medical Department (AMEDD) Center and School, Ft. Sam Houston, TX

HEALTHCARE EXPERIENCE

MEDICAL ASSISTANT: Hialeah Urgent Care and Family Clinic, Hialeah, FL   2004–Present
Serve a diverse patient population, beginning with triage and covering full range of urgent and ongoing care. Work cooperatively with physicians and other members of the healthcare team. Provide extensive patient education.
- Took on added responsibilities: taking X rays and EKGs, performing lab work, calling in medication renewals, and arranging consultations with specialists.
- Selected to train all new employees, identifying and filling in knowledge gaps to build overall staff capability.

PATIENT CARE ASSISTANT (CNA II): Miami-Dade Community Hospital, Miami, FL   2004–Present
On a combined medical/oncology unit, provide high level of care to patients—monitoring vital signs, bathing and tube-feeding patients, communicating patient status to the nursing team, and delivering end-of-life care with empathy and compassion.
- Recognized for ability to identify significant changes in status based on observation, intuition, and patient interaction.
- Effectively prioritized care during periods of staff shortages, dealing appropriately with patient concerns and complex medical issues.

CNA I, UNIT SECRETARY: South Florida Memorial Hospital, Miami, FL   2004–2005
Assisted nurses with care of critically ill patients on an emergency unit.
- Monitored cardiac monitors, interpreted rhythms, and notified nursing staff of changes in rhythm, oxygen saturation, respiratory rate, and blood pressure.
- As unit secretary, input physician orders into computer, answered phones, and paged physicians.

MEDICAL SPECIALIST: United States Army Reserves, Miami, FL   1998–2004
Provided preventative and emergency care including air and land evacuation of injured soldiers.
- Earned EMT certification.

EMERGENCY MEDICAL TECHNICIAN: Dade County Rescue Squad, Miami, FL   2001–2002

Fluent in Spanish. Proficient in a variety of computer applications.

6

Degree: AAS.
Job Target: Occupational therapist assistant.
Strategy: Capitalized on his relatively extensive internship experience.

JONATHAN P. SADOWSKI, OTA

1984 Miller Pass ▸ Linden, MI 48452 ▸ 810-555-2399 ▸ bdybldr@yahoo.com

EDUCATION

BAKER COLLEGE • Flint, Michigan
Associate of Applied Science — Occupational Therapist Assistant   2005
COTA Certification   June 2005

HIGHLIGHTS OF SKILLS AND EXPERIENCE

- ▸ Plan and implement treatments and activities appropriate to individual patients, helping them increase capacity and attain their highest levels of functional independence.
- ▸ Experience working with pediatric and adult patients in outpatient and inpatient settings, individually and in groups.
- ▸ Basic knowledge of Neuro-Developmental Treatment (NDT) and Proprioceptive Neuromuscular Facilitation (PNF).
- ▸ Incorporate knowledge of and experience with body-building techniques into OT practices.
- ▸ Assess and treat patients regarding these issues:
  - — Cognitive
  - — Social/behavioral
  - — Community integration
  - — Mobility and motor
  - — Sensory integration
  - — Activities of daily living (ADLs)
  - — Perceptual skills
  - — Communication
- ▸ Experience with patients with varying diagnoses:
  - — Brain injuries
  - — Hand injuries
  - — Cerebrovascular accidents
  - — Orthopedic
- ▸ Familiarity with these and other treatment methods:
  - — Iotophoresis
  - — Phonophoresis
  - — Electrical stimulation
  - — BTE
  - — Ultrasound

CLINICAL EXPERIENCE

GENESYS REGIONAL MEDICAL CENTER • Flint, Michigan
Student Intern [320 hours]   Jan.–Mar. 2005

HEARTLAND REHABILITATION SERVICES • Lapeer, Michigan
Student Intern [320 hours]   Oct.–Dec. 2004

HURLEY MEDICAL CENTER • Flint, Michigan
Student Intern [120 hours]   Sept.–Nov. 2004

MARION D. CROUSE INSTRUCTIONAL CENTER • Flint, Michigan
Student Intern [60 hours]   July–Aug. 2004

AFFILIATIONS

- ▸ AOTA (American Occupational Therapy Association)
- ▸ National Physique Committee *(for competitive bodybuilders)*

OTHER EXPERIENCE

JAY'S POTATO CHIPS • Flint, Michigan	**Route Driver**	2002–Present
EXPEDX PAPER & GRAPHICS • Flint, Michigan	**Shipping Clerk**	1999–2002
AIRBORNE EXPRESS • Lansing, Michigan	**Courier**	1996–1999
GM PROVING GROUNDS • Milford, Michigan	**Vehicle Test Driver**	1995–1996

References available on request

7

Degree: Certificate in Dental Hygiene.
Job Target: Dental hygienist.
Strategy: Capitalized on her experience in the dental field as a chair-side assistant.

Juanita P. Morales

3482 McCandlish Road
Grand Blanc, MI 48439
810-555-2396 • jpmsmiles@home.net

Profile

❖ Certification and training as **Dental Hygienist.**
❖ Experience as chair-side **Dental Assistant** in general and periodontal practices.
❖ Ability to earn **trust** and develop **rapport** with patients.
❖ Strong patient **assessment** and **education** skills.
❖ Training and experience in using **Prophy Jet** and **ultrasonic scalers.**

Dental Experience

CARO PERIODONTAL ASSOCIATES • Caro, MI	2005–Present
FAMILY DENTAL • Clarkston, MI	2001–2005
DR. ROGER ANDERSON • Rochester, MI	2000–2001
MACKIN ROAD DENTAL CLINIC • Lapeer, MI	1996–2000

Education

MOTT COMMUNITY COLLEGE • Flint, MI
Certificate in Dental Hygiene   2005
— Graduated in Top 10% of class
— Passed state and national exams
— Past President, MCC Dental Students Association

Selected Classes & Training

❖ "Infection Control in a Changing World"
❖ "Advanced Techniques in Root Planing and Instrument Sharpening"
❖ "AIDS: Oral Signs, Symptoms, and Treatments"
❖ "Periodontal Diseases in Children and Adolescents"
❖ "Periodontal Screening Record"
❖ "Strategies for Teamwork and Communication Skills"

Community Involvement

❖ International Institute — Event Assistant
❖ Spanish-Speaking Information Center — Volunteer Tutor
❖ Big Brothers/Big Sisters of Greater Flint — Big Sister

References available on request

Degree: AAS, Equine Training and Management.
Job Target: Equine trainer.
Strategy: Communicated specific horse-related knowledge gained through training and experience.

Michael A. Viner
44811 WCR 33, Pierce, CO 80650
(H) 970-238-1718   (C) 970-504-6184
viner@hotmail.com

EDUCATION

Associate of Applied Science in Equine Training and Management
Laramie County Community College, Cheyenne, Wyoming
2005

RELEVANT COURSEWORK

Basic Management and Training, Equine Science I and II, Advanced Horse Management
and Training, Equine Evaluation, Equine Breeding, Equine Health Management,
Advanced Training Techniques, Internship, Equine Sales and Service

EXPERIENCE

Training
- Halter-broke weanlings for ranches and individuals.
- Started colts under saddle.
- Taught ground manners to weanlings and yearlings.

Breeding
- Assisted with mare care and exercise.
- Prepared mares for breeding.
- Handled stallions in barn.

Management and Maintenance
- Successfully managed up to 45 employees for 12 years.
- Maintained health and breeding records.
- Administered vaccinations and de-wormers.
- Organized and managed barn.

EXPERIENCE HISTORY

Trainer/Handler	TR Paints and Quarter Horses, Laramie, Wyoming	2002–2003
Office Manager	Brooks and Associates, Cheyenne, Wyoming	2001–2002
Trainer/Handler	Happy Hollow Ranch, Pierce, Colorado	1995–1999
Manager	Dairy Queen, Pierce, Colorado	1988–2001

PROFESSIONAL AFFILIATIONS

Laramie County Community College Equine Show Team, Secretary, 2003–2004
Block and Bridle Executive Council, 2003–2004
Southern Oregon Horse Activities, Vice President, 1996–1997
Westernairs, 1978–1988

9

Degree: AAS, Hospitality Management.
Job Target: Management position at a major hotel.
Strategy: Showed transferable skills, solid work ethic, and academic accomplishments for this 54-year-old man recovering from major illness and looking for a second career. Demonstrated prior experience in management. Listed extensive honors and professional development training.

DONALD C. DUDEK

267 French Road   (315) 839-6504
Syracuse, New York 13135   DonCDude@att.net

OBJECTIVE: Position utilizing skills, training and experience in supervision and hospitality management.

SUMMARY:
- Demonstrated solid knowledge and hands-on skills in front office, lobby/front desk, room service, restaurant and housekeeping operations.
- Hired, trained, motivated, evaluated, disciplined, dismissed, promoted and supervised up to 60 employees.
- Scheduled personnel, oversaw purchasing and coordinated outside contracting.
- Revised tour planner's guide, updated database of tour guides and planners, scheduled appointments for international show, collected tourist information regarding local sites, planned itineraries and evaluated quality of services.
- Gained firsthand experience in all aspects of running and maintaining an upscale, high-occupancy hotel serving business and leisure clientele.
- Participated in banquet planning, preparation and execution.
- Assisted in a variety of marketing projects designed to promote tourism.
- Supervised full- and part-time staff comprising maintenance workers in a 325-bed hospital and major apartment complex.
- Maintained 184 apartment units with responsibility for plumbing, heating, air conditioning and electrical repairs.
- Utilized computer skills in WordPerfect, PowerPoint and Excel.

EDUCATION: Cazenovia College, Cazenovia, New York
Associate in Applied Science — Hospitality Management, 2005
Dean's List   GPA: 3.5

Courses included:

Introduction to Hospitality	Accounting Principles
Human Resource Management	Front Office Operation
Hospitality Management	Macroeconomics
Rooms Division Management	Urban Promotion and Marketing
Effective Business Communications	Cultural Diversity
Microcomputer Applications	Ethics
Food, Beverage and Banquet Operations	
Convention Sales, Trade Shows and Gaming Operations	

INTERNSHIPS: Syracuse Convention & Visitors Bureau, Syracuse, New York (3/2005–5/2005)
Intern in Travel and Tourism

Syracuse Marriott, Syracuse, New York (10/2004–12/2004)
Intern in Front Desk/Kitchen/Housekeeping

(continued)

(continued)

9

DONALD C. DUDEK   Page Two
(315) 839-6504 • DonCDude@att.net

ADDITIONAL *TRAINING:*	<u>Kaset International</u> — "The Foundation for Creating Loyal Customers," "Caring Responses for Extraordinary Service," "Understanding Behavior to Create Successful Service Encounters and Skills" and "Strategies and Choices for Handling Challenging Situations"
	<u>Syracuse University</u> — Emerging Leaders Forum with workshops in "Person-Centered Language" and "The Many Sides of People"
	<u>Fulton Community College</u> — Courses in building and maintenance management
	<u>Northgate Nursing Home</u> — Courses in "Supervisory Management Development," "Implementing Change" and "Assertiveness"
	<u>Service Engineering Associates</u> — Seminar in housekeeping management and supervision
	<u>New York State</u> — Class 2 HVAC License
HONORS:	President of Student Union Board, 2002–2004
	Phi Theta Kappa, International Scholastic Order
	Guest Speaker at Friends of Cazenovia Dinner
	Cazenovia Hospitality Student Scholarship
	Carrier Foundation Scholarship
	Certificate of Recognition for Service as Student Orientation Leader
EMPLOYMENT:	Colonie Apartments, Syracuse, New York (1987–2001) **Director of Maintenance**
	Northgate Nursing Home, Syracuse, New York (1986–1987) **Interim Director of Maintenance**
	Brown Barron Lounge, East Syracuse, New York (1984–1995) **Maintenance Manager/Bartender**
REFERENCES:	Furnished upon request.

10

Degree: Certificate in Computer Systems Technology.
Job Target: Computer systems technician/field service technician/help desk technician.
Strategy: Because job experience, although relevant, was only limited part-time work, emphasized recent education and coursework more heavily.

ARMAND J. AMAR

555 Juniper Way, Ojai, California 93023 — (805) 555-1212
armandamar@lycos.com

CAREER PROFILE

♦ **Computer Technician / Field Service Technician / Help Desk Technician**
♦ **Certification backed by pertinent industry experience.**
♦ **Additional skills include the ability to manage multiple projects, interface effectively with technical and lay staff, and deliver excellent customer service.**

TECHNICAL SKILLS SUMMARY

Successful completion of classroom projects and on-the-job training, including ground-up construction of PCs and installation of local area networks.

HARDWARE	SOFTWARE
Installation, Configuration, and Upgrading	MS Office, Outlook, FrontPage
Diagnosing and Troubleshooting	Symantec Norton Antivirus
Preventative Maintenance	BASIC for DOS
Motherboards, Processors, Memory	HTML
Drives and Printers	
Basic Networking	
Fiber Optic & Cat5 Cabling Systems	

EDUCATION

Technology Development Center, Ventura, California (WASC accredited)
♦ Certified Computer Systems Technologist (A+ PC Technician equivalent) — 31 weeks
♦ Graduated with honors 4/2005
Moorpark College, Moorpark, California — 2004
♦ Office Information Systems, 50 semester hours with a 4.0 GPA.

CAREER HISTORY

Customer Engineering Technician (Part-Time)   2004–Present
Tandon Technologies, Simi Valley, California

Customer-service and field-maintenance expert for a recognized leader in PC systems design. Installation, maintenance, repair, service, and inspection of electronic equipment such as motherboards, processors, controllers, and hard-floppy-SCSI drives. Help-desk responsibilities include client training, real-time remote diagnostics, repair, and quality control.
♦ Customer feedback revealed 100% satisfaction in latest performance review.

CHAPTER 6

Resumes for Internship and Co-op Applicants

Resume Number	Degree	Job Target
11	BS, Communications	Internship in media production
12	BA, Advertising	Internship in advertising with direction in creative strategy and graphic design
13	BA, Communication Studies	Communications internship
14	BS, Exercise and Sports Science	An internship in the sports industry
15	BS, Marketing and Management Information Systems	An internship position with a large corporation
16	BS, Accounting	Accounting co-op position
17	BS, Management (marketing minor)	Construction industry internship in the U.S.
18	BFA, Interior Design	Contract design internship
19	BS, Fashion Merchandising	Internship in fashion (open to any area)
20	BS, Biology/Chemistry	Research internship in the life sciences industry
21	BS, Political Science	Congressional internship
22	BA, Public Relations	Congressional internship
23	BS, Government and Public Policy	Internship related to her major
24	BA, Criminal Justice	FBI Honors Internship Program
25	BS, Chemical Engineering	Relevant internship or co-op job
26	BS, Chemical Engineering	Chemical engineering co-op

11

Degree: BS, Communications.
Job Target: Internship in media production.
Strategy: Demonstrated consistent record of leadership, initiative, and achievement supported by relevant work experience in media production, modeling, and sales. High school information is included (on page 2) because it is relevant to the current goal and supports the strategy.

Corinne Sanderson

Permanent Address		**School Address**
119 Old Stone Trail		139 Bay State Road
Guilford, CT 06437	csanderson@bu.edu	Boston, MA 02115
203-248-0973		617-505-1594

Goal

Internship: Summer 2005
Public Relations / Marketing / Media Production

Skills

Media Production: Two hands-on summer internships with a multimedia producer of major corporate programs and events.

Presentation and Communication: Comfortable speaking before groups and in business settings. Model, spokesperson, guide, and peer advisor. Strong writing and editing skills.

Leadership: Repeatedly took on leadership roles in school and community activities. Demonstrated initiative, drive, and ability to manage multiple priorities.

People Skills: At my best when interacting with others and working in a team environment.

Education

Boston University, Boston, MA
BS Communications — anticipated 2006
Concentrations: Public Relations / Film & Television

Leadership

Admissions Representative: Chosen through competitive interview process to work with Admissions Office and represent Boston University to prospective students.
- Greet and assist visitors and prospective students as front-desk representative for Admissions Office; weekly assignment.
- Lead tours for visiting high school students and their families and for visiting alumni during Reunion Weekend.
- Served on Recruitment Team; interviewed potential admissions representatives.
- Conducted recruitment events at Cheshire Academy, Connecticut, 2004.

Alumni Bridge: Recommended by faculty member and approved through alumni interview process.
- Volunteer at special alumni events such as new student receptions, athletic events (home and away), and Reunion Weekend.
- Chosen for Recruitment Team; interviewed prospective members.
- Nominated and elected to Executive Board position — VP of Publicity, 2005

Membership Public Relations Student Society of America (PRSSA)

Volunteer Special Olympics Volunteer, 2003, 2004, 2005

Experience

Media Production Internship

Production Assistant, Shoreline Productions, Madison, CT, Summers 2003, 2004
Participated in every aspect of producing corporate media programs for major events. In fast-paced, demanding work environment, performed tasks from PowerPoint programming and tape dubbing to running errands, serving as production crew, and modeling for corporate promotions. Also assisted with office administrative duties.
- **Major projects:** Major corporate convention for $1 billion Mega Products Company (2003 and 2004) and corporate event for Good Stuff, Inc., a $100 million direct-sales company (2004).
- **Media production duties:** Creating and editing PowerPoint presentations; programming TVL; scanning; researching footage; dubbing tapes; propping sets; operating TelePrompTer; assisting with production footage.
- **Requested to return** for third summer internship.

11 *(continued)*

Corinne Sanderson
Page 2

csanderson@bu.edu

Home: 203-248-0973
School 617-505-1594

Experience

Modeling
Sales

(continued)

Model, East Coast Talent, West Haven, CT, 2001–Present

Sales Associate, Ann Taylor, South Bend, IN, 2004–Present
Sales Associate, The Gap, Meriden, CT, 2001–2003

High School

Cheshire Academy, Cheshire, CT
Graduated with Distinctive Honors, 2004

Academic Honors

National Honor Society, inducted 2003

French Honor Society, President

Second Place, French, Connecticut Scholastic Achievement Test (team competition)

Center for the Advancement of Academically Talented Youth / Johns Hopkins University
- Chosen in junior high school based on academic achievement and promise; participated for 6 years.

Founders Award in History

Faculty Award in Languages (French)

Leadership

Elected to Student Council, 2 years

Prom Committee, 3 years; Co-chair, senior year

Yearbook Editor, senior year

Peer Counselor

Volunteer

School-based: Educational Assistance Program (classroom aide for local elementary school); annual Book Drive for schools in underprivileged neighborhoods; Famine Relief fund-raising initiative

Community: American Heart Association, Madison Hill Nursing Home, Shoreline Association for Retarded and Handicapped (SARAH)

Special Project: SARAH Ambassador: Delivered presentations at more than a dozen area schools to promote participation in programs benefiting SARAH and the people it serves.
- Influenced the launching of SARAH chapters at 7 schools.
- Named "Ambassador of the Year" (among 20 Ambassadors) for outstanding achievement in community service.

Athletics / Modeling / Travel

Varsity soccer player — 4 years

Dance — jazz, tap, ballet, pointe

Midwestern Talent Expo — Model (placed in all 3 categories entered)

Travel abroad — Australia, most of Europe, Ghana

12

Degree: BA, Advertising.
Job Target: Internship in advertising with direction in creative strategy and graphic design.
Strategy: Elevated his candidacy by highlighting his background, which includes business experience as well as college classes. Included interests in skiing, wakeboarding, and in-line skating to promote him as a risk-taker with a thirst for adventure.

Franklyn North

Permanent address:	northtofrank@wmu.edu	*Current Address:*
9669 N. Heatherbrook		1221 University Avenue
Bloomfield, MI 48335	*portfolio available at:*	Kalamazoo, MI 49008
248.555.6101	FrankNorth.com	616.555.0169

Current Focus	INTERNSHIP — Business/Advertising with core direction in Creative Strategy, Account Planning, and Graphic Design
Competencies	Highly proficient computer skills in Adobe Photoshop, Illustrator, PageMaker; Microsoft Word, PowerPoint, Excel applications; and Internet business strategies
	Web page development and design skills
	Advertising Communications • Brand Strategy • Creative Services • Electronic Media • Market Research • Radio & Television Media • Press Releases • Advanced Mass Media • Marketing Statistics • Consumer Research • Creative Writing • Branding

---

EDUCATION

Western Michigan University; Kalamazoo, Michigan
Major: **Advertising** – Bachelor of Arts degree *(anticipated)* 12/2006
Curriculum includes: **Graphic Design/Studio Art**

EXPERIENCE

Bradley Entertainment Productions; Kalamazoo, Michigan
Creative & Design Director, 9/2004–present
Design, develop, and produce advertising material and promotional tools for nonprofit student-run business promoting entertainment groups.
- Developed business identity logos for the company and bands; designed graphics for advertising promotions.

Groundwater Enterprises, Inc.; Royal Oak, Michigan
Internship, 6/2003–8/2003
Designed websites and updated Internet-based graphics for company that provided Business Continuity services and expertise. Assigned to Now&Again.com account.
- Designed business website including navigation strategies. Developed all logos, graphics, icons, and routing.

ACTIVITIES

Member – American Advertising Federation; Western Michigan University, 2002–present
Held position in the creative department developing ideas and advertisements. Campaign work also conducted in the community relations department. Responsible for organizing fund-raising efforts and social events.

Member – Alpha Tau Omega Fraternity, Epsilon Eta Chapter
Attained positions as House Social Coordinator and Philanthropy Chair

OTHER INFORMATION

Involved in snow skiing, water skiing, wakeboarding, in-line skating, and mountain biking. Highly knowledgeable and accomplished in weight training, fitness, and nutrition. Skilled in drawing, painting, ceramics, and sculpture. Talented guitar player.

13 **Degree:** BA, Communication Studies.
Job Target: Communications internship.
Strategy: Highlighted business and customer-service skills; de-emphasized haircutting expertise without sacrificing her creativity.

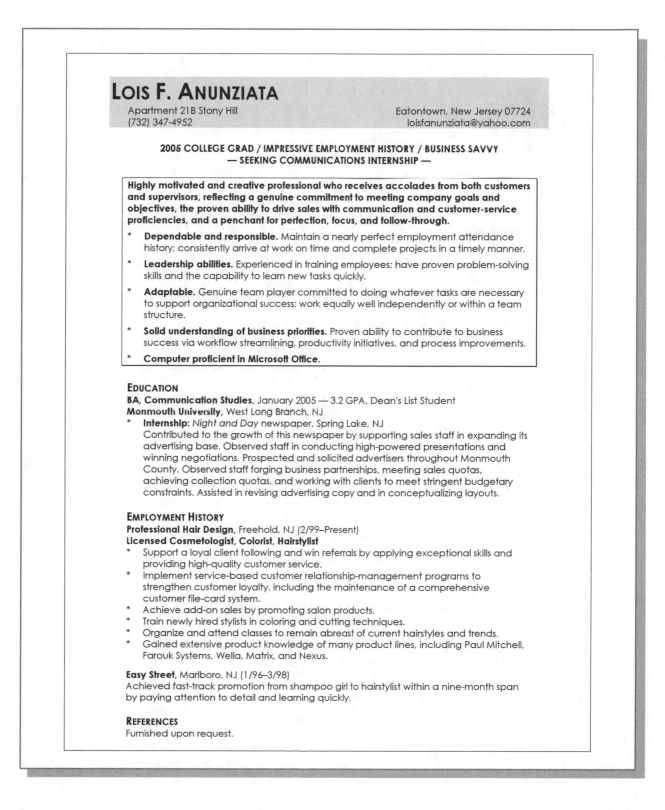

LOIS F. ANUNZIATA

Apartment 21B Stony Hill   Eatontown, New Jersey 07724
(732) 347-4952   loisfanunziata@yahoo.com

2005 COLLEGE GRAD / IMPRESSIVE EMPLOYMENT HISTORY / BUSINESS SAVVY
— SEEKING COMMUNICATIONS INTERNSHIP —

Highly motivated and creative professional who receives accolades from both customers and supervisors, reflecting a genuine commitment to meeting company goals and objectives, the proven ability to drive sales with communication and customer-service proficiencies, and a penchant for perfection, focus, and follow-through.

* **Dependable and responsible.** Maintain a nearly perfect employment attendance history; consistently arrive at work on time and complete projects in a timely manner.

* **Leadership abilities.** Experienced in training employees; have proven problem-solving skills and the capability to learn new tasks quickly.

* **Adaptable.** Genuine team player committed to doing whatever tasks are necessary to support organizational success; work equally well independently or within a team structure.

* **Solid understanding of business priorities.** Proven ability to contribute to business success via workflow streamlining, productivity initiatives, and process improvements.

* **Computer proficient in Microsoft Office.**

EDUCATION
BA, Communication Studies, January 2005 — 3.2 GPA, Dean's List Student
Monmouth University, West Long Branch, NJ
* **Internship:** *Night and Day* newspaper, Spring Lake, NJ
  Contributed to the growth of this newspaper by supporting sales staff in expanding its advertising base. Observed staff in conducting high-powered presentations and winning negotiations. Prospected and solicited advertisers throughout Monmouth County. Observed staff forging business partnerships, meeting sales quotas, achieving collection quotas, and working with clients to meet stringent budgetary constraints. Assisted in revising advertising copy and in conceptualizing layouts.

EMPLOYMENT HISTORY
Professional Hair Design, Freehold, NJ (2/99–Present)
Licensed Cosmetologist, Colorist, Hairstylist
* Support a loyal client following and win referrals by applying exceptional skills and providing high-quality customer service.
* Implement service-based customer relationship-management programs to strengthen customer loyalty, including the maintenance of a comprehensive customer file-card system.
* Achieve add-on sales by promoting salon products.
* Train newly hired stylists in coloring and cutting techniques.
* Organize and attend classes to remain abreast of current hairstyles and trends.
* Gained extensive product knowledge of many product lines, including Paul Mitchell, Farouk Systems, Wella, Matrix, and Nexus.

Easy Street, Marlboro, NJ (1/96–3/98)
Achieved fast-track promotion from shampoo girl to hairstylist within a nine-month span by paying attention to detail and learning quickly.

REFERENCES
Furnished upon request.

14

Degree: BS, Exercise and Sports Science.

Job Target: An internship in the sports industry.

Strategy: Used a format that will catch attention at job fairs and stand out in a stack of several hundred applications. The left table highlights volunteer experience with some prestigious golf and college organizations.

Allison A. Everett

936 Lincoln • Ames, IA 50014
Phone: (515) 249-5655 • Cell: (515) 290-2222
Alverett996@yahoo.com

Sports-Related Activities

National Cyclone Club Tent Welcoming Host Fall 2004

Allianz Championship Golf Tournament Office Staff Fall 2004

ISU Sports Camps Counselor Summer 2004

Hy-Vee Women's Golf Classic Media Relations Runner May 2004

ISU Athletic Department & National Cyclone Club Intern May–August 2004

Riverbend Golf Course Jr. Golf League Volunteer Summer 2003

Riverbend Golf Course Couples' League Co-President Summer 2003

Ballard-Huxley Community Schools District Golf Champion 2000

Ballard-Huxley Community Schools Cross-Country Manager 2000

Education

BS, Iowa State University, Ames, IA (anticipated 2006)
Exercise and Sports Science / Sport Management
- Currently enrolled in Sport Management core classes
- Sport Management Club member

Computer Skills

Microsoft Word, Excel, PowerPoint
(Experience preparing and executing large mail-merges)

Work History

Allianz Championship Golf Tournament, Des Moines, IA
OFFICE STAFF VOLUNTEER (August–September 2004)
- General office assistance; stuffing envelopes for mass mailings and checking ticket orders.

Iowa State University, Athletic Department, Ames, IA
INTERNSHIP (May–August 2004)
- Worked with Varsity Club to increase membership.
- Updated database, typed letters, and prepared mailings.

SPORTS CAMP COUNSELOR (June 2004)
- Supervised 20–40 sports camp participants during two golf camps and one basketball camp. Oversaw dormitory stay; ensured timely arrival at camp and meals.
- Developed solid relationships with coaches and staff, including Julie Manning, Golf Coach.

Hy-Vee Women's Golf Classic, Des Moines, IA
MEDIA RELATIONS RUNNER (May 2004)
- Relayed information from leader board to media continuously throughout tournament.
- Monitored media interviewing schedule with golf personalities.

Professional Property Management, Ames, IA
RENTAL CONSULTANT (February–May 2004)
- Answered phone and booked appointments to show rental apartments; prepared lease contracts and paperwork.

Dr. Tricia J. Johnson, Iowa City, IA
NANNY (July 2003–January 2004)
- Performed daily child-care duties and light housekeeping for two children. Provided transportation to and from school and other activities.

15

Degree: BS, Marketing and Management Information Systems.
Job Target: An internship position with a large corporation.
Strategy: Highlighted the levels of responsibility in work experiences, eagerness to gain experience in many areas, and ability to manage many activities—drew out skills an employer wants to see.

Bridgett Dearborn

dear3@mail.com

Home Address	Telephone
109 E. Maple St.	Home: (219) 866-6000
Rensselaer, IN 47978	School: (219) 865-1021

Objective

A corporate internship in Management, Marketing, Information Systems

Education

Saint Joseph's College; Rensselaer, IN
Bachelor of Science in Management, Marketing, Informational Systems (MMIS)   Minor in Accounting
Anticipated graduation: May 2006   GPA: 3.48/4.0

Work Experience

Intern: Saint Joseph's College Career Center; Rensselaer, IN—August 2003–current
- Student liaison for Career Fest—communicate and market the benefits of participating in the annual career fair to students, faculty, and alumni.
- Develop marketing strategies and communications to student body and SJC constituents on Career Center services, special events, and activities.
- Develop and maintain Web pages for Career Center Web site.

Manager: McDonald's; Rensselaer, IN—February 2000–current
- Open and close the store, which involves counting and recording deposits up to $4,000.
- Have developed communication and leadership skills pertinent to working in a customer-service business as a leader.
- Determined placement and promotion of Point of Purchase (POP) displays in an effort to attract customer attention.

Associate: National Company; Rensselaer, IN—Summer 2003
- Trained in multiple departments and took initiative to learn the various stages of product development.
- Worked in a team of two, frequently producing 25% more than team of three on other shift.
- Invited by upper management at corporate level to apply for internship at corporate headquarters in North Carolina.
- Company chairperson for company's first participation in the American Cancer Society's Relay for Life. Secured more than 27% employee participation in this community event.

Extracurricular Activities

- Vice President, sophomore class—2004–2005
- College Democrats—2003–2005 (Treasurer—2004)
- Co-captain of team for American Cancer Society's Relay for Life—2003–2005
- Judiciary Task Force Committee member
- Students In Free Enterprise—2003–2005 (advertising committee chairperson—2004–2005)
- SJC Investment Club—2002–2004
- "Observer" (school newspaper)—2003–2004 (circulation manager—2003)
- Student Union Board, advertising chair—2004

Career portfolio available upon request

16

Degree: BS, Accounting.
Job Target: Accounting co-op position.
Strategy: Emphasized coursework and experience as treasurer of fraternity.

Chang Jan Li

862 Trafalgar Court
Rochester, New York
Phone: (585) 359-2109   E-mail: cjli@yahoo.com

objective

A challenging cooperative education assignment with a public accounting firm.

education

May 2006
(Anticipated)

Bachelor of Science, Accounting
Rochester Institute of Technology; Rochester, New York
Dean's List; GPA: 3.25/4.00
Outstanding Transfer Scholarship Winner / Trustee Scholarship Winner

significant courses

— Auditing	— Operations Management
— Tax Accounting	— Complex Business Organizations
— Cost Accounting	— Corporate Finance (I & II)
— Financial Reporting & Analysis (I, II, III)	— Management Science
— Not-for-Profit/Government Accounting	— Statistics

May 2003

Associate of Applied Science, Business Administration
Monroe Community College; Rochester, New York
Dean's List — Three Semesters; GPA: 3.5/4.0

activity

Treasurer, Alpha Beta Gamma Honorary Fraternity
— Collect payments and process disbursements.
— Prepare balance sheets and financial statements.
— Submit financial reports to national headquarters and student government.
— Prepare the annual budget for submission to student government.
— Reconcile bank statements.
— Provide financial information to auditor.

**computer
literacy**

MS Windows, Word, Excel, PowerPoint, and Access; Minitab

experience

Summer 2004

Driveway Sealing Technician, College Guys, Inc.; Henrietta, New York
Applied protective coatings to residential driveways and commercial parking areas.
— Edged driveways and performed other preparation work.
— Interfaced with customers to ensure satisfaction.

Summer 2002
Summer 2001

Assembly Line Operator, Federal Automotive; Rochester, New York
Served as part of 10-member team accountable for assembly of V-6 throttle bodies.
— Met daily production quotas.
— Conducted QC inspections of finished pieces.

1999–2002

Head Waiter, Jade Dynasty; Webster, New York
Oversaw the activities of up to four servers.
— Trained servers in procedures and customer-service skills.
— Assigned workstations and side duties to servers; scheduled breaks.
— Resolved operational problems and customer-satisfaction issues.
— Waited on patrons and attended to their needs.

References Available upon Request

17

Degree: BS, Management (marketing minor).
Job Target: Construction industry internship in the U.S.
Strategy: Emphasized the student's experience in previous internships with a foreign construction company. To overcome potential negative perception of his prior experience with a family-owned business in Brazil, drew out valuable experience from his three internships, one with a large, international theater company. The family-owned status of the construction business became irrelevant.

THOMAS M. GOMEZ

7105 Gulf Breeze Circle, Apt. 12C, Tampa, FL 33602 • (813) 971-5916 • tmgomez@aol.com

---

OBJECTIVE: Complete a marketing or management internship with a U.S. construction firm.

EDUCATION

BS Management, Marketing Minor (Candidate), Southwest Florida College, Tampa, FL   May 2006
Relevant Course Work: Advanced Marketing Research
Collaborated with a team to develop a business plan for an information-technology consulting firm.
- ❖ Researched competitors and products, conducted a survey, and created the marketing plan.
- ❖ Received recognition for completing the best project and for conducting the best presentation.

PROFESSIONAL EXPERIENCE

BERTONE CONSTRUCTION, INC., São Paulo, Brazil   2003, 2004
*(Performed two summer **internships,** totaling seven months, with construction company of 1,800 employees that specializes in residential, road, bridge, and governmental construction.)*
- ❖ Analyzed the results of various surveys on construction quality and customer service; surveys were distributed to current and prospective clients to assist the company in penetrating new geographic markets.
- ❖ Developed and implemented various improvements for the corporate Web site, as follows:
  - ▪ Created a page to display company plans, achievements, recognition, and changes.
  - ▪ Established a toll-free customer service line and added the number to the Web site.
  - ▪ Ensured that the "homes for sale" list was updated weekly to delete "sold" properties.
- ❖ Assisted the Vice President of Human Resources with interviewing internship candidates.
- ❖ Participated in researching product pricing among Bertone's 200 vendors for supplies such as cement, steel, electrical appliances, elevators, computers, and other construction materials.
- ❖ Observed the process for updating headquarters on daily progress at 25 construction sites.

WORLDWIDE THEATER COMPANY, Miami, FL   2002
*(Completed a two-month **internship** with the world's second-largest theater company, which operates theaters throughout the U.S. as well as in Latin America, Europe, and Asia.)*
- ❖ Worked with the directors of the legal, construction, real estate, and marketing departments.
- ❖ Observed contract negotiations with vendors for domestic and international construction.
- ❖ Developed an understanding of legal restrictions governing overseas trade.
- ❖ Trained in writing letters of intent, selecting construction sites, and determining theater size.
- ❖ Attended a meeting of 50 managers from throughout the U.S. to conduct strategic planning toward the goals of increasing service offerings and improving the theaters' seating and architecture.
- ❖ Observed all aspects of selecting movies for specific theaters based on location and audience, and became familiar with film-studio negotiations to rent films for multiple venues.

COMPUTER SKILLS   Proficient in MS Word, Excel, and PowerPoint; and Lotus Notes.

LANGUAGES   Fluent in English, Portuguese, and Spanish.

AFFILIATION   National Association of Hispanic Accountants

18

Degree: BFA, Interior Design.
Job Target: Contract design internship.
Strategy: The objective highlights the value of having both design knowledge and business experience (this individual returned to school after completing her first bachelor's degree and working in marketing for several years). The functional approach maps her relevant skills to her achievements from previous employment, her current studies, and her own initiative to make and sell functional art.

Heather Jones

(212) 980-8424 • 100 East 75th Street #2A, New York, NY 10000 • hjones@yahoo.com

Objective

A **Contract Design Internship** utilizing communication and organizational skills in a team-oriented environment. Qualified by a unique blend of design knowledge and a business administration background.

Education

The Interior Design Institute, New York, NY
Bachelor of Fine Arts, Interior Design—expected May 2006
Dean's List Honors, 3.7 GPA

University of Massachusetts, School of Management, Amherst, MA
Bachelor of Science, Business Administration—2001
Dean's List Honors; Major—Marketing, Minor—Advertising

Related Skills & Career Achievements

Creativity & Design	• Rigorous formal training in color theory, perspective, textiles & finishes, construction documents & drafting, materials & methods of construction, codes, residential design, historical styles, art history, architectural design, design history. • Designed and sold functional art to local stores. • Collaborated on the design of advertising and direct-mail pieces.
Project Management	• Organized promotional events for Paramount that increased interest in the films. • Managed trafficking of insertion orders and creative materials for print publications.
Client & Vendor Relations	• Readily inspired confidence of Small Advertising's clients. Numerous media-placement, public-relations, and graphic-design suggestions were accepted and implemented. • Increased traffic 23% at the Australian Maritime Museum by conceiving and executing a campaign to educate the local hospitality industry about new, interactive exhibits. Initiated a hands-on art/play area to make the museum more family-oriented. • Consulted one-on-one with students to resolve financial accounts for housing.
Computer Applications	• Proficient in AutoCAD 2000. • Highly proficient in Windows and Macintosh applications for word processing, spreadsheets, presentations, database management, and Internet navigation.

Career Chronology

Jr. Media Director, Small Advertising Agency, New York, NY	2002–2004
Paramount College Promotions Representative, Film Advertising, Boston, MA	2001
Student Accounts Assistant, University of Massachusetts Housing Office, Amherst, MA	2000–2001
Marketing Promotions Assistant, Australian Maritime Museum, Perth, Australia	2000

Professional Affiliation

ASID, Student Chapter

19

Degree: BS, Fashion Merchandising.
Job Target: Internship in fashion (open to any area).
Strategy: Highlighted small areas of hands-on experience and let personality and enthusiasm shine through. Used an eye-catching format to draw attention to the resume and therefore its contents. Made every effort to display personality.
Outcome: Secured internship with Marc Jacobs and Louis Vuitton.

Elizabeth Young

2403 Whitesboro Way - Austin, Texas 78750
512-349-1412 • eyoung@hotmail.com

Objective

An Internship position in the fashion industry that will utilize my education, enthusiasm, experience, and passion for style and merchandising in an opportunity that promotes growth and learning.

Education

B.S., Fashion Merchandising, Southwest Texas State University, San Marcos — completion Dec. 2005

Studio Makeup Academy, Hollywood, CA — 2003

Palomar Institute of Cosmetology, San Marcos, CA — 2003

Qualifications

- Licensed Esthetician — State of Texas, number 1222161.
- Experienced film makeup artist recognized for work on 2 full-length features and 1 short film.
- Organized and managed successful promotional event for up-and-coming musical talent.
- Strong knowledge of fashion design methods and technologies.
- Advanced education in fashion design, fashion merchandising, and marketing.
- PC Proficient: MS Word, MS Excel, MS PowerPoint, and Internet navigation.
- Possess basic German language skills.

Related Experience

Leasing Intern, *Trizec Hahn* — 1999–2000
Collected, organized, and presented retailer data in the planning and development of shopping centers and malls nationally. Created informational spreadsheets for supervisors and development of trade show portfolio. Assisted with organization of materials, promotional items, and displays for Trizec Hahn's ICSC (International Council of Shopping Centers) convention attendance.

Junior Apparel Consultant, *Trizec Hahn* — 2000
Consulted with executive developer on junior fashion purchasing and shopping experiences. Provided personal insight, experiences, and preferences to assist with redevelopment and target market shift of mall.

Event Coordination / Promotions, *Convoy* — 1999
Organized CD release party for Convoy (formerly known as Dishwater) to promote release of band's first soundtrack. Managed total event from conception through cleanup, including location, on-site personnel, catering, sales of CDs, and event promotion.

Film Makeup Artist / Stylist, *Various Titles and Directors* — 1996–1997
Provided makeup artistry and styling for 2 full-length motion picture films and 1 award-winning short film. Worked in various roles to gain overall knowledge and experience within the film industry.

Additional Experience

Operations Clerk, *Austin American Statesman* — 2002–2003

Cashier / Customer Service, *Central Market* — 2001–2002

Caregiver, *Therapeutic Equestrians* — 1994

Portfolio and References Available upon Request • Willing to Travel

20

Degree: BS, Biology/Chemistry.
Job Target: Research internship in the life sciences industry.
Strategy: Highlighted technical skills in the laboratory, exceptional leadership activities, and unique opportunities in which he has participated that demonstrate his interest and high academic achievements.

RON W. CONRAD
rwc221@yahoo.com

<u>Campus Address</u>
Saint Joseph's College
P.O. Box 3421
Rensselaer, IN 47978
(219) 866-6000

<u>Permanent Address</u>
2121 N. Winter Ave.
Indianapolis, IN 46205
(317) 412-8962

————**Research internship with a life sciences company or medical program**————

EDUCATION

Saint Joseph's College, Rensselaer, IN
Bachelor of Science in Biology/Chemistry; December 2005
G.P.A. 3.89/4.00
Dean's List, all 4 years

Relevant course work:
Comparative Vertebrate Anatomy/Lab, Microbiology/Lab, Human Medical Physiology,
Genetics/Lab, Histology, Physics/Lab, Advanced Microbiology

RESEARCH EXPERIENCE

Independent Research, Spring 2004
St. Joseph's College, Dr. Carol Walbaum, Rensselaer, IN
- DNA analysis using PCR and 3D Gel Electrophoresis

Minority Medical Education Program, Summer 2003
Fisk/Vanderbilt Universities, Nashville, TN
- Participated in problem-based learning sessions with Vanderbilt University medical students. Shadowed Dr. Kyle Mangoles in neurology to observe surgical procedures and techniques.

Pediatric Gastroenterology Research Assistant, Summer 2002
I.U. Medical School/Riley Hospital, Dr. Charles Groff, Indianapolis, IN
- Set up independent study on the prevalence of H. pylori in African Americans in Indianapolis using ELISA test.

HONORS & AWARDS

Outstanding General Chemistry Student, Saint Joseph's College, 2002
Trustee's Award for the Natural Science Division, Saint Joseph's College, 2003
National Football Foundation and College Football Hall of Fame Scholar Athlete
- **1 of 16 given nationally each year for exceptional academic performance, leadership, athletic ability, and citizenship**
Senior of the Year, Saint Joseph's College, 2005
Honors Scholarship, Saint Joseph's College
Minority Student Leadership Scholarship, Saint Joseph's College
Realizing the Dream Award (first-generation college students, Independent Colleges of Indiana)

ACTIVITIES

Indiana Academy of Science Meeting
Saint Joseph's College Minority Student Union (MSU) — President 2001–2005
- Developed an efficient and direct communication link among the minority students, the administration, and the majority students on campus.
- Co-coordinator of all MSU events, including Black History Month.
Academic Cabinet—Student representative on cabinet
NCAA Division II Football and Track
Saint Joseph's College Gospel Choir

21

Degree: BS, Political Science.
Job Target: Congressional internship.
Strategy: Played up political involvement as a student.

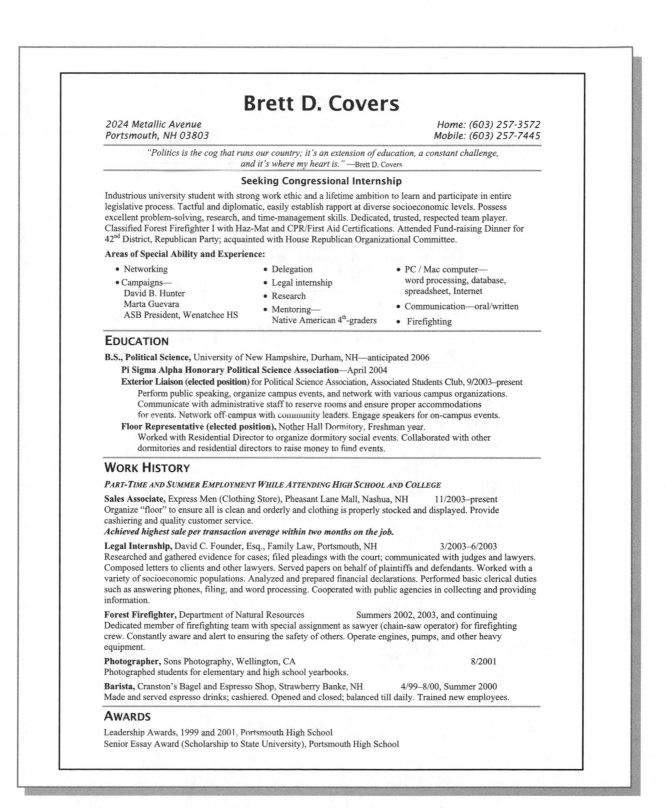

Brett D. Covers

2024 Metallic Avenue
Portsmouth, NH 03803

Home: (603) 257-3572
Mobile: (603) 257-7445

*"Politics is the cog that runs our country; it's an extension of education, a constant challenge,
and it's where my heart is."* —Brett D. Covers

Seeking Congressional Internship

Industrious university student with strong work ethic and a lifetime ambition to learn and participate in entire legislative process. Tactful and diplomatic, easily establish rapport at diverse socioeconomic levels. Possess excellent problem-solving, research, and time-management skills. Dedicated, trusted, respected team player. Classified Forest Firefighter I with Haz-Mat and CPR/First Aid Certifications. Attended Fund-raising Dinner for 42nd District, Republican Party; acquainted with House Republican Organizational Committee.

Areas of Special Ability and Experience:

- Networking
- Campaigns—
  David B. Hunter
  Marta Guevara
  ASB President, Wenatchee HS

- Delegation
- Legal internship
- Research
- Mentoring—
  Native American 4th-graders

- PC / Mac computer—
  word processing, database,
  spreadsheet, Internet
- Communication—oral/written
- Firefighting

EDUCATION

B.S., Political Science, University of New Hampshire, Durham, NH—anticipated 2006

Pi Sigma Alpha Honorary Political Science Association—April 2004

Exterior Liaison (elected position) for Political Science Association, Associated Students Club, 9/2003–present
Perform public speaking, organize campus events, and network with various campus organizations. Communicate with administrative staff to reserve rooms and ensure proper accommodations for events. Network off-campus with community leaders. Engage speakers for on-campus events.

Floor Representative (elected position), Nother Hall Dormitory, Freshman year.
Worked with Residential Director to organize dormitory social events. Collaborated with other dormitories and residential directors to raise money to fund events.

WORK HISTORY

PART-TIME AND SUMMER EMPLOYMENT WHILE ATTENDING HIGH SCHOOL AND COLLEGE

Sales Associate, Express Men (Clothing Store), Pheasant Lane Mall, Nashua, NH   11/2003–present
Organize "floor" to ensure all is clean and orderly and clothing is properly stocked and displayed. Provide cashiering and quality customer service.
Achieved highest sale per transaction average within two months on the job.

Legal Internship, David C. Founder, Esq., Family Law, Portsmouth, NH   3/2003–6/2003
Researched and gathered evidence for cases; filed pleadings with the court; communicated with judges and lawyers. Composed letters to clients and other lawyers. Served papers on behalf of plaintiffs and defendants. Worked with a variety of socioeconomic populations. Analyzed and prepared financial declarations. Performed basic clerical duties such as answering phones, filing, and word processing. Cooperated with public agencies in collecting and providing information.

Forest Firefighter, Department of Natural Resources   Summers 2002, 2003, and continuing
Dedicated member of firefighting team with special assignment as sawyer (chain-saw operator) for firefighting crew. Constantly aware and alert to ensuring the safety of others. Operate engines, pumps, and other heavy equipment.

Photographer, Sons Photography, Wellington, CA   8/2001
Photographed students for elementary and high school yearbooks.

Barista, Cranston's Bagel and Espresso Shop, Strawberry Banke, NH   4/99–8/00, Summer 2000
Made and served espresso drinks; cashiered. Opened and closed; balanced till daily. Trained new employees.

AWARDS

Leadership Awards, 1999 and 2001, Portsmouth High School
Senior Essay Award (Scholarship to State University), Portsmouth High School

22

Degree: BA, Public Relations.
Job Target: Congressional internship.
Strategy: Showcased skills and accomplishments in a functional format to demonstrate levels of achievement appropriate to a Congressional intern.
Outcome: Secured the position.

CLAY WHITE

University Address:
3412 32th Street
Lubbock, Texas 79410
(806) 780-2666

claywhite@hotmail.com

Permanent Address:
4114 99th Street
Lubbock, Texas 79423
(806) 794-3221

OBJECTIVE
Congressional Internship for spring 2006

QUALIFICATIONS
A dynamic and accomplished university student with leadership, general office, and sales experience. Selected to the highest public-relations position for students. Elected to numerous leadership positions. Possess extensive communication skills.

Public Relations and Communication
- o   Selected to the Chancellor's Ambassadors as a junior; one of 30 juniors and seniors chosen to facilitate communication with university donors at social functions.
- o   One of two from each fraternity pledge class to serve on the Junior Greek Council Public Relations Office.
- o   Provided information for the yearbook and newspaper as the Cardinal Key Publications Chairperson.
- o   Elected as Alumni Secretary for Phi Delta Theta; planned and executed the homecoming reception for more than 150 students and alumni; responsible for all aspects of the founder's day banquet; compose and send newsletters two times yearly to more than 1,000 alumni.
- o   One of six active members chosen to the Standards Board to guide and police activities of the more than 150 members and 50 pledges.
- o   High School: Mr. Lubbock, Prom King, and Student PTA Representative.

Leadership
- o   One of 20 students selected to attend and receive leadership training by the Texas Tech University administrators and deans at the Emerging Leaders Retreat.
- o   Voted president of fraternity pledge class and facilitated communications between actives and pledges.
- o   Camp counselor and lifeguard for pre-teenage children; 500 children per session.
- o   Selected as Freshman Greek Man of the Year based on grades and activities.
- o   High School: Boy's State Nominee, President of the Senior Class, National Honor Society, City-wide Youth Leadership Workshop Facilitator, church Youth Council, Teen of the Month (three times).

General Office and Management
- o   Purchasing clerk: answered phone, entered purchase orders, served as runner, and performed general duties
- o   Computer: excellent keyboarding skills; proficiency in Microsoft Word and Excel
- o   Inventory: bar-code and inventory millions of dollars of fixed assets
- o   Accounts receivable and payable with lawn business

Sales and Customer Service
- o   Door-to-door sales of book packages averaging $60–$200 per sale, working 80 hours weekly.
- o   Budgeted time and money and made a $4,500 profit for the summer.
- o   Purchased, developed, and managed a lawn service for three years.

(continued)

22 *(continued)*

CLAY WHITE   claywhite@hotmail.com

EDUCATION

Texas Tech University, Lubbock, Texas   2002 to Present
- o B.A. Degree projected for completion 2006 in **Public Relations** with a Marketing Minor
- o 3.44 GPA

Honors
- o Golden Key National Honor Society
- o Alpha Lambda Delta
- o Phi Eta Sigma
- o Dean's Honor List (two times)
- o Cardinal Key
- o High School: National Honor Society, Booster Club Scholarship

EMPLOYMENT

Inventory Clerk, Lubbock Independent School District, Lubbock, Texas	2002 to Present
Salesman, Southwestern Company, Rock Hill, South Carolina	Summer 2004
Camp Counselor and Lifeguard, Camp Ozark, Mt. Ida, Arkansas	Summer 2002
Purchasing Clerk, Lubbock Independent School District, Lubbock, Texas	Summer 2001
Co-owner, White Lawn Service, Lubbock, Texas	1999 to 2001

COMMUNITY ACTIVITIES

Volunteer approximately 30 hours each semester for the United Way, Food Bank, Highway Clean-up Campaign, and American Red Cross (blood donor)

High school: volunteered for United Way, Food Bank, and American Red Cross

INTERESTS

Team
- o Intramural football and softball
- o High school: varsity baseball (two years), All-District First Baseman, City League Baseball Sportsmanship Award

Other
- o Member: Young Republicans and Tech Snow Sports Club
- o Church youth sponsor, mentoring junior-high and high-school students

23

Degree: BS, Government and Public Policy.
Job Target: Internship related to her major.
Strategy: Distinct sections focusing on student leadership, student government, and fellowship experiences are designed to attract the attention of government organizations. Goal is addressed as part of the summary statement.

ELAINE M. STEWART

1788 Burlington Blvd., Apt. 356 • Fairfield, CT 97554 • tel: 203.335.6634 • emstewxt@yahoo.com

SUMMARY

Accomplished, well-rounded college professional seeking an internship in government and public policy. Enthusiastic and energetic contributor to student government and mentoring programs, requiring leadership, problem-solving, and cross-cultural communications strengths. Computer and Internet savvy.

EDUCATION

FAIRFIELD UNIVERSITY, Fairfield, CT, anticipated graduation May 2005
• Pursuing B.S. degree in Government and Public Policy; GPA: 3.87

Courses in International Studies

U.S. Foreign Relations (1890 to the present), Moot Court Honors Class (researching current Supreme Court cases and role-playing as justices or attorneys), Government and Political Communication, Government and Political Policy Process.

Scholarships / Honors

• Recipient of **Aramark Fellowship,** Spring 2005
Program designed to tap highly motivated, talented students who represent the next generation of leaders; provides training on governmental processes.

• Recipient of **Academic Excellence Scholarship,** 2002–2005
• Selected for **Collegium V—Fairfield University's Honors Program**

LEADERSHIP / ORGANIZATIONAL ACTIVITIES

Chair, Academic Affairs Committee—Student Government Association (2004–present)
♦ Instrumental in various projects, including surveying students and persuading the administration to implement new foreign-language curriculum (Mandarin Chinese, Arabic, and Vietnamese). Currently involved in other initiatives such as Advanced Placement credit for selected classes and establishing a campus radio station.

Senator, Executive Committee—Student Government Association
♦ Twice elected Senator, 2004–2005 and 2003–2004. Collaborate with the President, Vice President, and other Senate Chairs to establish effective processes/procedures both within the committee and in partnering with other campus organizations.

Vice Chair, Multicultural and Minority Affairs—Student Advisory Council (2004)
♦ Researched university system policies regarding international students and study-abroad programs, with recommendations presented to the Board of Regents.

Orientation Team Mentor—New Students Program (2004)
♦ Completed preparatory class that included leadership skills training. Participated in the coordination of all orientation programs to facilitate transition of freshman, transfer, and graduate students to the university, as well as at the freshmen camp and Emerging Leadership Program. Served as mentor to 5 students and assisted them with transition/academic issues.

FELLOWSHIP

Special Assistant—UNITED NATIONS INFORMATION CENTRE, Washington, DC (Spring 2005)

♦ Awarded **Aramark Fellowship** as 1 of 2 from Fairfield University. Produced reports on Congressional hearings, conferences, and lectures relating to United Nations activities.
♦ Researched nonprofit organizations applying for non-governmental organization (NGO) status with the UN and prepared information updates on the UN conference on Sustainable Finance.

EMPLOYMENT

SAT Tutor—SCORE PREP, Stamford, CT (2003–Present)

♦ Provide private math/verbal SAT tutoring, which includes coaching on Score Prep methods, relaxation skills, vocabulary, and basic math formulas.
♦ Effectively tutored 35 students to date, including individuals with dyslexia and ADD/ADHD. Efforts have resulted in increased scores of 100 points or more on each section.

24

Degree: BA, Criminal Justice.
Job Target: FBI Honors Internship Program.
Strategy: Pulled out the relevant skills and achievements in a separate column on the left for impact. "Highlights" section sets the stage for the reader to perceive her as an "achiever."

MARIA TERESITA GOMEZ

OBJECTIVE: FBI Honors Internship Program

HIGHLIGHTS OF QUALIFICATIONS
☑ Self-motivated, disciplined individual with an intense desire to succeed.
☑ Able to achieve results independently and as a cooperative team member.
☑ Successfully developed and implemented aerobic programs for all athletic levels.
☑ Resourceful, creative, and diligent. Noted for consistent professional manner.

LEADERSHIP
- As Freshmen Orientation Leader, addressed groups of incoming freshmen on academic requirements and college life, and assisted them in registration process for 3 orientations.

- In the Marathon Township Police Department Intern Program, entrusted with collecting evidence, such as fingerprints, and accurately cataloguing it in police database. Assisted in speed surveys in the ride-along program.

FITNESS PROGRAM COACH
- Personally instructed and motivated groups in aerobic exercises (3 classes weekly with 30 students) for 2 private fitness centers.

- As Exercise Coach at Dennison College, oriented new members to gym, tailoring the basic program to meet their varying levels and goals. Supervised and evaluated 10 work-study students in gym. Monitored gym members' fitness level progress and made recommendations for improvement.

PERSONAL ACHIEVEMENTS
- Achieved Dean's List status for 4 years.

- Won title as Dennison Women's Body-Building Champion for 2004.

- Elected President of Police Explorers during high school.

EDUCATION
Bachelor of Arts (B.A.) anticipated May 2005
Criminal Justice and Administration and Planning,
Dennison College of Criminal Justice, New York City

Certifications: Water & Boat Safety, Brown Belt (Karate)

EMPLOYMENT HISTORY
Freshman Orientation Leader   2001–2005
and Exercise Coach
Dennison College, New York City

Intern, Marathon Township Police Dept.   2001
Marathon Township, NJ

Aerobics Instructor   1999–2001
Pump Iron Gym, Hillsborough, NJ
Synergy Spa, Princeton, NJ

COMPUTER SKILLS
MS Windows, MS Office (Word, Excel, PowerPoint),
MS Outlook, WordPerfect, Internet, email

LANGUAGES
Proficient in Spanish—conversation, reading, and writing.
Knowledge of French and Portuguese.
Currently studying Chinese.

PROFESSIONAL MEMBERSHIPS
Aerobic Association International, member since 1999
International Sports Medicine Assoc., member since 1999

Present Address: 355 W. 101th Street, New York, NY 10025 ▪ (212) 765-5555 ▪ mariagomez@juno.com
Permanent Address: 65 Michael Lane, Hillsborough, NJ 08844 ▪ (908) 281-3981

25

Degree: BS, Chemical Engineering.
Job Target: Relevant internship or co-op job.
Strategy: The Relevant Experience & Skills section allows this individual to show areas of strength from past employment that are contributing factors to success in the engineering field.

DERRICK S. THOMAS

903 Osage Trail • Manhattan, Kansas 66502 • H: 785-246-3030 • CENGINEER@aol.com

OBJECTIVE	To obtain an internship or co-op position while completing my degree in chemical engineering.
HIGHLIGHTS OF QUALIFICATIONS	• Highly organized and dedicated, with a positive attitude. • Resourceful; skilled in analyzing and solving problems. • Good written, verbal, and interpersonal communications. • Ability to prioritize; complete multiple tasks under stressful situations. • Proficient in Microsoft Office (Word, PowerPoint, Excel, Access), Lotus 1-2-3, WordPerfect, e-mail, and Internet resources. • Fluent in Russian, Serbian, and Croatian.
RELEVANT EXPERIENCE & SKILLS	**Research & Analysis** • Trained in interception, transcription, and translation of foreign voice transmissions throughout Germany, Russia, and the United States. • Experienced in collecting, recording, and distributing secure intelligence information. • Demonstrated ability to operate intercept receivers to include radio telephones, multichannel systems, and recording equipment. • Possess a Top Secret Security Clearance granted by the United States Army and the Department of Defense. **Supervision & Training** • Supervised daily activities of personnel, quickly shifting priorities as requested by upper management. • Provided professional staff training in the areas of new techniques, safety, equipment use, and quality control. **Customer Service & Communications** • Effectively interacted with a wide range of diverse, culturally varied individuals; established and maintained positive interaction with the general public in customer-service capacities. • Successfully prepared, scheduled, and conducted specialized security training, briefings, and surveys to enhance the security of supported units.
EDUCATION	**Bachelor of Science: Chemical Engineering** Expected May 2006 Kansas State University, Manhattan, Kansas **Graduate,** Defense Language Institute, Monterey, California
WORK HISTORY	**Military Linguist and Analyst,** United States Army 1993 to 2002

26

Degree: BS, Chemical Engineering.
Job Target: Chemical engineering co-op.
Strategy: Made this young man stand a notch above others with (1) logo creativity, (2) special skills learned from past three co-ops, and (3) proven leadership in collegiate extracurricular activities. These skills carry over into the workplace and would certainly be addressed in a cover letter.
Outcome: Successful in securing well-paying co-op employment.

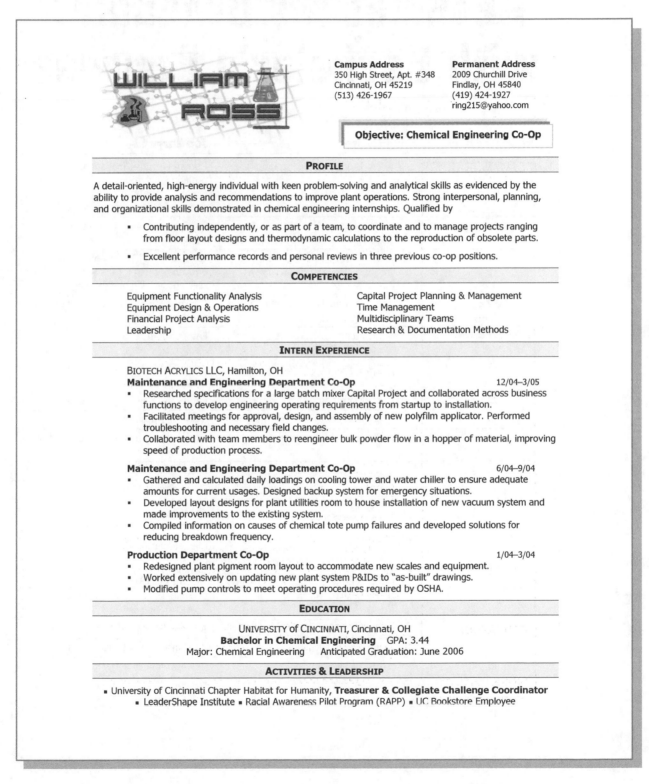

WILLIAM ROSS

Campus Address	**Permanent Address**
350 High Street, Apt. #348	2009 Churchill Drive
Cincinnati, OH 45219	Findlay, OH 45840
(513) 426-1967	(419) 424-1927
	ring215@yahoo.com

Objective: Chemical Engineering Co-Op

PROFILE

A detail-oriented, high-energy individual with keen problem-solving and analytical skills as evidenced by the ability to provide analysis and recommendations to improve plant operations. Strong interpersonal, planning, and organizational skills demonstrated in chemical engineering internships. Qualified by

- Contributing independently, or as part of a team, to coordinate and to manage projects ranging from floor layout designs and thermodynamic calculations to the reproduction of obsolete parts.
- Excellent performance records and personal reviews in three previous co-op positions.

COMPETENCIES

Equipment Functionality Analysis	Capital Project Planning & Management
Equipment Design & Operations	Time Management
Financial Project Analysis	Multidisciplinary Teams
Leadership	Research & Documentation Methods

INTERN EXPERIENCE

BIOTECH ACRYLICS LLC, Hamilton, OH
Maintenance and Engineering Department Co-Op   12/04–3/05
- Researched specifications for a large batch mixer Capital Project and collaborated across business functions to develop engineering operating requirements from startup to installation.
- Facilitated meetings for approval, design, and assembly of new polyfilm applicator. Performed troubleshooting and necessary field changes.
- Collaborated with team members to reengineer bulk powder flow in a hopper of material, improving speed of production process.

Maintenance and Engineering Department Co-Op   6/04–9/04
- Gathered and calculated daily loadings on cooling tower and water chiller to ensure adequate amounts for current usages. Designed backup system for emergency situations.
- Developed layout designs for plant utilities room to house installation of new vacuum system and made improvements to the existing system.
- Compiled information on causes of chemical tote pump failures and developed solutions for reducing breakdown frequency.

Production Department Co-Op   1/04–3/04
- Redesigned plant pigment room layout to accommodate new scales and equipment.
- Worked extensively on updating new plant system P&IDs to "as-built" drawings.
- Modified pump controls to meet operating procedures required by OSHA.

EDUCATION

UNIVERSITY of CINCINNATI, Cincinnati, OH
Bachelor in Chemical Engineering   GPA: 3.44
Major: Chemical Engineering   Anticipated Graduation: June 2006

ACTIVITIES & LEADERSHIP

- University of Cincinnati Chapter Habitat for Humanity, **Treasurer & Collegiate Challenge Coordinator**
- LeaderShape Institute ▪ Racial Awareness Pilot Program (RAPP) ▪ UC Bookstore Employee

CHAPTER 7

Resumes for Graduates with Bachelor's Degrees

Resume Number	Degree	Job Target
27	BA, Business Administration	Human resources/management training position (This resume and resume 28 were written for the same individual seeking two different job targets.)
28	BA, Business Administration	Retail management (see resume 27 for this individual)
29	BS, Construction Engineering	Sales position (This resume and resume 30 were written for the same individual seeking two different job targets.)
30	BS, Construction Engineering	Construction engineering position (see resume 29 for this individual)
31	BA, Communication Sciences and Disorders	Entry to graduate school
32	BA, General Education	Admission to Master of Education program
33	BS, Marketing	Entry-level marketing associate
34	BS, Marketing	Marketing position
35	BS, Sports Management	Sports marketing position for a major sports league
36	BA, Natural Science	Pharmaceutical sales
37	BA, Marketing	Pharmaceutical sales
38	BS, Marketing	Sales
39	BA (in progress)	Retail sales (while going to school)
40	BS, Business Administration	Marketing position with a pro sports team
41	BS, Business Administration	Public relations or marketing
42	BA, Spanish/French	Communications/public relations/ sales/customer service
43	BS, Communications	Ad copywriter or account executive
44	BA, Communications	Local media or national TV network
45	BA, Architecture	Architect in a large city
46	BA, Interior Design	Position with a trend leader in the home design industry
47	BFA	A position in a fine-arts museum with future growth to director level
48	BS, Elementary Education	Elementary school teacher
49	BA, Education	High-school history, political science, or geography teacher

Resume Number	Degree	Job Target
50	BS, Health and Physical Education	Phys. ed. teacher or fitness coach/trainer
51	BA, Sociology	Social researcher
52	BA, Social Work/Communication	Social work (adolescent counseling, prevention, intervention)
53	BA, Psychology	Employment in human service field while working on postgraduate degree
54	BA, Gerontology	Geriatric care/management
55	BA, Psychology and Sociology, minor in Criminal Justice	A position in the criminal justice field
56	BS, Criminal Justice (degree pending)	Victim/witness program coordinator
57	BS, Biological Sciences, and BS, Psychology	Crime scene investigator/field investigator
58	BS, Pathologist's Assistant	Pathologist's assistant
59	BS, Agricultural Studies	A position in agribusiness
60	BS, Biology	Professional biology career
61	BS, Civil Engineering	Wastewater civil engineer
62	BS, Chemical Engineering	Entry-level chemical engineering position
63	BS, Technology, major in Mechanical Design Technology	Mechanical design in the automotive industry
64	BS, Management Computer Information Systems	Help desk position
65	BS, Applied Science	Systems analyst
66	BS, Computer Science	Systems analyst/programmer
67	BS, Accounting	Entry-level accounting position
68	BS, Management Information Systems	MIS position
69	Bachelor of Commerce	Corporate accounting position
70	BS, Marine Business	Primarily marine business, but also interested in investment/financial analysis or market research
71	BA, Political Science	Investment banking/financial services
72	BS, Business Administration	A position in finance
73	BS, Business Management	A position in finance
74	BS, Economics	Retail management
75	BA, Human Resources	HR position
76	BS, Communications, emphasis in Human Relations	Specific position with a specific organization: graduate hall director at Northwestern University

27

Degree: BA, Business Administration.
Job Target: Human resources/management training position.
Strategy: Culled relevant HR experience from five years in retail, and then used side headings to highlight relevant areas of education and experience.

Christopher Dell

29 Highland Avenue
Stoneham, MA 02180
chrisdell@attglobal.net
781-749-2059

GOAL

Management Training opportunity with emphasis in Human Resources.

SUMMARY OF QUALIFICATIONS

- Bachelor's degree in Business Administration, with concentration in management and additional coursework in organizational behavior.
- Track record of advancement based on proven capabilities, work ethic, and enthusiasm.
- Management experience in a fast-paced retail environment.
- Chosen to train all new employees and new managers for 12-store retail district.
- Able to effectively supervise and motivate staff to high performance levels.
- Understand bottom-line priorities and the importance of customer satisfaction.

EDUCATION
December 2005

Boston College, Chestnut Hill, MA
Bachelor of Arts in Business Administration   Area of Emphasis: Management

Relevant Coursework

Accounting	*Organizational Management*	*Organizational Behavior*
Economics	*Small Business Management*	*Operations Management*
Finance	*Administrative Personnel Systems*	*First Line Supervisor*
Business Law	*Quantitative Methods for Business*	*Introduction to Computers*
Statistics	*High Performance Teams in Business*	

Accomplishments

- Personally financed 100% of college education through full-time employment; completed bachelor's degree in 4½ years.
- Won Coach's Award as member of track team, freshman year.

EXPERIENCE
2000–Present

BLOCKBUSTER VIDEO—Promoted through 5 levels to current position as second-in-command at the busiest location in the Boston area. Recognized for abilities in training, managing, and motivating staff; providing excellent customer service; and demonstrating initiative and responsibility.

Senior Assistant Manager, Woburn, MA
Train and manage customer service staff and oversee store operations to ensure customer satisfaction, operating efficiency, and compliance with corporate procedures. Handle and resolve customer questions and complaints. Help manage store revenue; handle cash and balance totals. Maintain well-organized inventory and keep customer service staff on track with ongoing operational duties. Manage entire store during manager's absence.

Human Resources and Training

- Assist with interviewing and participate in hiring decisions.
- With store manager, selected as regional training team for a newly launched corporate training program. Personally train all new employees for 12-store North Shore district through week-long program of on-site instruction, observation, and testing; also train new managers in a 3-week program.
- Developed a wide range of training and motivational methods to build on strengths and improve weaknesses of individual employees.

Customer Service

- Communicate customer-service focus to staff, working hard to keep lines short, inventories clean and well stocked, and staff focused on courtesy and helpfulness.
- Developed new organizational system for fast, error-free restocking of returned videos.

Staff Supervision

- Create effective supervisory relationship with each employee; able to adapt management style to best motivate individual staff members.

Degree: BA, Business Administration.
Job Target: Retail Management.
Strategy: For this second resume for the same individual (see resume 27), reversed order of education and experience because employment was directly related to the career target.

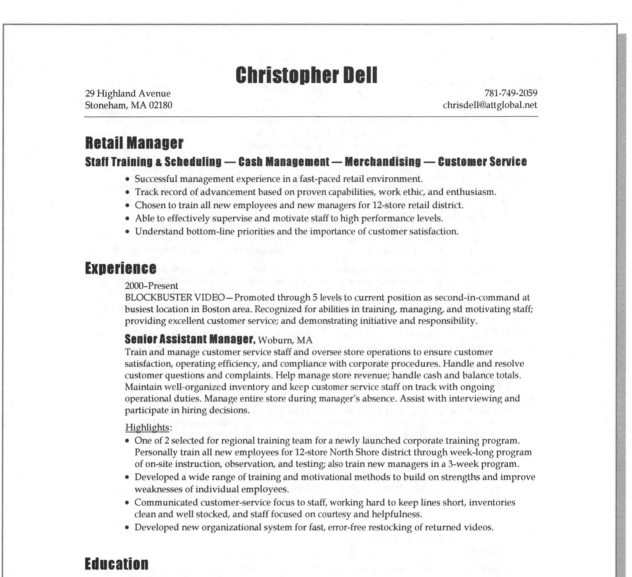

Christopher Dell

29 Highland Avenue
Stoneham, MA 02180

781-749-2059
chrisdell@attglobal.net

Retail Manager
Staff Training & Scheduling — Cash Management — Merchandising — Customer Service

- Successful management experience in a fast-paced retail environment.
- Track record of advancement based on proven capabilities, work ethic, and enthusiasm.
- Chosen to train all new employees and new managers for 12-store retail district.
- Able to effectively supervise and motivate staff to high performance levels.
- Understand bottom-line priorities and the importance of customer satisfaction.

Experience

2000–Present
BLOCKBUSTER VIDEO—Promoted through 5 levels to current position as second-in-command at busiest location in Boston area. Recognized for abilities in training, managing, and motivating staff; providing excellent customer service; and demonstrating initiative and responsibility.

Senior Assistant Manager, Woburn, MA
Train and manage customer service staff and oversee store operations to ensure customer satisfaction, operating efficiency, and compliance with corporate procedures. Handle and resolve customer questions and complaints. Help manage store revenue; handle cash and balance totals. Maintain well-organized inventory and keep customer service staff on track with ongoing operational duties. Manage entire store during manager's absence. Assist with interviewing and participate in hiring decisions.

Highlights:
- One of 2 selected for regional training team for a newly launched corporate training program. Personally train all new employees for 12-store North Shore district through week-long program of on-site instruction, observation, and testing; also train new managers in a 3-week program.
- Developed a wide range of training and motivational methods to build on strengths and improve weaknesses of individual employees.
- Communicated customer-service focus to staff, working hard to keep lines short, inventories clean and well stocked, and staff focused on courtesy and helpfulness.
- Developed new organizational system for fast, error-free restocking of returned videos.

Education

BOSTON COLLEGE, Chestnut Hill, MA
Bachelor of Arts in Business Administration, December 2005
Area of Emphasis: Management

Relevant Coursework:

Accounting	Organizational Management	Administrative Personnel Systems
Economics	Organizational Behavior	First Line Supervisor
Finance	Small Business Management	Quantitative Methods for Business
Business Law	Operations Management	High Performance Teams in Business

Accomplishments:
- Personally financed 100% of college education through full-time employment; completed bachelor's degree in 4½ years.
- Won Coach's Award as member of track team, freshman year.

29

Degree: BS, Construction Engineering.
Job Target: Sales position. (This resume and resume 30 were written for the same individual seeking two different job targets.)
Strategy: Highlighted entrepreneurial ventures showing measurable sales results; downplayed engineering details of education, projects, and internships.

JORDAN JONES

3834 39TH Street
Lubbock, TX 79413   jjones50@aol.com

Home: 806.788.1111
Mobile: 806.239.1555

QUALIFICATIONS PROFILE
Sales, Business, and Leadership

Talented, resourceful, and dedicated professional offering a unique combination of professional skills. Experienced in developing entrepreneurial businesses and customer relationships. Enthusiastic and detail-oriented. Competitive, decisive, and committed to professional growth and opportunity. Experience includes

- Strategic Planning & Business Development
- Competitive Market Positioning
- Marketing & Sales Development
- Team Building & Leadership

- Business Vision & Strategy
- Customer Development & Relationships
- Special Projects Management
- Numbers Management & Estimating

"He (Jordan) has been successful in both... businesses, which he built from the ground up. Jordan is not a stranger to a hard day's work. He will be an asset to any quality organization."
                                                    —Kirk Curtis, Director of Marketing, A Group

---

EDUCATION

Bachelor of Science, Construction Engineering, Texas Tech University, Lubbock, TX, Spring 2005
- Worked throughout college career and earned a 3.1 GPA.
- Recognized on Dean's List, Spring 2004.
- Awarded three scholarships.

Presentations:
- Developed and presented a business and marketing plan for a mobile car wash.
- Planned and presented as a team member a project developed for a local business.
- Researched and presented a project in PowerPoint format, demonstrating the resolution of a problem for a business.

Specialized Courses:
- Computer Programming
- Contracts & Specifications
- Cost Estimating
- Project Management

- Statistical Methods
- Cost & Profit Analysis
- Professional & Business Communications

Honor graduate, Coronado High School (CHS), Lubbock, Texas • May 2001
- Lettered two years, Varsity Basketball; received All-Academic Athlete Award
- Participant: National Honor Society and Bell Crew Spirit Squad

"Jordan is a winner in every sense of the word."
                                                    —Barry Knight, CHS Head Basketball Coach

EXPERIENCE

Owner / Operator
Jordan Jones Mobile Car Care, Lubbock, TX • 2002 to Present
After selling a former business, developed a second entrepreneurial venture, a mobile car wash company.

- Developed more than 25 regular clients.
- Maintain excellent client relationships with a 100% satisfaction rate.
- Drove business to more than $5K in profits annually.

29 *(continued)*

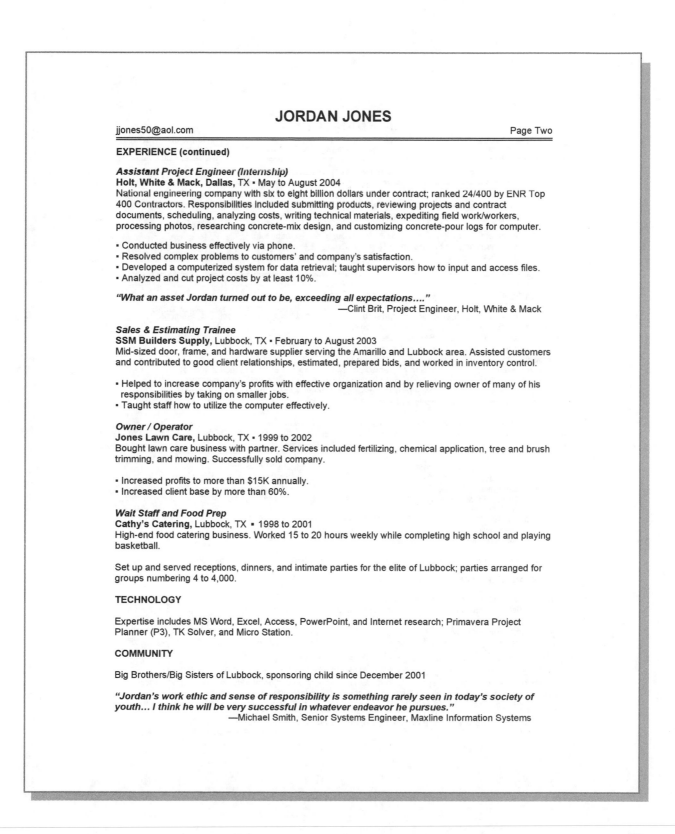

JORDAN JONES

jjones50@aol.com   Page Two

EXPERIENCE (continued)

Assistant Project Engineer (Internship)
Holt, White & Mack, Dallas, TX ▪ May to August 2004
National engineering company with six to eight billion dollars under contract; ranked 24/400 by ENR Top 400 Contractors. Responsibilities included submitting products, reviewing projects and contract documents, scheduling, analyzing costs, writing technical materials, expediting field work/workers, processing photos, researching concrete-mix design, and customizing concrete-pour logs for computer.

▪ Conducted business effectively via phone.
▪ Resolved complex problems to customers' and company's satisfaction.
▪ Developed a computerized system for data retrieval; taught supervisors how to input and access files.
▪ Analyzed and cut project costs by at least 10%.

"What an asset Jordan turned out to be, exceeding all expectations...."
—Clint Brit, Project Engineer, Holt, White & Mack

Sales & Estimating Trainee
SSM Builders Supply, Lubbock, TX ▪ February to August 2003
Mid-sized door, frame, and hardware supplier serving the Amarillo and Lubbock area. Assisted customers and contributed to good client relationships, estimated, prepared bids, and worked in inventory control.

▪ Helped to increase company's profits with effective organization and by relieving owner of many of his responsibilities by taking on smaller jobs.
▪ Taught staff how to utilize the computer effectively.

Owner / Operator
Jones Lawn Care, Lubbock, TX ▪ 1999 to 2002
Bought lawn care business with partner. Services included fertilizing, chemical application, tree and brush trimming, and mowing. Successfully sold company.

▪ Increased profits to more than $15K annually.
▪ Increased client base by more than 60%.

Wait Staff and Food Prep
Cathy's Catering, Lubbock, TX ▪ 1998 to 2001
High-end food catering business. Worked 15 to 20 hours weekly while completing high school and playing basketball.

Set up and served receptions, dinners, and intimate parties for the elite of Lubbock; parties arranged for groups numbering 4 to 4,000.

TECHNOLOGY

Expertise includes MS Word, Excel, Access, PowerPoint, and Internet research; Primavera Project Planner (P3), TK Solver, and Micro Station.

COMMUNITY

Big Brothers/Big Sisters of Lubbock, sponsoring child since December 2001

"Jordan's work ethic and sense of responsibility is something rarely seen in today's society of youth... I think he will be very successful in whatever endeavor he pursues."
—Michael Smith, Senior Systems Engineer, Maxline Information Systems

30

Degree: BS, Construction Engineering.
Job Target: Construction engineering position (see resume 29).
Strategy: Highlighted engineering details of education and projects; brought internship experience to the fore and downplayed entrepreneurial ventures.

JORDAN JONES

3834 39TH Street   Home: 806.788.1111
Lubbock, TX 79413   jjones50@aol.com   Mobile: 806.239.1555

CONSTRUCTION ENGINEER

Motivated, talented professional with the ability to plan, develop, and complete projects efficiently. Excellent time-management and human-relationship skills. Anticipate completion of BS in Construction Engineering spring 2005. Qualifications include

- Problem Resolution
- Teambuilding & Leadership
- Hands-on Experience
- Customer Relationships
- Quality & Productivity Improvement
- Engineering & Project Management

EDUCATION

Bachelor of Science, **Construction Engineering,** Texas Tech University, Lubbock, TX, Spring 2005
- Worked throughout college career and earned a 3.1 GPA.
- Recognized on Dean's List, Spring 2004.
- Successfully completed Fundamentals of Engineering Exam, Fall 2004.
Presentations:
  - Estimated, scheduled and presented group project to owner for a cafeteria addition.
  - Developed and presented a business and marketing plan for a mobile car wash.
  - Presented in PowerPoint format a project that demonstrated the successful resolution of a construction-specific problem.
Awarded:
  - West Texas Home Builders Scholarship, 2001 to Present
  - National Associated General Contractors Scholarship, Spring 2001 to Present
  - College of Engineering Scholarship, Spring 2004 to Present
Specialized Courses:
  - Construction Management
  - Contracts & Specifications
  - Engineering Design
  - Professional & Business Communications
  - Computer Programming
  - Statistical Methods
  - Cost Estimating
  - Cost & Profit Analysis

Honor graduate, Coronado High School (CHS), Lubbock, Texas, May 2001
- Lettered two years Varsity Basketball; received All-Academic Athlete Award
- Participant: National Honor Society and Bell Crew Spirit Squad

"Jordan is a winner in every sense of the word." —Barry Knight, CHS Basketball Coach

RELEVANT EXPERIENCE

Assistant Project Engineer (Internship)
Holt, White & Mack, Dallas, TX • May to August 2004
National engineering company with six to eight billion under contract; ranked 24/400 by ENR Top 400 Contractors. Responsibilities included submitting products, reviewing projects and contract documents, scheduling, analyzing costs, writing technical materials, expediting field work/workers, processing photos, researching concrete-mix design, and customizing concrete-pour logs for computer.

- Analyzed and cut costs for project by at least 10%.
- Developed a computerized system for data retrieval; taught project engineers how to input and access files.
- Resolved complex technical problems and conducted business effectively via phone.
- Developed, maintained, and expedited the schedule for a small phase of a large construction project.

"What an asset Jordan turned out to be, exceeding all expectations for a summer intern...."
                                    —Clint Brit, Project Engineer, Holt, White & Mack

30 *(continued)*

JORDAN JONES

jjones50@aol.com   Page Two

Sales & Estimating Trainee (Internship)
SSM Builders Supply, Lubbock, TX • February to August 2003
Mid-sized door, frame, and hardware supplier serving the Amarillo and Lubbock area. Estimated, prepared bids, worked in inventory control, assisted customers, and contributed to good client relationships. Became proficient in material take-off from contract documents, plans, and specifications. Taught staff how to utilize the computer effectively.

• Increased company's ability to take on more work through effective organization and relieving owner of many of his responsibilities.

ADDITIONAL WORK EXPERIENCE

Owner/Operator
Jordan Jones Mobile Car Care, Lubbock, TX • 2002 to Present
Developed a mobile car wash business with 25 regular clients and $5K profits annually.

• Selected equipment and assembled car wash trailer.
• Maintain excellent client relationships with a 100% satisfaction rate.

Owner
Jones Lawn Care, Lubbock, TX • 1999 to 2002
Bought lawn care business. Services included fertilizing, chemical application, tree and brush trimming, and mowing.

• Increased client base by more than 60%, drove profits to more than $15K yearly.

"Jordan's work ethic and sense of responsibility is something rarely seen in today's society of youth… I think he will be very successful in whatever endeavor he pursues."
—Michael Smith, Senior Systems Engineer, Maxline Information Systems

TECHNOLOGY

Expertise includes Primavera Project Planner (P3), TK Solver, Micro Station; MS Word, Excel, Access, PowerPoint, and Internet research.

ASSOCIATIONS / COMMUNITY

Student Member, Association of General Contractors
Member, Society of Engineer Technologists
Participate in Big Brothers/Big Sisters of Lubbock, sponsoring the same child since December 2001

"I would highly recommend Jordan Jones to any construction company with which he would seek employment."
—Clint Brit, Project Engineer, Holt, White & Mack

31

Degree: BA, Communication Sciences and Disorders.
Target: Entry to graduate school.
Strategy: Created a unique one-page resume using visuals to target field of study (audiology).

SAMANTHA COSSUM

352-424-6633
cossum@email.net

1483 Long Drive
Gainesville, FL 32622

"You will become as small as
your controlling desire; or as
great as your dominant
aspiration." —*James Allen*

Articulate and personable **COMMUNICATION SCIENCES AND DISORDERS** scholar distinguished by...

- Effective communication, listening, and interpersonal skills
- A strong customer focus, with attention to detail and excellent follow-through
- The ability to work independently or as part of a team
- A unique combination of analytical and creative competencies in approaching and resolving challenges
- Computer proficiency

EDUCATION

Bachelor of Arts, CSD—2005
University of Florida, Gainesville, Florida

- Graduated with honors, 3.96/4.0 GPA
- Recipient of a 4-year Florida Academic Scholars Award
- Named to the President's Honor Roll every semester
- CLAS Anderson Scholar of High Distinction

ACADEMIC MEMBERSHIPS

National Society of Collegiate Scholars
Golden Key National Honor Society

EMPLOYMENT

Office Assistant

John Smith, Esq., Gainesville, Florida—since August 2005
Keith Long, M.D., Brandon, Florida—Summer 2004
Allen Carlisle, C.P.A., Brandon, Florida—Summer 2003

Resident Assistant

University of Florida, Division of Housing
Gainesville, Florida—January 2004 to May 2005

- Murphree Area Special Recognition Award, Spring 2005
- Trained in crisis intervention, team building, conflict mediation, and confrontation and assertiveness

32

Degree: BA, General Education.
Target: Admission to Master of Education program.
Strategy: Conveyed dedication through extensive volunteer activities and relevant employment experiences.

CARA PENNY

2222 22nd Street, Mooney, WA 90001
(555) 888-5555
e-mail: cpenny@hotmail.com

OBJECTIVE

Master of Education Program —Student Personnel Administration

PROFILE

Industrious university student presents a track record of responsibility and achievement. Demonstrated desire and ability to motivate and encourage student development and interest in education. Adaptable, flexible, dedicated team player with proven leadership capabilities recognized for ability to generate enthusiasm and instill confidence in others. Strong public relations and presentation skills, both written and spoken. Computer literate.

"Cara has always impressed me as a woman who is talented, personable, and dedicated to whatever she puts her mind to. She is motivated to be successful in all her endeavors." —Director of Athletics

EMPLOYMENT RECORD

Women's Basketball Student Assistant Coach, Mooney Washington University   6/03–present
Assist head and assistant coaches, including coaching, counseling, and inspiring young women on the team. Strategize, plan practices, instruct breakdown drills, deliver pep talks. Review game videos to assess play tactics. Scout potential recruits. Provide transportation to and from airport.

Nanny to Two Preschool-age Children, private family, Mooney, Washington   1/04–present
Mornings only, Monday through Friday, provide general care-taking—create and implement activities, prepare food, and provide transportation.

Girls' Basketball Camp Assistant Director, Mooney Washington University   Summers 2003–present
Direct and manage 32 coaches and 400 students. Teach Mass Demos—instruct, speak, and demonstrate basketball techniques and strategies. Act as liaison for program participants and parents. Provide information, resolve conflicts, and solve wide range of problems—personal, structural, premises, and more.

Women's Basketball Camp Registrar, Mooney Washington University   4/01–10/01
Accepted and processed more than 500 applications for MWU Basketball Camp. Created registration database in Excel for tracking applicants, deposits, balances due, etc. Oversaw financial transactions totaling $150,000 for camp—administered petty cash in coordination with other departments. Effectively communicated with applicants and potential applicants face-to-face and by phone.

Assistant to Administrative Assistant, Mooney Washington University   6/00–10/00
Answered telephones using Northern Telecom PBX system. Distributed mail, filed, typed. Assisted with preparation for Viking Night Fundraiser that generated $70,000.

VOLUNTEER SERVICE	AWARDS AND HONORS
Facilitate MWU Girls' Basketball Clinics	MWU Coaches Award 2003, one of only two awarded
Presentations to Campfire Girls and county elementary schools on the importance of staying in school and the relevance of athletics	Elected to Tournament Teams
	Captain of MWU Women's Basketball Team
Testimonials at MWU Athletic Department-sponsored scholarship lunches and breakfasts	CEMORE Captain Humanities Award, 1996
	NCAA II Final Four, 2002–2003
MWU Athletic Department Representative on NAKAMA 2000 Leadership Panel	NCAA II Sweet Sixteen, 2001–2002
Speaker at Mascot Night 2003 Annual Auction	Homecoming Queen, Mooney High School, 1998

EDUCATION

B.A., General Education, Mooney Washington University, Mooney, Washington, June 2004

33 **Degree:** BS, Marketing.
Job Target: Entry-level marketing associate.
Strategy: Used academic projects and independent experience of starting a dot-com business to position this new graduate as someone with the knowledge and experience to be successful.

DANIEL LENNON

2 Oriental Crossway 25-A • Brentwood, NY 11717 • (631) 402-3009 • dlbmd@mall.net

Seeking an entry-level position in the capacity of

MARKETING ASSOCIATE

Offer a Bachelor's degree in marketing, diverse experience, and a solid understanding of marketing strategies illustrated through academic projects and an Internet venture that continues to develop and test theoretical marketing strategies and business management skills in the areas of

– Conceptual Planning	– Web-Based Marketing	– Advertising Campaigns
– Strategy Development	– Market Penetration	– Media/Client Relations
– Project Management	– Competitive Analysis	– Ad Copy Creation

EDUCATION

Bachelor of Science, Marketing, 2005
STATE UNIVERSITY OF NEW YORK AT OLD WESTBURY

— Academic Research Projects —

Conducted a case study on National (Long Island) and International (Russia) markets to determine the feasibility of import and export operations with a focus on

economics • consumer populations • cultural influences • communications • demographic infrastructure • product mix • target marketing and penetration • warehousing • distribution • brand awareness • advertising strategies (television, radio, print, Internet, billboard, co-op, and direct mailings).

Conducted a case study on Microsoft Corporation vs. Netscape to determine the ethical sale and marketing of Internet browsers. Formulated an argument and presented data to support decision in Microsoft Corporation's favor based on the Sherman Anti-trust Act of 1896.

EXPERIENCE

Marketing • Sales • Customer Service

Marketing Manager, Big Mall Direct, Brentwood, NY   8/03–present
- Conceptualized the development and launch of bigmalldirect.com, an e-commerce–driven consumer and business-to-business Internet-based shopping mall offering a range of retail products and services.
- Cost-effectively increase site visibility through reciprocal link programs with local and national partner sites as well as print advertising. Achieved a 25% increase in traffic from November to close of 2004.
- Retained a web developer to build site; independently manage all aspects of site maintenance.

Licensed Stock Broker (Series 63 and 7), Garnett Barger, Glen Cove, NY   5/01–8/02
- Sold MidCap and aggressive/high-risk stocks through generation of up to 600 daily outbound sales calls to prospective pharmaceutical, software, and Internet-based client investors.
- Assessed clients' short-term financial goals to reduce investment risks and maximize financial gains.

Customer Service Representative (NE Region), US Auto Insurance, Westbury, NY   5/00–5/01
- Processed customer-service requests for a broad range of changes in automobile policy status.
- Achieved a 99% customer retention rate as a result of customer needs assessments and quality service.
- Interfaced with claims, sales, underwriting, fraud investigation, and special requests departments to ensure proper communications and timely, accurate processing of claims.

34 **Degree:** BS, Marketing.
Job Target: Marketing position.
Strategy: Drew on the combination of education and work ethic, highlighting skills employers are looking for such as communication and leadership.

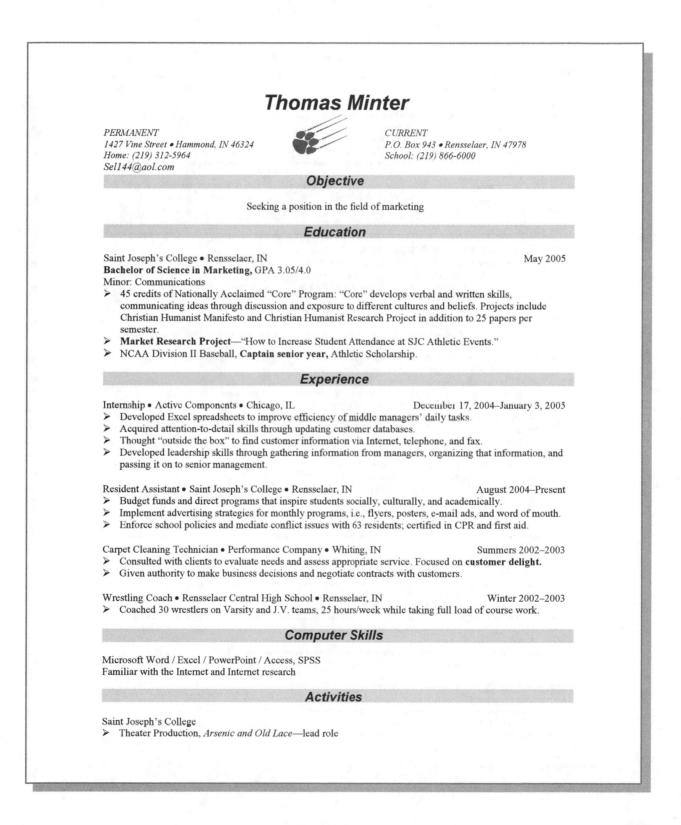

Thomas Minter

PERMANENT
1427 Vine Street • Hammond, IN 46324
Home: (219) 312-5964
Sel144@aol.com

CURRENT
P.O. Box 943 • Rensselaer, IN 47978
School: (219) 866-6000

Objective

Seeking a position in the field of marketing

Education

Saint Joseph's College • Rensselaer, IN   May 2005
Bachelor of Science in Marketing, GPA 3.05/4.0
Minor: Communications
➤ 45 credits of Nationally Acclaimed "Core" Program: "Core" develops verbal and written skills, communicating ideas through discussion and exposure to different cultures and beliefs. Projects include Christian Humanist Manifesto and Christian Humanist Research Project in addition to 25 papers per semester.
➤ **Market Research Project**—"How to Increase Student Attendance at SJC Athletic Events."
➤ NCAA Division II Baseball, **Captain senior year,** Athletic Scholarship.

Experience

Internship • Active Components • Chicago, IL   December 17, 2004–January 3, 2005
➤ Developed Excel spreadsheets to improve efficiency of middle managers' daily tasks.
➤ Acquired attention-to-detail skills through updating customer databases.
➤ Thought "outside the box" to find customer information via Internet, telephone, and fax.
➤ Developed leadership skills through gathering information from managers, organizing that information, and passing it on to senior management.

Resident Assistant • Saint Joseph's College • Rensselaer, IN   August 2004–Present
➤ Budget funds and direct programs that inspire students socially, culturally, and academically.
➤ Implement advertising strategies for monthly programs, i.e., flyers, posters, e-mail ads, and word of mouth.
➤ Enforce school policies and mediate conflict issues with 63 residents; certified in CPR and first aid.

Carpet Cleaning Technician • Performance Company • Whiting, IN   Summers 2002–2003
➤ Consulted with clients to evaluate needs and assess appropriate service. Focused on **customer delight.**
➤ Given authority to make business decisions and negotiate contracts with customers.

Wrestling Coach • Rensselaer Central High School • Rensselaer, IN   Winter 2002–2003
➤ Coached 30 wrestlers on Varsity and J.V. teams, 25 hours/week while taking full load of course work.

Computer Skills

Microsoft Word / Excel / PowerPoint / Access, SPSS
Familiar with the Internet and Internet research

Activities

Saint Joseph's College
➤ Theater Production, *Arsenic and Old Lace*—lead role

Degree: BS, Sports Management.
Job Target: Sports marketing position for a major sports league.
Strategy: Overcame the challenge of average academic performance and lack of paid work experience by highlighting the highly visible internships she was able to line up, where she had strong accomplishments.

SHOSHANA R. LESKY

9254 Guilford Road ➤ Hamburg, NY 14737   716.345.2366 ➤ lesky21@aol.com

PROFILE

♦ Pending college graduate with strong academic skills and hands-on experience planning and implementing programs, projects, and public-relations events.

♦ Represent companies intelligently and professionally; excellent customer-service, public-relations, and leadership qualities.

♦ Strong organizational skills; take initiative in identifying ways to streamline tasks and meet deadlines on or ahead of schedule.

♦ Computer competent: demonstrated ability using Microsoft Word, Excel, Access, and PowerPoint; conducting Internet research; using office e-mail; formatting HTML.

EDUCATION

BS Sports Management, Buffalo State College, Buffalo, NY   May 2005

INTERNSHIP ASSIGNMENTS AND ACHIEVEMENTS

Sports Management Program, Buffalo State College, Buffalo, NY   2004–present

♦ Reported to the Director of Sports Management; earned a reputation as a dependable and hardworking student.

♦ Systematically streamlined the process for assigning, tracking, and evaluating student interns while cutting required paperwork virtually in half:
  – Reviewed packet of required forms to eliminate anything unnecessary or redundant.
  – Adapted weekly time sheets to a more efficient monthly system.
  – Oversaw the formatting of all paperwork in HTML so that forms could be accessed, completed, and printed directly from the Web site.

♦ Assisted with refining the student transfer component of the Sports Management degree:
  – Researched academic competencies required at other schools.
  – Compared competencies to equivalent Buffalo State classes.
  – Made recommendations to the director on ways to better serve transfer students.

Department of Student Affairs, Buffalo State College, Buffalo, NY   2000–2001

♦ Provided part-time support to the Dean of Students, interacting professionally with various academic departments and students.

♦ Independently managed registration for the annual Buffalo Run 5K Race:
  – Maintained a database of the 500+ race participants.
  – Oversaw formatting the database to post on the Web site.
  – Assisted with managing event activities the day of the race.
  – Met time-sensitive deadlines in posting racing outcomes to the Web.

Sales and Marketing Department, Buffalo Destroyers, Buffalo, NY   2003–2004

♦ Competently handled multiple tasks, in the office and at the games, demonstrating exceptional customer-service and phone skills and a willingness to learn new things.

♦ Effectively resolved problems with season ticket distribution, using patience, perseverance, and ability to deal with dissatisfied customers to ensure delivery of nearly 5,000 returned tickets in time for season opening.

♦ Received and processed phone and ticket-window requests for game-day and season tickets, while learning to use a "Ticketmaster" computer system to access arena seating.

♦ Read and sorted e-mail from fans; responded or forwarded to the appropriate department for response; maintained a database of customer comments.

Department of Promotions, Buffalo Blizzards, Buffalo, NY   2002–2003

♦ Professionally represented the team during various game-day activities, promotions, and public presentations.

♦ Engaged game spectators to participate in half-time shows; organized activities and coordinated distribution of promotional awards.

♦ Assisted with alcohol-/drug-free presentations by team players at area elementary schools.

♦ Supported the office Administrative Assistant in routine tasks, including creating office correspondence and maintaining a database.

EXTRACURRICULAR AND LEADERSHIP ACTIVITIES

Captain of the Women's Inaugural Soccer Division III
Resident Assistant and President of Resident Student Council
President of the Sports Management Club
Upperclassmen Senator for Student Government

36

Degree: BA, Natural Science.
Job Target: Pharmaceutical sales.
Strategy: Highlighted science coursework (because the individual had a BA rather than BS degree) and leadership skills; downplayed student athletic trainer internship (an area he was initially interested in pursuing).

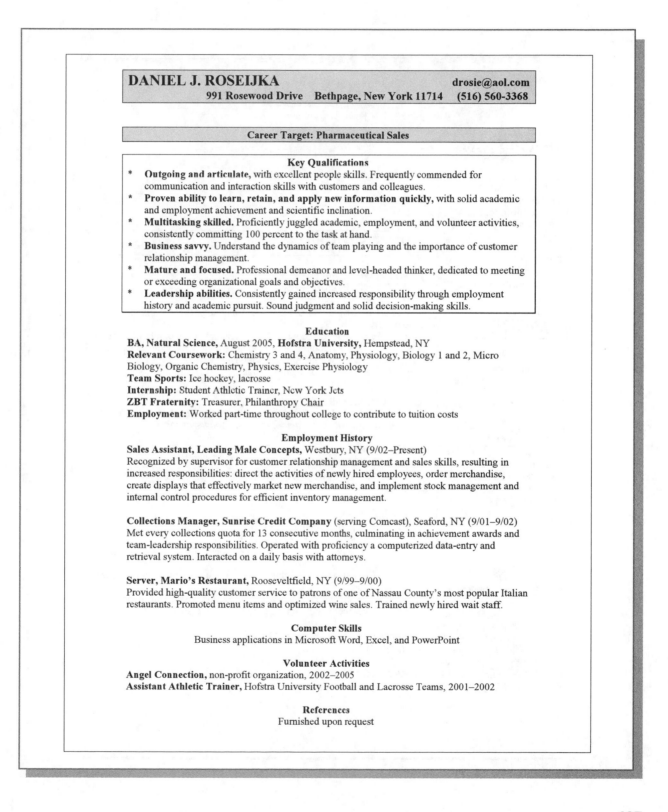

DANIEL J. ROSEIJKA   drosie@aol.com
991 Rosewood Drive   Bethpage, New York 11714   (516) 560-3368

Career Target: Pharmaceutical Sales

Key Qualifications

* **Outgoing and articulate,** with excellent people skills. Frequently commended for communication and interaction skills with customers and colleagues.
* **Proven ability to learn, retain, and apply new information quickly,** with solid academic and employment achievement and scientific inclination.
* **Multitasking skilled.** Proficiently juggled academic, employment, and volunteer activities, consistently committing 100 percent to the task at hand.
* **Business savvy.** Understand the dynamics of team playing and the importance of customer relationship management.
* **Mature and focused.** Professional demeanor and level-headed thinker, dedicated to meeting or exceeding organizational goals and objectives.
* **Leadership abilities.** Consistently gained increased responsibility through employment history and academic pursuit. Sound judgment and solid decision-making skills.

Education

BA, Natural Science, August 2005, **Hofstra University,** Hempstead, NY
Relevant Coursework: Chemistry 3 and 4, Anatomy, Physiology, Biology 1 and 2, Micro Biology, Organic Chemistry, Physics, Exercise Physiology
Team Sports: Ice hockey, lacrosse
Internship: Student Athletic Trainer, New York Jets
ZBT Fraternity: Treasurer, Philanthropy Chair
Employment: Worked part-time throughout college to contribute to tuition costs

Employment History

Sales Assistant, Leading Male Concepts, Westbury, NY (9/02–Present)
Recognized by supervisor for customer relationship management and sales skills, resulting in increased responsibilities: direct the activities of newly hired employees, order merchandise, create displays that effectively market new merchandise, and implement stock management and internal control procedures for efficient inventory management.

Collections Manager, Sunrise Credit Company (serving Comcast), Seaford, NY (9/01–9/02)
Met every collections quota for 13 consecutive months, culminating in achievement awards and team-leadership responsibilities. Operated with proficiency a computerized data-entry and retrieval system. Interacted on a daily basis with attorneys.

Server, Mario's Restaurant, Rooseveltfield, NY (9/99–9/00)
Provided high-quality customer service to patrons of one of Nassau County's most popular Italian restaurants. Promoted menu items and optimized wine sales. Trained newly hired wait staff.

Computer Skills
Business applications in Microsoft Word, Excel, and PowerPoint

Volunteer Activities
Angel Connection, non-profit organization, 2002–2005
Assistant Athletic Trainer, Hofstra University Football and Lacrosse Teams, 2001–2002

References
Furnished upon request

37

Degree: BA, Marketing.
Job Target: Pharmaceutical sales.
Strategy: Created an attention-getting resume for a new grad seeking a position in a very competitive field. Focused on education as well as sales experience and accomplishments, obtained in internships and work experience.

OLIVER TRENT

555 Fifth Avenue
Duluth, Minnesota 55777
(218) 879-5555
Email: olivertrent@yahoo.com

EDUCATION

UNIVERSITY OF MINNESOTA, Duluth
Bachelor of Arts—2005
Major: **Communications**
Minor: **Marketing**

NOTTINGHAM TRENT UNIVERSITY, NOTTINGHAM, ENGLAND
Study Abroad—Summer 2004

AWARDS

- Mayo Clinic Scholarship
- Arrowhead Award: Outstanding Student in a student organization, MN Board of Regents

COMMUNITY

- Habitat for Humanity, assisted in building a house.
- Channel One Food Shelf, stock shelves.
- Blanket Duluth.

"Committed on a personal and professional level to achieve and set higher goals."

EXPERIENCE

May 2004–Present
ACCOUNT EXECUTIVE
Mount Rose Publishing
Sell advertising for the University of Minnesota, Duluth, telephone directory.

- Service existing accounts. Contact potential customers by telephone and arrange appointments. Negotiate contracts, occasionally bartering services. Upsell advertising whenever possible.
- Arrange graphic designs manually.
- Handle billing.

ACCOMPLISHMENTS
Contact potential clients more than once, often resulting in a sale that otherwise would not be made, through persuasive selling.

2003–Present
SALES REPRESENTATIVE
No Limitz Snowboard Company
Sell snowboards.

2001–Present
(Certified Professional) SKI INSTRUCTOR
Ghost Mountain Ski Resort, Duluth, MN
- Part of hiring process of new ski instructors. Train new hires and evaluate their performance.
- Teach advanced-level classes. Persuade students to continue their ski lessons.
- Receive additional instruction from Ski Instructors of America.
- Provide information and sell products at pro shop.

September–November 2002
INTERN
UMD University Relations
Wrote and edited magazine articles, bi-weekly newsletter, telephone directory, and news releases.

37 *(continued)*

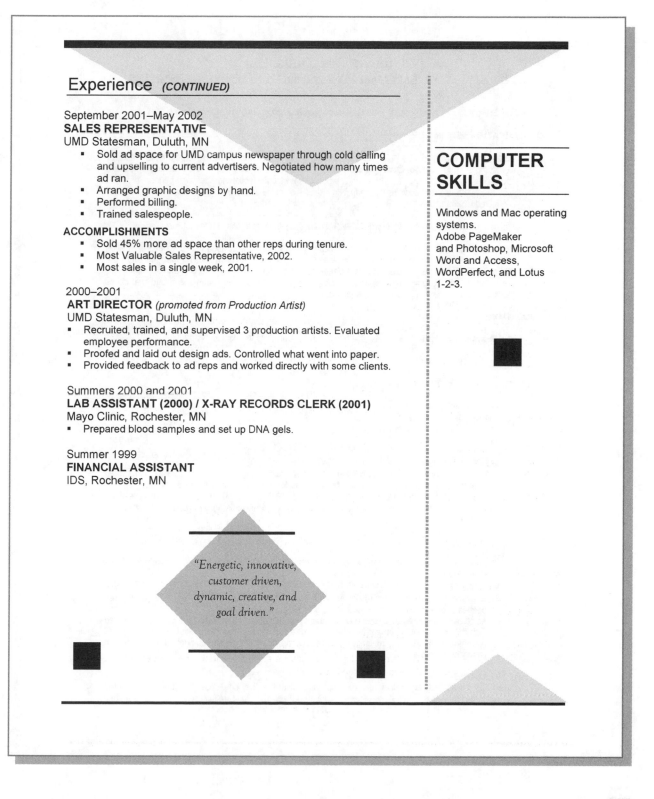

Experience *(CONTINUED)*

September 2001–May 2002
SALES REPRESENTATIVE
UMD Statesman, Duluth, MN
- Sold ad space for UMD campus newspaper through cold calling and upselling to current advertisers. Negotiated how many times ad ran.
- Arranged graphic designs by hand.
- Performed billing.
- Trained salespeople.

ACCOMPLISHMENTS
- Sold 45% more ad space than other reps during tenure.
- Most Valuable Sales Representative, 2002.
- Most sales in a single week, 2001.

2000–2001
ART DIRECTOR *(promoted from Production Artist)*
UMD Statesman, Duluth, MN
- Recruited, trained, and supervised 3 production artists. Evaluated employee performance.
- Proofed and laid out design ads. Controlled what went into paper.
- Provided feedback to ad reps and worked directly with some clients.

Summers 2000 and 2001
LAB ASSISTANT (2000) / X-RAY RECORDS CLERK (2001)
Mayo Clinic, Rochester, MN
- Prepared blood samples and set up DNA gels.

Summer 1999
FINANCIAL ASSISTANT
IDS, Rochester, MN

COMPUTER SKILLS

Windows and Mac operating systems.
Adobe PageMaker and Photoshop, Microsoft Word and Access, WordPerfect, and Lotus 1-2-3.

"Energetic, innovative, customer driven, dynamic, creative, and goal driven."

38

Degree: BS, Marketing.
Job Target: Sales.
Strategy: Emphasized sales internship; industry knowledge (he was interested in targeting the audiovisual industry); professional sales training (he'd financed an intensive, two-day AMA sales training program himself); and job experience as a bartender, server, and trainer to relate to his objective.

SHANE T. MCDOUGALL

9219 Holmes Drive, Apt. 15 • Blacksburg, VA 24060 • (540) 513-2064 • shanemcdougall@access.net

OBJECTIVE: Professional sales position within the ***audiovisual equipment/system industry.***

QUALIFICATIONS SUMMARY:

Sales Intern—Worked at API, a firm specializing in the sales and marketing of computer modular workstations and ***audiovisual equipment.*** Participated in two-week sales-training program, encompassing role-playing activities and product knowledge. Following training period, provided customers with updated audiovisual product literature. Also made cold calls; prepared sales proposals and conducted telemarketing.

Industry Knowledge—Subscribe to *Presentations* magazine, an audiovisual trade journal.

Professional Sales Training—Took American Management Association's "Fundamental Selling Techniques for the New or Prospective Salesperson," an intensive, two-day, hands-on introduction to the art of selling. Course covered pre-call planning, prospecting, building rapport and commitment, presentation skills, reading buyer signals, handling objections, establishing commitment, and trial closes (April 8–9, 2004). Personally paid for this program.

EDUCATION:

B.S. Marketing, Virginia Polytechnic Institute and State University, Blacksburg, VA, 2005

Computer Skills: Microsoft Office (Word, PowerPoint); Internet savvy.

RELATED EMPLOYMENT EXPERIENCE:

Bartender—Houlihan's, Blacksburg, VA	4/03–Present
Bartender—The Firehouse Pub, Snowshoe, VA	10/02–4/03
Bartender—Rock Ola Café, Farmington, VA	1/01–9/01
Server—Rock Ola Café, Farmington, VA	5/00–1/01

SALES/INITIATIVE
- Won three contests for selling the most dinner specials among 15 servers/waitpersons. Promoted from server to bartender within one month at upscale, Irish-motif, Blacksburg restaurant.
- Recognized as *Employee of the Month* (August 2001) among 50 to 60 employees, based on performance above and beyond one's normal accountabilities. Assumed tasks of training and orienting new employees.
- Acknowledged as *Employee of the Month* (November 2000) among 50-plus employees; criteria included arriving on time, receiving no customer complaints, and assuming additional non-assigned responsibilities.
- Completed the 2003 New York City Marathon.

MANAGEMENT
- Implemented twice-daily liquor count, which substantially reduced liquor costs at Rock Ola. Also opened and/or closed restaurant, handling daily accounting (receipts).
- Acted as on-duty manager (was the only employee, except for the manager and owner, designated with this responsibility) at restaurant in the largest ski-resort market in the Southeast. Participated in informal discussions, making recommendations regarding menu changes that resulted in changeover from a gourmet deli to a full-scale dinner menu.

TRAINING
- Served as Certified Trainer for new employees. With this "key employee" designation, conducted screening and pre-interviews of prospective employees and group-training sessions for servers and bartenders. Provided with autonomous authority in resolving major customer problems.

39

Degree: BA (in progress).
Job Target: Retail sales (while going to school).
Strategy: Immediately established that she is experienced in retail sales, with an outstanding performance record; an achiever who pushes the envelope, whether competing for retail sales or being awarded a foreign exchange student slot (the only one chosen out of 50 applicants). Used Outward Bound experience to show high stamina and energy, and ability to handle changing situations.

	KATALINA SANDERS
OBJECTIVE	**Sales Associate—Retail Sales**
PROFILE	☑ College student with more than 4 years of retail sales experience. ☑ Professional and approachable manner. Talent for identifying customers' needs and presenting solutions that drive purchases. ☑ Highly motivated team player—willing to take on added responsibilities. ☑ Proven skills in problem solving and customer relations. Fluent Spanish.
COMPUTER	Microsoft Windows and Word, retail sales databases, Internet, e-mail
WORK HISTORY	**SENTIMENTS,** Randallstown Center, Randallstown, MD 2004–present **Sales Associate** Provide sales, merchandising, and customer service to upscale clientele in 700-square-foot card and stationery retail store. ▪ Successfully interact with more than 50 customers daily, achieving $300 to $500 in sales per day. Upsell and cross-sell products, ensuring customer satisfaction. Assigned managerial authority for opening store. ▪ Cultivate cooperative, team-oriented relationships with 10 co-workers and managers, assisting with custom orders and demanding customers. **CENTER STORE,** Magnolia Mall, Magnolia Heights, MD 2001–2004 **Senior Sales Associate** (Children's and Electronics Departments) Conducted inventory, merchandising, pricing, sales, and customer service of children's clothing, video games, and toys in 3,000-square-foot department. Worked in teams of 2–3 sales associates/managers, as well as alone. ▪ Promoted to Senior Sales Associate. Given open and close authority for store. Assisted in quarterly inventory-assessment program. ▪ Sold $1,000 in merchandise daily, serving 50–80 customers per day. Proofed cash drawer (including credit card sales) with low error rate. ▪ Developed loyal clientele and increased sales through personal attention to customers' needs. Resolved customer complaints diplomatically.
EDUCATION	Bachelor of Arts (in progress), Baltimore State University, Baltimore, MD Diploma, Magnolia Heights High School, Magnolia Heights, MD—2001
ACTIVITIES	Foreign Student Exchange Program—Seville, Spain Summer 2001 Chosen from 50 candidates; traveled throughout Spain. Outward Bound, The Appalachian Trail (Maryland) October 1999 Participated in week-long wilderness experience in a group of 10 students.

14 Magnolia Lane, Baltimore, MD 12345 ▪ (410) 825-5555 ▪ ksanders@mail.com

40

Degree: BS, Business Administration.
Job Target: Marketing position with a pro sports team.
Strategy: Capitalized on an internship with a financial services company, as well as his coaching and athletics experience.

TERRY S. CARRIGAN

207 Cherokee Drive
Hendersonville, TN 37075

Home (615) 264-2863
Campus (901) 587-7735

Career Focus — SALES & MARKETING

- May 2005 college graduate with a keen interest in professional sales and marketing career. Committed to continued learning and the improvement of business-related skills.

- Strong communication, interaction, and relationship-building skills acquired through experience as sales and marketing intern and through customer-service positions, volunteer work, team sports, and coaching activities.

- Computer experience includes Microsoft Office (Word, Excel) in a Windows XP environment. Confident in learning and using new business applications.

EDUCATION

B.S. BUSINESS ADMINISTRATION / MARKETING .... May 2005
University of Tennessee, Knoxville

WORK EXPERIENCE

INTERN .... Summer 2004
Chase Manhattan Financial Group, LLC—Brentwood, Tennessee

- Generated sales leads through aggressive cold calling from database of 1,100 companies. Developed list of 160+ leads and contacts that were forwarded to General Agent for follow-up. Accompanied General Agent on select appointments to observe sales style.
- Delivered well-received presentation to General Agent outlining prospect companies, contacts, renewal dates, and success rate comparison between 2002 and 1999 business directories.
- Used Internet sourcing (Monster.com) to recruit employee candidates for the Nashville area. Directed qualified yet out-of-area prospects to appropriate region of the state for follow-up.
- Attended intensive 3-day Career School to further develop sales skills. Topics included generating leads, prospecting for potential clients, and understanding the total sales process.

PHARMACY TECHNICIAN 2001–2003
Wal-Mart Pharmacy—Gallatin, Tennessee (2003)
R & R Prescription Shop—Hendersonville, Tennessee (2001–2002)

- Assisted pharmacists with reading and preparing prescriptions, compounding, counting pills, and filing insurance claims.
- Acquired significant experience in customer relations through direct contact with customers.

ACTIVITIES

VOLUNTEER: Worked with Alpha Tau Omega fraternity to raise $20,000 for Saint Jude's Children's Research Hospital (2003). Participated in Appalachian Service Project in West Virginia (2001).

COACH: Successfully coached intramural sorority basketball team to 2000 championship. Three years of experience as Assistant Coach in AAU Boys Basketball (1999–2002).

ATHLETE: Participated in tennis and basketball throughout high school and college plus intramural football in college. Achieved state ranking in tennis (1999–2001) and advanced to Tennessee State Tennis Tournament (2000–2001).

Degree: BS, Business Administration.
Job Target: Public relations or marketing.
Strategy: Used his history of success in the restaurant industry as a real asset toward attaining his job goal.

DAVID M. ARNONE

♦ ♦ ♦ ♦ ♦

1645 South Woodmont Drive, Apartment B21 ▪ Columbia, SC 29407
(843) 769-6929 ▪ arnon29407@msn.com

CAREER OBJECTIVE

Public Relations ▪ New Business Promotion ▪ Staff Training

PROFILE

- More than six years of experience working with the public in the customer-service-driven restaurant environment
- Gifted with a persuasive, congenial personality and a proven talent for building and maintaining positive rapport with diverse populations
- Demonstrate creativity; initiative; good judgment; and the ability to clearly and simply express thoughts, verbally and in writing
- Possess a working knowledge of basic computer skills, including Microsoft Office, WordPerfect, Lotus, COBOL, and the Internet
- Have a respect and appreciation for the organizational structure of a business and the level of detail necessary to maximize profits and foster a reputation for success
- Competitive, yet flexible; willing to travel

EDUCATION

BS, **Business Administration,** University of South Carolina, Columbia, SC   Graduation 2005

EMPLOYMENT

Server/Trainer, T-Bonz, Columbia, SC   2002 to present
- Competently manage multiple job responsibilities in a high-volume, fast-paced dining establishment, which caters to businesspeople, college students, and tourists. Serve up to 150 customers per shift; assist with the hands-on training of new hires.
- Foster repeat customers by consistently providing quick, well-timed, and professional service.
- Particularly adept at responding to customers' complaints by engaging them in arriving at acceptable solutions that address their concerns while minimizing lost profits.
- Have earned a reputation among co-workers and managers as a valuable and competent employee:
  - Known to be fair, honest, and willing to help others when needed.
  - Effectively mediate and resolve issues between management and staff.
  - Trusted with closing responsibilities.
  - Effectively handle the busy weekend shift, which generates $20,000 to $25,000 in sales.
- Assumed leadership in redesigning the restaurant menu board, working closely with a graphic designer to create a more graphic, aesthetically pleasing, permanent display.

Server/Kitchen Manager, Mosby's Restaurant, Richmond, VA   1999 to 2002
- Hired as a server for this family restaurant while attending high school. Took over responsibilities of Kitchen Manager, including scheduling and supervising eight to ten kitchen employees. Maintained inventory, placing orders of up to $3,000 per week.

42

Degree: BA, Spanish/French.
Job Target: Communications/public relations/sales/customer service.
Strategy: Used testimonials from instructors and employers demonstrating work ethic, enthusiasm, and ability to communicate and motivate others to action, with the goal of overcoming somewhat "unrelated" college degree and work history (she had no previous sales training or experience).

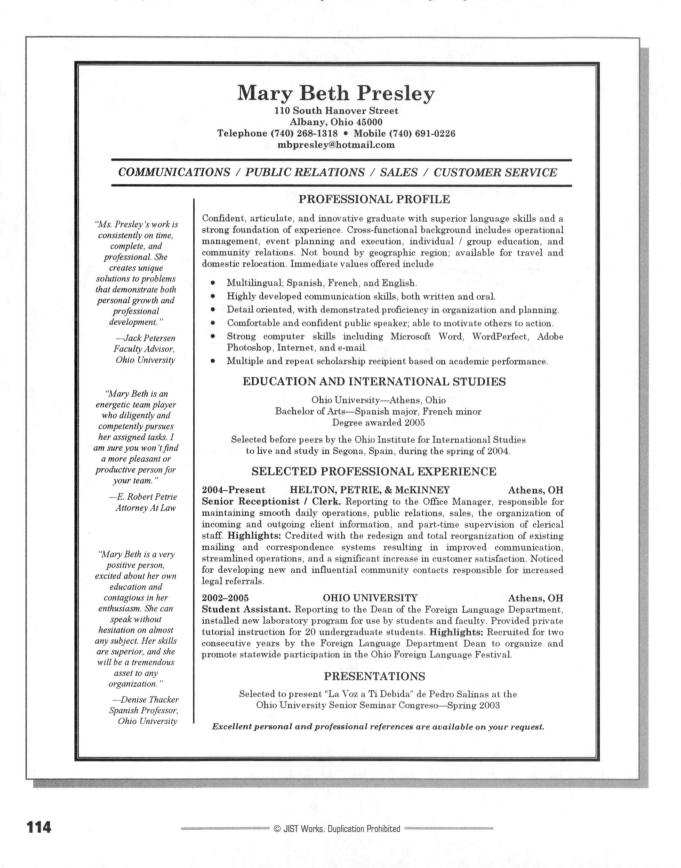

Mary Beth Presley

110 South Hanover Street
Albany, Ohio 45000
Telephone (740) 268-1318 • Mobile (740) 691-0226
mbpresley@hotmail.com

COMMUNICATIONS / PUBLIC RELATIONS / SALES / CUSTOMER SERVICE

PROFESSIONAL PROFILE

"Ms. Presley's work is consistently on time, complete, and professional. She creates unique solutions to problems that demonstrate both personal growth and professional development."

*—Jack Petersen
Faculty Advisor,
Ohio University*

Confident, articulate, and innovative graduate with superior language skills and a strong foundation of experience. Cross-functional background includes operational management, event planning and execution, individual / group education, and community relations. Not bound by geographic region; available for travel and domestic relocation. Immediate values offered include

- Multilingual; Spanish, French, and English.
- Highly developed communication skills, both written and oral.
- Detail oriented, with demonstrated proficiency in organization and planning.
- Comfortable and confident public speaker; able to motivate others to action.
- Strong computer skills including Microsoft Word, WordPerfect, Adobe Photoshop, Internet, and e-mail.
- Multiple and repeat scholarship recipient based on academic performance.

EDUCATION AND INTERNATIONAL STUDIES

"Mary Beth is an energetic team player who diligently and competently pursues her assigned tasks. I am sure you won't find a more pleasant or productive person for your team."

*—E. Robert Petrie
Attorney At Law*

Ohio University—Athens, Ohio
Bachelor of Arts—Spanish major, French minor
Degree awarded 2005

Selected before peers by the Ohio Institute for International Studies
to live and study in Segona, Spain, during the spring of 2004.

SELECTED PROFESSIONAL EXPERIENCE

2004–Present   HELTON, PETRIE, & McKINNEY   Athens, OH
Senior Receptionist / Clerk. Reporting to the Office Manager, responsible for maintaining smooth daily operations, public relations, sales, the organization of incoming and outgoing client information, and part-time supervision of clerical staff. **Highlights:** Credited with the redesign and total reorganization of existing mailing and correspondence systems resulting in improved communication, streamlined operations, and a significant increase in customer satisfaction. Noticed for developing new and influential community contacts responsible for increased legal referrals.

"Mary Beth is a very positive person, excited about her own education and contagious in her enthusiasm. She can speak without hesitation on almost any subject. Her skills are superior, and she will be a tremendous asset to any organization."

*—Denise Thacker
Spanish Professor,
Ohio University*

2002–2005   OHIO UNIVERSITY   Athens, OH
Student Assistant. Reporting to the Dean of the Foreign Language Department, installed new laboratory program for use by students and faculty. Provided private tutorial instruction for 20 undergraduate students. **Highlights:** Recruited for two consecutive years by the Foreign Language Department Dean to organize and promote statewide participation in the Ohio Foreign Language Festival.

PRESENTATIONS

Selected to present "La Voz a Ti Debida" de Pedro Salinas at the
Ohio University Senior Seminar Congreso—Spring 2003

Excellent personal and professional references are available on your request.

43 Degree: BS, Communications.
Job Target: Ad copywriter or account executive.
Strategy: Highlighted two internships and related college experience in a strong functional skills section.

ANDREA SNOW
(704) 537-9820
andsnow@aol.com

7128-F Raindrop Lane   Charlotte, North Carolina 28227

OBJECTIVE

A position as copywriter, account executive, or related entry-level position within the creative department of an advertising/public relations firm or radio/TV station.

EDUCATION

B.S., Communication, Ohio University, Athens, OH, 2005—graduated *Summa Cum Laude*

AREAS OF RELATED EXPERIENCE

PUBLICITY—*Clark Communications*, Columbus, OH
* Wrote press releases for biographical sketches highlighting individual career advancement, published in the *Columbus* (Ohio) *Dispatch.*
* Created and wrote personality sketches appearing in *OADMEC,* a professional medical association newsletter.

VIDEOTAPE EDITING—*A. C. Robertson Advertising, Inc.*, Port St. Lucie, FL
* Served as Creative Director for 30-second spot for county political candidate, completing project within management's mandated two-hour deadline. Edited interview copy; selected clips from interview tape.

PRODUCTION/AGENCY OPERATIONS—*A. C. Robertson Advertising, Inc.*
* Proofread and critiqued final creative materials for agency's self-marketing video; discovered and corrected error that would have impaired copyright value.
* Scheduled interviews for models used in print campaign for health-care client.
* Acquired skills in client negotiation, budget management, and adherence to deadlines. Attended client meetings.

ADVERTISING SALES—*Clark Communications*
* Solicited and sold advertising space for *BikeOhio,* a magazine targeted to cyclists. Set up co-op advertising for clients.

PRESENTATIONS—*Ohio University*
* As Chairperson, Communications Week, introduced speakers for internship panel and coordinated audience question-and-answer session among 300 participants.

WORK HISTORY/ACTIVITIES

Casa Gallardo Mexican Restaurant, Charlotte, NC   October 2002–May 2005
Waitress—Opened bar; trained new bar staff in setup procedures.

A. C. Robertson Advertising, Inc., Port St. Lucie, FL   September 2004–December 2004
Clark Communications, Columbus, OH   June 2003–August 2003
Intern

Modern Office Machines, Charlotte, NC   August 2002–October 2002
Sales Representative—Sold Canon fax machines.

Newscaster—WLHD campus radio station; member, Pat Hall's Dance Class; Charlotte Jaycees; various honors/awards for academic achievement, Ohio University.

44

Degree: BA, Communications.

Job Target: Local media or national TV network.

Strategy: Straightforward presentation of qualifications, experience, and education that will accompany a written approach to media companies and direct readers to her Web site, which contains video samples and a dynamic Web resume.

Note: This is one of the few professions in which it's acceptable to include a photograph—because appearance can be considered a bona fide job qualification.

SEAN MARTIN

161832 South 600 West
Idaho Falls, Idaho 83401
208.522.0000
Email: smartin@email.com

QUALIFICATIONS

- ◆ Four years of successful broadcast news and reporting on campus.
- ◆ Proficient use of linear and nonlinear equipment and DVC Pro cameras.
- ◆ Outstanding writing, editing, shooting, producing, reporting, and enterprising stories.
- ◆ Able to lead, motivate, and promote team-building among co-workers.
- ◆ Creative, enthusiastic, outgoing, dependable, hardworking, and dedicated.

EXPERIENCE

KIDX / CAMPUS NEWS 8, Idaho Falls, Idaho
Intern Anchor ◆ *Intern Reporter* ◆ *Intern Producer*
October 2003 to Present

Anchor and produce weekend newscasts—the weekend news program on campus. Daily assignments include developing the lead story and presenting "live" news coverage.

KDIE / NEWS 59, Pocatello, Idaho
Intern Reporter ◆ *Photographer*
June 2003 to September 2003

Field-reported for nightly newscasts in addition to shooting video and writing and editing packages, VOs, VO/SOTs, and teases generated for air.

CNN, Atlanta, Georgia
Environment Unit Intern
September 2002 to May 2003

Researched potential environmental stories for daily CNN news broadcasts as well as for weekly Network Earth program, organized satellite interviews, produced CNN feature news story, and participated in editing and post-production sessions.

EDUCATION

Idaho State University, Pocatello, Idaho
Bachelor of Arts Degree in Communications, June 2005. GPA 3.86

Georgia State Junior College, Atlanta, Georgia
General Education Courses, 2002–2003.

VIDEO SAMPLES / WEB RESUME

www.seanmartin.com

45

Degree: BA, Architecture.
Job Target: Architect in a large city.
Strategy: Captured key skills using a sleek presentation unlike any others: The resume, along with an outstanding portfolio of Web designs and more, was stored on a CD-ROM and sent in a classy folder with a cover letter.

BRIAN KITTS

Permanent Address:
3226 Lexington Drive
Findlay, OH 45840
(419) 423-1952

Campus Address:
5262 Brown Road, Apt. #18
Kent, OH 44240
(330) 461-3040
kittsba@yahoo.com

Seeking position as ... Architectural Designer

✷ Digital-Based Architectural Media Development & Design ✷
A Team Player with Excellent Interpersonal Skills

PROFILE

A detail-oriented, high-energy individual with strong creative and technical skills as evidenced by the ability to provide innovative practical design solutions utilizing ...

Photo Realistic Rendering & Animation	Architectural Design
Photo Manipulation	Graphics Design/Layout
3D Virtual & Physical Modeling	Project Management
Multimedia Presentation Development	Computer IT Services

EDUCATION

KENT STATE UNIVERSITY, Kent, OH
Bachelor *of* Arts, School *of* Architecture Degree

Graduation: May 2005
GPA: 3.7

DESIGN/MEDIA EXPERIENCE & INTERNSHIPS

KENT STATE UNIVERSITY ARCHITECTURE LAB, *Lab Consultant,* Kent, OH   2003–PRESENT
- Instruct and implement computing resources for students.
- Monitor usage of computer lab and maintain facilities.

DIGITAL i LTD., *Independent Contracting Intern,* Kent, OH   SUMMER 2004
- Performed three-dimensional modeling for Apollo Homes Corporation.
- Generated three-dimensional animations/virtual walkthroughs for Kelly Corporation.

PERSONAL PHOTO SERVICE, INC., *Digital Photography Assistant,* Kent, OH   SUMMER 2004
- Constructed, operated, and maintained high-end workstations.
- Performed image manipulation and graphic-design consulting.

MARATHON/ASHLAND, LLC, *Graphics Department Intern,* Findlay, OH   SUMMER 2003
- Created national corporate advertisements.
- Performed image manipulation, document cropping, and file exportation.

ACTIVITIES & AFFILIATIONS

Architectural Mentoring Program
Kent State University Architectural Advisory Council,
    Student Representative
Kent State University Steel Drum Band

> "Brian has the ability to perform at a high level within a team environment and to maintain his sense of individuality and personal drive."
> Larry Williams
> Supervisor, Digital i Ltd.

COMPUTER TECHNOLOGIES

Environments: Microsoft Windows 2000, XP, and NT
Languages: BASIC, Visual C++, PASCAL
PC Software: 3dsMAX 4.0, Form_Z Modeling, AutoCAD 2000
               Adobe Photoshop 6.0, Illustrator 9.2, Premier 5.0, PageMaker 8.0
               MacroMedia Flash 5.0, Director 8.0, Dreamweaver 3.0
               Microsoft Office: Word, Excel, PowerPoint

46 **Degree:** BA, Interior Design.
Job Target: Position with a trend leader in the home design industry.
Strategy: Designed a visually compelling resume to attract attention from a highly desired employer in a competitive industry.

Jacqueline P. Jones

459 Pine Valley Circle ☐ Idaho Falls, Idaho 83406 ☐ (208) 528-0770 ☐ (208) 521-0945 Cell ☐ E-mail: dezynr@email.com

CAREER OBJECTIVE
Residential, Showroom, and Office Interior Design

PROFESSIONAL SUMMARY
- More than six years of experience in family-owned interior design business.
- Successful in selling a variety of interior design products by establishing good rapport with clients, determining their needs, and making recommendations on products based on competent knowledge.
- Have established clientele including contractors, businesses, and private individuals.
- Won Best Decorated Home—Builder's Show 2003.
- Organized, scheduled, and marketed events and shows for automobiles and RVs.
- Decorated campers, trailers, and motor homes for trade shows.
- Redesigned a 30,000-square-foot showroom and won Second Place in Display Competition.

PROFESSIONAL SKILLS
- Expertise in coordinating wallpaper, window treatments, floor coverings, tile, accessories, and overall design.
- Highly motivated, resourceful, and can get the job done.
- Excellent customer service and public relations.
- Prompt, reliable, dependable, and willing to learn.
- General office skills including answering multi-line telephone system and operating copy, facsimile, and other office machines.
- Computer literate—experience in Word, Excel, DesignCAD, AutoCAD, Illustrator, Quark, Photoshop, Visio, Internet, and e-mail.

WORK EXPERIENCE
INTERIORS BY DESIGN, Idaho Falls, Idaho. May 2000–Present (Part-time). Family-owned business.
Designer Trainee. 2004–Present. Produce floorplans and designs for homes, offices, and commercial space. Work with clients to determine color schemes, lighting, window treatments, accessories, wallpaper, and overall design.

Salesperson. 2002–2004. Sold a variety of wallpaper, carpet, linoleum, furniture, and accessories. Made office visits and in-home visits to assess customer needs. Placed orders and tracked sales.

Inventory Stocker/Receptionist/Cashier. 2000–2002. Answered multi-line phone system, directed calls, balanced cash drawer, and made bank deposits. Regrouped and organized wallpaper and accessories to make them easier to locate.

EDUCATION
Idaho State University, Pocatello, Idaho
Bachelor of Arts Degree in Interior Design, January 2006

47

Degree: BFA.
Job Target: A position in a fine-arts museum with future growth to director level.
Strategy: Emphasized valuable and highly relevant internships; created interesting visual design. Note the reference to the online portfolio.

Margo L. Kramer

2520 Main Street • Townsville, MA 01583 • (508) 355-1034 • pixperfect@cs.com

Objective

To apply photography education along with freelance and internship experience in a studio or fine-arts institution.

Education

Bachelor of Fine Arts, May 2005   The Art Institute of Boston, Boston, MA
   Photography major
   Portfolio scholarship award for "Rails" Series, 2002

Internships

The Image Maker, Boston, MA   A non-profit photography gallery
   Assistant to Director during auction and member selection for exhibits. Independently built and maintained an accurate mailing list.

The Art of Life, Inc., Boston, MA   A custom black-and-white photofinishing, matting, and framing studio
   Applied photography techniques to assist with retouching/spotting of finished fine-art photographs for gallery inventory and professional darkroom clients. Acquired experience and became proficient in matting and framing fine-art photographs. Utilizing computer skills, scanned photographs and entered pertinent data relative to individual photographs into database, creating a foundation for the existing photographic database.

Exhibits

   Gallery 601, "Behind the Scenes Portfolio"
   Equinox Grille, "Mixed Media"
   Water Street Café, "Thanksgiving Parade"
   Kougeaus Gallery, "Waiting" (from "Rails" series; selected photography)
   First Impression Gallery, "Student Exhibit"

Publications

   Old House Interiors............................ Stylist/Photo Assistant, "Bates Mansion 2004"
   Gallery Guide .... Advertisement for Kougeaus Gallery Exhibition
   Art Institute of Boston........................ Awards Brochure, "Connections"

Additional

Experienced with medium-format photography and digital photography for portraits, documentaries, and special events, including weddings, birthdays, and anniversaries. Additional experience includes extensive knowledge of textures and patterns for visual display.

Funded education working in local restaurant and as freelance photographer, stylist, and garden planner.

Portfolio available   www.margosart.com/portfolio

48

Degree: BS, Elementary Education.
Job Target: Elementary school teacher.
Strategy: Used appropriate fonts and graphics to help this new teacher's resume stand out. Created clever "ABCDE" profile. Detailed student-teaching experience to effectively convey teaching abilities.

ANNE C. ELLIS

H: 360-445-1256

210 Candlewood Court • Lacey, Washington 98509 • acellis@earthlink.com

OBJECTIVE

A position as an **Elementary School Teacher** that will utilize strong teaching abilities to create a nurturing, motivational, and stimulating learning environment to help children achieve their potential.

PROFILE

A highly motivated, enthusiastic, and dedicated educator who wants all children to be successful learners.
"Believe in the impossible"; continually research educational programs and procedures to benefit students.
Committed to creating a classroom atmosphere that is stimulating and encouraging to students.
Demonstrated ability to consistently individualize instruction, based on students' needs and interests.
Exceptional ability to establish cooperative, professional relationships with parents, staff, and administration.

EDUCATION

B.S. in Elementary Education, Troy State University, Dothan, Alabama   May 2005
• Summa Cum Laude • President's Honor List • Kappa Delta Phi
• National Collegiate Education Award Winner
• Who's Who Among Students in American Universities and Colleges
• Participated in the Test for Teaching Knowledge field project, 2001
A.A. in Arts and Sciences, Pierce College, Tacoma, Washington   2001

CREDENTIALS

Elementary Education   Washington License (K–8)—Alabama License (K–6)

STUDENT TEACHING

Student Teacher—Grade 1, Harrand Creek Elementary School, Enterprise, Alabama   Fall 2004
Completed 200 hours of hands-on teaching in a first-grade classroom. Utilized children's literature to teach and reinforce reading, writing, grammar, and phonics. Coordinated and taught math lessons and activities. Collaborated with teacher in planning, preparing, and organizing thematic units. Observed the use of teaching techniques to meet the needs of visual, kinesthetic, and auditory learners for all subject areas. Assisted in the quarterly grading.

STUDENT INTERN EXPERIENCE (60 hours)

2nd Grade, Reading, Clover Park Elementary School, Dothan, Alabama
4th Grade, Reading, Science & Social Studies, Headland Elementary School, Dothan, Alabama
4th Grade, Math, EastGate Elementary School, Dothan, Alabama
5th Grade, Art & Social Studies, EastGate Middle School, Ozark, Alabama
1st Grade, Reading Tutor for student at-risk program, Troy State University, Alabama

RELATED EXPERIENCE

Director, Kinder-Care Learning Centers, Lacey, Washington   1996 to 1998
Oversaw day-to-day operations of child care center for 65 children. Ensured all local, state, and federal rules and regulations were adhered to.

AFFILIATIONS

Member, National Council for Exceptional Children
Leader, Girl Scouts of America

49

Degree: BA, Education.
Job Target: High-school history, political science, or geography teacher.
Strategy: Combined all relevant teaching experience (even though it is unpaid) in one section to demonstrate substantive teaching experience despite new-grad status.

EDUARDO DIAZ

2104 E. 12th St. #7 ▪ Fremont, NE 68025 ▪ (402) 464-8460 ▪ e-mail: eduardo@uno.edu

EDUCATION

University of Nebraska at Omaha   Expected graduation: May 2005
- ☑ Bachelor of Arts in Education — Social Science 7–12 Field Endorsement
- ☑ Cumulative GPA: 3.97/4.0 — Dean's List 7 consecutive semesters from Fall 2001–Fall 2004

CORE COMPETENCIES

Teaching and training experience both in schools and in business. Competent, results-oriented instructor able to motivate students of differing abilities to achieve their potential.
- ☑ Certified to Teach: History, Political Science, Geography, Economics, Sociology, Psychology
- ☑ Strengths: Integrated Curriculum, Multicultural, Service Learning, Special-Needs Students
- ☑ Classroom Media: PowerPoint, Internet Research, Microsoft Word

TEACHING EXPERIENCE

Student Teacher, Grades: 7–12   Auburn Public Schools, Auburn, NE   2005
- ☑ Taught World History, American History, American Government, and Sociology to 100 students.
- ☑ Instructed students on how to research political parties, develop platforms, and debate ideas.

Student Practicum, Grades: 7–8   Hildreth Middle School, Fremont, NE   2003
- ☑ Created and taught unit on Louisiana Purchase to 20 students.
- ☑ Planned and implemented service-learning project to increase awareness of economically disadvantaged persons.

Master-Level Tutor, Undergraduates   University of Nebraska at Omaha   2003–2004
- ☑ Certified by International College Reading and Learning Association.
- ☑ Tutored students in History, Political Science, Sociology, and Geography.
- ☑ Trained new tutors at workshops.

Student Mentor, Grade: 8   Central Catholic High School, Fremont, NE   2003–2004
- ☑ Tutored student with AD/HD in English, Math, Science, and History.
- ☑ Implemented creative learning techniques that resulted in student passing exams.

WORK EXPERIENCE

Shift Manager/Crew Member   Mexican Fiesta, Fremont, NE   2000–present
- ☑ Managed up to five employees, including hiring, training, and scheduling.
- ☑ Balanced daily receipts and deposited cash at bank.

PROFESSIONAL ACTIVITIES

Presented *Atlantic Conflict* paper at Phi Alpha Theta National Conference in San Antonio   2004
Phi Alpha Theta (History Honor Society): Vice President, 1 year   2002–present
History Club: President, 2 years   2002–present
History Department liaison to incoming freshmen   2004
Phi Eta Sigma (Freshman Honor Society)   2001–2002

CREDENTIALS ON FILE

Office of Career Services, University of Nebraska at Omaha, Omaha, NE 68182 ▪ (402) 554-8501

50

Degree: BS, Health and Physical Education.
Job Target: Phys. ed. teacher or fitness coach/trainer.
Strategy: Used functional categories in a "Core Competencies" list to show the ability to teach and develop curriculum at elementary, middle-school, and high-school levels.

Kris Grayson

255 Cameron Street, Harrisburg, PA 17126 ▪ Phone: (717) 783-2002 ▪ E-mail: kgrayson@rcn.com

CAREER PROFILE & OBJECTIVE

Outgoing health and physical-education teacher and coach with extra year of study in kinesiology. Proven experience teaching, coaching, and organizing health-related groups and events at schools and other settings. Effectively motivate all-aged students, from elementary to high school; plan and organize health activities and classes; coach youth sports teams; and manage health events in school and other settings. Reputation for reliability, professionalism, planning, teaming, and interpersonal skills.

Objective: *A position as either a high-school-level phys-ed teacher or a fitness coach/trainer working with adults or youth in a corporate setting.*

CORE COMPETENCIES

COURSE PLANNING & TEACHING
Planned a syllabus and daily lessons, and taught a physical education and health curriculum for grades kindergarten through eight.

Temporary Teacher (Grades 6–8) Middletown Middle School—Middletown, PA (early fall quarter, 2005)
Temporary Teacher (Grades K–5) Hershey Elementary School—Hershey, PA (late fall quarter, 2005)

ATHLETIC COACHING & TEAM DEVELOPMENT
Managed team, game events, and coordination with competing teams. Coached and encouraged the development of athletic skills and sportsmanship for two female sports teams.

Athletic Coach, Middletown High School (Spring/Fall 2005)
- Coached 8th-grade girls' lacrosse team during spring season.
- Coached 8th-grade girls' field hockey team during fall season.

COUNSELING & FACILITATION
Did special projects while attending school to complete a five-year degree, as follows:

Camp Counselor, Cumberland Summer Camp—Cumberland, PA (Summer 2004)
- Facilitated and oversaw daily activities of children aged 11–17 at summer camp.
- Planned music, sports, and other activities to balance learning with fun.

Special Olympics Facilitator, Dauphin County Special Olympics—Harrisburg, PA (Winter/Spring 2002)
- Coordinated/oversaw activities of male and female students aged 10–21.
- Assisted students one-on-one during ski lessons.

Office/Computer Support, On-Call Success—Harrisburg, PA (May 2002–Present)
- Provided on-call office and computer support and developed Internet/software skills.

EDUCATION & AFFILIATION

B.S., Health and Physical Education (Kinesiology), YORK COLLEGE—York, PA (Jan 2006)
(Teaching certification pending)

Computer Skills: MS Word, Excel, and PowerPoint; Windows XP and 2000

Member, **PSAHPERD** (PA State Assn. for Health, Phys. Ed., Recreation & Dance), Since Jan 2003
Member, **AAHPERD** (American Alliance for Health, Phys. Ed., Recreation & Dance), Since May 2003

51

Degree: BA, Sociology.
Job Target: Social researcher.
Strategy: Highlighted common threads in this all-over-the-board experience from internships, the Peace Corps, and post-college assignment to position her as having the social, analytical, and multilingual skills needed to do social research—even though she had never performed this job.

J.B. BRUSSEL

187 Ash Street, Brooklyn, NY 11222 • (718) 349-2002 • jbbrussel@hotmail.com

OBJECTIVE
To perform social research that benefits a community-based or multilingual program.

PERSONAL PROFILE
Multilingual survey researcher with five+ years of internships/volunteerism in the nonprofit sector. Community- and diversity-minded, with excellent analytical and interpersonal skills. Familiar with various methods of social research and interviewing. Speak and read Spanish, Portuguese, German, and African Creole.

PROFESSIONAL EXPERIENCE
PROGRAM ANALYST (The Grant Monitoring Association—New York, NY)   **2005–PRESENT**
- **Provide internal quality assurance** by collecting, evaluating, and analyzing data from various criminal justice programs for federal contract-client.
- **Ensure continued grant funding** by writing monthly, quarterly, annual, and ad hoc reports to government funding agencies.
- **Track program status in relation to contractual goals** by designing and maintaining data-collection mechanisms such as variance and deliverables spreadsheets and summary reports.
- **Brief executive staff** on client satisfaction and results of program evaluations.

PEACE CORPS INSTRUCTOR: SECOND LANGUAGES (Senegal, Africa)   **2003–2004**
- **Helped alleviate national teacher shortage** by teaching English as a Second Language for high-school students in Senegal.
- **Heightened student learning through exposure to dynamic learning methods.** Planned lessons, wrote original texts, and created comprehensive instructional packages appropriate for multiple learning levels.
- **Increased sustainable resources** available to students by overseeing the creation of a resource "bank" that contained books, tutorials, newspapers, and basic school supplies.

INTERNSHIPS   **2001–2003**
- **Assisted a major project to integrate family services** offered by the Family Planning Service (San Juan, Puerto Rico). Interviewed family-service providers throughout Puerto Rico and published report on the needs and opportunities for integrated services.
- **Assisted day-to-day operations of a children's shelter/crisis-intervention center** (Hamburg, Germany) and compiled statistics for annual report.
- **Taught urban, bilingual, at-risk middle school students.** Designed and led a full educational curriculum and recreational program for grades 4–6 (San Jose, Costa Rica).
- **Publicized an urban youth organization to the media,** general community, and potential supporters. Wrote and designed brochure for the organization (Urban Youth Initiatives in Rhode Island).
- **Coordinated fund-raising visits** for New York inner-city children who visited and studied with families in 25 regions of the U.S., for the Inner City Children's Fund. Maintained regular contact with chairpersons in each region and 50 city agencies.

EDUCATION & TRAINING
B.A. *cum laude,* **Sociology,** minor in Hispanic/German studies   **2005**
(Rhode Island College—Providence, RI)
   Selected as participant in the International Studies Program by the U.S. Dept. of Education.
   Senior Social Projects: *1) Family Services in Puerto Rico and Rhode Island in Light of the Puerto Rican Family Structure and Culture, and 2) The Impact of Welfare Reform in Rhode Island: A Preliminary Study*
Language, technical, and cross-cultural training (Peace Corps—Africa)   **SUMMER 2003**
Semester abroad (Die Universitat Hamburg—Germany)   **SPRING 2002**
Semester abroad (Universidad de Costa Rica—Costa Rica)   **FALL 2001**
Computer skills: MS Office, Windows, Internet research, and grant management

52 **Degree:** BA, Social Work/Communication.
Job Target: Social work (adolescent counseling, prevention, intervention).
Strategy: Highlighted academic honors/accomplishments and experiences, both paid and volunteer, that are related to counseling and crisis management.

Mary F. Esposito

17 TOWNSAND RD. ★ ALBANY, NY 12208
518-447-3746 / 518-456-2365
MESPOSITO@YAHOO.COM

SUMMARY

Recent **Social Work/Communications** graduate with excellent academic and counseling skills seeks a professional position allowing for continued opportunity to support and assist adolescents. Extensive exposure to prevention, intervention, and emergency-response programs has provided a solid foundation of experience and strength.

ACADEMIC ACCOMPLISHMENTS

Social Work/Communications ~ BA ~ SUNY Albany, Albany, NY ~ May 2005

★ Dean's List ~ GPA 3.43, National Honor Society, *Who's Who Among American College Students*

YOUTH-RELATED EMPLOYMENT

Director of Teen Programs ~ The Albany YMCA ~ Albany, NY ~ 2001–present

★ Provide guidance and support to pre-teen and teen members by listening and advising. Issues involve peer concerns, questioning of values, parental conflict, and academic frustrations.
★ For the Teen Summer Camp, arranged activities that included canoeing, indoor rock climbing, in-line skating, visits to museums, and a weekend trip to Boston.

Youth Tennis Instructor ~ City of Albany Tennis Camp ~ SUNY Albany ~ Albany, NY ~ 1999–2001

★ Instructed children ages 8 through 18 with differing levels of tennis skill. Teaching methods included individual instruction as well as drills, games, and matches designed to improve the participants' tennis skills.

COUNSELING FIELD WORK

Watervliet Junior High School ~ Watervliet, NY ~ 2004

★ Tutored, mentored, and counseled students assigned by the **Guidance Department.**
★ Worked with the Mentoring and Adventure Programs in an effort to teach communication and team building.

Albany Police Department ~ **Domestic Violence Services Unit** ~ Albany, NY ~ 2003

★ Interviewed crime victims and complainants, took statements, spoke with witnesses, made victim referrals to support and assistance programs, and otherwise assisted officers assigned to the unit.

COMMUNITY INVOLVEMENT

ACT ~ **AIDS Communicating to Teens** ~ Troy, NY ~ 2001–present

★ Perform in improvised skits designed to educate audience members about AIDS and how it is transmitted. Stress tolerance and compassion toward those afflicted with HIV and AIDS.

ADDEM ~ **Albany Diocesan Drug Education Ministry** ~ Albany, NY ~ 2000–2002

★ Counseled and mentored elementary students to encourage good choices regarding substance abuse.

Voorheesville Fire/EMS Department ~ Voorheesville, NY ~ 2000–present

★ **Firefighter and EMT (NYS certified).** Responded to more than 100 fire and EMS calls in 5 straight years.

53

Degree: BA, Psychology.
Job Target: Employment in human service field while working on postgraduate degree.
Strategy: Created a strong profile to sum up qualifications and strengths; emphasized diverse employment while pursuing a degree to communicate work ethic.

PILAR A. JERASIMO
■ Human Service / Psychology Professional

4922 Church Street, Apt. 24
Nashville, Tennessee 37203

615.255.6223 cell ▪ pilar@yahoo.com

■ PROFILE

Ambitious professional with strong work ethic; substantial knowledge of behavioral and emotional disorders among men, women, and children; and treatment plan design experience.

Hands-on leader, driven by eagerness to help others, and able to assess complex situations and formulate solutions. Motivated and effective communicator who learns quickly, develops expertise, and produces immediate contributions to people, teams, and organizations.

■ EDUCATION

Bachelor of Arts, Psychology (Magna Cum Laude)   2005 Graduate
VANDERBILT UNIVERSITY; Nashville, Tennessee
Coursework included Childhood Psychopathology, Abnormal Psychology, Psychology of Women, Multicultural Communications, Racial and Ethnic Diversity, and numerous other Human Service courses.

■ CAREER EXPERIENCE

Volunteer Aide   1999 to Current
LINCOLN MEMORIAL ELEMENTARY SCHOOL; Hendersonville, Tennessee
Work one-on-one with first and second graders in classroom setting providing guidance with projects and math, spelling, and reading skills; several students suffer from various behavioral and emotional problems, including ADD, ADHD, and ODD.

Intern   2004 to 2005
THE CHILDREN'S SANCTUARY; Nashville, Tennessee
Co-led group-therapy sessions, tutored and assisted residents with homework assignments, reviewed daily journals and logs, wrote words of encouragement in journals, and participated in weekly treatment-team meetings.
▪   Earned perfect job evaluation.

Volunteer   1999 to 2003
ST. MARY HOSPITAL EMERGENCY ROOM; Nashville, Tennessee
Assisted nurses and staff; communicated with and consoled patients and their families; transported blood to and from lab for nurses and doctors.

■ EMPLOYMENT WHILE FINANCING EDUCATION

Dance Instructor   1996 to Current
NEW YORK DANCE STUDIO; Hendersonville, Tennessee
Lead students through various levels of training, coordinate rehearsals and performances for national competitions, encourage and motivate students to discover strengths and talents, and meet with parents regarding their children's well being.

Office Manager   2001 to 2002
HENDERSONVILLE FAMILY HEALTHCARE CLINIC; Hendersonville, Tennessee
Evaluated patient charts and recorded various diagnoses under direction of doctor, participated in resolving patient medical and financial issues, mediated interactions between dentist and patients, and counseled high-anxiety child and adult patients.

Cruise Staff Member / Featured Dancer   2000 to 2001
NORWEGIAN CRUISE LINES; Miami, Florida
Guided guests through excursions, assisted physically challenged guests embarking and debarking ship, and reduced and resolved guest complaints.

54

Degree: BA, Gerontology.
Job Target: Geriatric care/management.
Strategy: Avoided looking like a "transplant" or a recent college graduate by putting her college address at the bottom and only her local address at the top (she wanted to return to her hometown to start her career).

KATHRYN R. REDPATH

1350 Edgewood Drive
Tampa, FL 37906

813-727-0671
kredpath@yahoo.com

SUMMARY OF QUALIFICATIONS

- ❑ Compassionate and professional—dedicated to providing quality care to the aging.
- ❑ Successful leader, equally effective as member of a team.
- ❑ Extensive education and hands-on experience with geriatric populations.
- ❑ Highly organized—able to accomplish multiple objectives.

EDUCATION

B.A., Gerontology, 2005—University of South Florida, Tampa, FL
Major GPA 4.0; cumulative GPA 3.87

Honors:
Dean's List of Scholars, Sigma Phi Omega Gerontological Honor Society,
National Society of Collegiate Scholars, Golden Key National Honor Society

Selected course work:

Geriatric Case Management	Business Management in an Aging Society
Physical Changes in Later Life	Disability and Society
Death and Dying	Gerontological Counseling

INTERNSHIPS

Case Manager Intern, Fall 2005
Providence Senior Services, Tampa, FL

- ❑ Developed care plans focused on keeping client in home and as self sufficient as possible.
- ❑ Coordinated in-home services with appropriate agencies.
- ❑ Conducted initial assessments and quarterly and annual reviews.
- ❑ Worked with specialty programs including Home Care for the Elderly (HCE), Alzheimer's Diseases Initiative (ADI), and Assisted Living Waiver.

Eldercare Program Intern, Fall 2004
Catholic Charities, Tampa, FL

- ❑ Created, organized, and supervised activities for an Alzheimer's respite program designed to give caregivers personal time while providing meaningful activities for patients.
- ❑ Developed and implemented a special volunteer-education program to train volunteers in the care of and interaction with Alzheimer's patients.
- ❑ Facilitated Alzheimer's support group for client caregivers.

Assistant to Geriatric Care Manager, Summer 2004
Lifespan Services, Inc., Tampa, FL

- ❑ Selected to supervise in-home visits of family members with Alzheimer's patient (mother) with aim to educate them on the disease and how it has affected the patient.
- ❑ Provided detailed written progress reports to case manager.

ADDITIONAL EXPERIENCE

Worked 25–30 hours per week during college career:
Server, Chili's Restaurant, Tampa, FL
Data processor, H.D. Osborne & Associates

South Carolina contact information: 210 Salem Dr., Southeast, SC 29631   864-657-7701

Degree: BA, Psychology and Sociology, minor in Criminal Justice.
Job Target: A position in the criminal justice field.
Strategy: Made the most of education, relevant coursework, and general knowledge of criminal justice; highlighted relevant volunteer experience.

AMANDA CARTER

307 Oglesby Court
Hendersonville, TN 37075

Home: (615) 824-5629
Email: carter_ac@yahoo.com

Career Focus—CRIMINAL JUSTICE

Position in Criminal Justice where education, initiative, and a desire to serve
will be of value in administering and safeguarding criminal and judicial processes.

Qualifications Summary

- Recent college graduate with career interest in criminal justice. Familiar with the concepts of justice, due process, criminal behavior, and criminal rehabilitation.
- Strong communication, interaction, and relationship-building skills acquired through work experience and volunteer activities.
- Computer experience with Windows-based software (Word, Excel) and online Internet research. Confident in learning and using new technology and computer applications.

Education

UNIVERSITY OF KENTUCKY—Lexington

BACHELOR OF ARTS
May 2005

Dual Major—Psychology and Sociology
Minor—Criminology

Coursework
Highlights:

Criminology—Criminal Law—Penology
Juvenile Delinquency—Deviant Behavior

Work Experience

TEACHER .... 2004 to Present
Children's World, Inc.—Hendersonville, TN

- Provide daily child care for toddlers ages 18 to 24 months in an active learning environment.
- Supervise children during playtime. Interact with parents delivering and picking up children.

KID'S COACH .... 2002 to 2003
Discovery Zone—Goodlettsville, TN

- Coordinated and supervised age-appropriate games and activities for children's birthday parties and other special events.
- Kept events running smoothly through effective problem-solving and good decision-making.

SECRETARY / OFFICE ASSISTANT .... Summers 1999 to 2001
Regent Manufacturing Co., Inc.—Portland, TN

- Provided general office support, including answering phones, filing, and accepting deliveries.

Volunteer Activities

- Observed behavior and interaction of children at Kentucky Safe Adoption agency. Reviewed case files and sat in on parenting classes.
- Traveled to Mexico and Costa Rica on youth mission trips. Coordinated VBS activities and helped with construction of new church facility.
- Provided office assistance to Hendersonville Chamber of Commerce (2004).

56
Degree: BS, Criminal Justice (degree pending).
Job Target: Victim/witness program coordinator.
Strategy: Emphasized internships, work experience, and bilingual skills.

Mary Short

1247 Sands Drive
Columbia, MD 21045

410.239.0987
Mshort@yahoo.com

CAREER FOCUS

Victim/Witness Program Specialist

PROFILE

Highly skilled coordinator offering the following expertise, competencies, and technical proficiencies:

· Legal Issues	· Case Management	· Problem Solving Abilities
· Legal Research	· Program Coordination	· Superior Organizational Skills
· Constitutional Rights	· Administration Management	· Excellent Interpersonal Skills
· Depositions	· Official Liaison	· Quality Customer Service
· QuickBooks	· Adaptable	· Sensitive to Critical Deadlines
· MS Word, Excel, PowerPoint	· Dependable	· Bilingual (Spanish)

- Two years of direct experience as an advocate and coordinator for Witness/Victim programs. Assist individuals in understanding their rights and entitlements. Represent the division and respond to general and specific inquiries regarding varied types of hearings.

- Work with complex laws governing Grand Theft and Witness/Victim programs and carefully analyze, explain, and apply appropriate laws when guiding or assisting clients. Respond directly to inquiries, demonstrating excellent oral and written communications skills.

- Collect documentary evidence to present to attorneys; ensure victims and witnesses are available for pre-file meetings; process and maintain detailed records and case files.

- Absorb, retain, and recall large amounts of data and information.

PROFESSIONAL EXPERIENCE

Internship. Part time during the school year, full time in summers.
Felony Screening Paralegal/Victim-Witness Coordinator   2002 to 2005
State Attorney's Office, MD

- Conduct telephone interviews of victims who did not witness a crime or do not know the defendant. These crimes involve burglary into a dwelling, structure, or vehicles or a crime dealing with forgery, uttering, or theft of personal documents or property.

- Victim/Witness Advocate Coordinator: Impart strong legal and administrative support to Assistant State Attorneys managing a caseload for victims and witnesses. Coordinate felony cases that are pending trial. Apply a working knowledge of the complete cycle that a victim or witness must complete to resolve cases.

- Coordinate and maintain detailed and accurate calendars for three Assistant State Attorneys including meetings, victim and witness conferences held at the office, and court dates.

- Maintain accurate client files and assure the availability of victims, witnesses, and law enforcement agents for meetings, pretrial conferences, and court appearances.

(continued)

56 *(continued)*

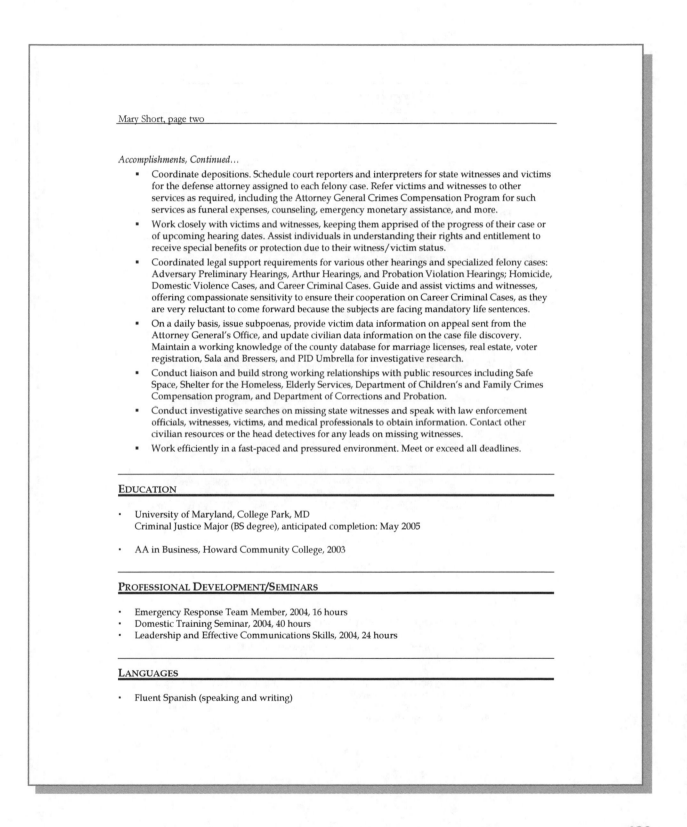

Mary Short, page two

Accomplishments, Continued...

- Coordinate depositions. Schedule court reporters and interpreters for state witnesses and victims for the defense attorney assigned to each felony case. Refer victims and witnesses to other services as required, including the Attorney General Crimes Compensation Program for such services as funeral expenses, counseling, emergency monetary assistance, and more.
- Work closely with victims and witnesses, keeping them apprised of the progress of their case or of upcoming hearing dates. Assist individuals in understanding their rights and entitlement to receive special benefits or protection due to their witness/victim status.
- Coordinated legal support requirements for various other hearings and specialized felony cases: Adversary Preliminary Hearings, Arthur Hearings, and Probation Violation Hearings; Homicide, Domestic Violence Cases, and Career Criminal Cases. Guide and assist victims and witnesses, offering compassionate sensitivity to ensure their cooperation on Career Criminal Cases, as they are very reluctant to come forward because the subjects are facing mandatory life sentences.
- On a daily basis, issue subpoenas, provide victim data information on appeal sent from the Attorney General's Office, and update civilian data information on the case file discovery. Maintain a working knowledge of the county database for marriage licenses, real estate, voter registration, Sala and Bressers, and PID Umbrella for investigative research.
- Conduct liaison and build strong working relationships with public resources including Safe Space, Shelter for the Homeless, Elderly Services, Department of Children's and Family Crimes Compensation program, and Department of Corrections and Probation.
- Conduct investigative searches on missing state witnesses and speak with law enforcement officials, witnesses, victims, and medical professionals to obtain information. Contact other civilian resources or the head detectives for any leads on missing witnesses.
- Work efficiently in a fast-paced and pressured environment. Meet or exceed all deadlines.

EDUCATION

- University of Maryland, College Park, MD
  Criminal Justice Major (BS degree), anticipated completion: May 2005

- AA in Business, Howard Community College, 2003

PROFESSIONAL DEVELOPMENT/SEMINARS

- Emergency Response Team Member, 2004, 16 hours
- Domestic Training Seminar, 2004, 40 hours
- Leadership and Effective Communications Skills, 2004, 24 hours

LANGUAGES

- Fluent Spanish (speaking and writing)

57

Degree: BS, Biological Sciences, and BS, Psychology.
Job Target: Crime scene investigator/field investigator.
Strategy: Showcased dual qualifications in biological science techniques and psychology knowledge, both desirable for her job target. Listed specific coursework to detail knowledge in scientific techniques and psychology.

Maggie Sarkoff

888 Mantle Drive, Kansas City, MO 64114
Phone: (816) 724-5785
Email: msarkoff@pcbell.net

CRIME SCENE INVESTIGATOR/FIELD INVESTIGATOR

EDUCATION

University of Kansas–Lawrence
B.S., BIOLOGICAL SCIENCES, May 2005
B.S., PSYCHOLOGY, December 2004
Cumulative GPA: 3.5

BIOLOGICAL SCIENCES

- BIOLOGY – Microbiology, Human Anatomy, Cellular Biology, Genetics, Immunology, Virology, Zoology, Botany, and Ecology.

- ORGANIC CHEMISTRY – Focused on nomenclature, reactions, and properties of alkanes, alkenes, alkynes, aromatic compounds, alcohols, ethers, aldehydes, ketones, carboxylic acids, and their derivatives. Utilized thin-layer chromatography, distillation, filtration, NMR, IR, and mass spectroscopy in simple and multi-step syntheses for purification and identification.

- QUANTITATIVE CHEMICAL ANALYSIS – Application of gravimetric, volumetric, colorimetric, and electroanalytical determinations.

- OBSERVED AND STUDIED – Electron microscopy, scanning electron microscopy, fluorescence microscopy, Western blot, Northern blot, Southern blot, PCR, gel electrophoresis, ELISA, SDS-PAGE, spectrophotometer, mass spec, and culturing of microorganisms for identification and purification. Highly proficient in light microscopy.

- ENGINEERING PHYSICS – Developed a fundamental understanding of mechanics, with an emphasis on kinematics, dynamics, and statics. Acquired working knowledge of the properties of electricity, magnetism, and light.

PSYCHOLOGY

- ABNORMAL AND CLINICAL PSYCHOLOGY – Anxiety disorders, depression, schizophrenia, bipolar personality disorders, and gender and sexuality disorders. Used DSM-IV as tool to diagnose disorders. Demonstrated the uses and limitations of intelligence testing.

- NEUROSCIENCE AND COGNITIVE NEUROSCIENCE – Anatomy of the brain and its relationship to speech, visual development, spatial acuity, neural plasticity, smell, taste, perception, basic life functions, left brain vs. right brain, and clinical disorders and diseases.

Page 1 of 2

57 *(continued)*

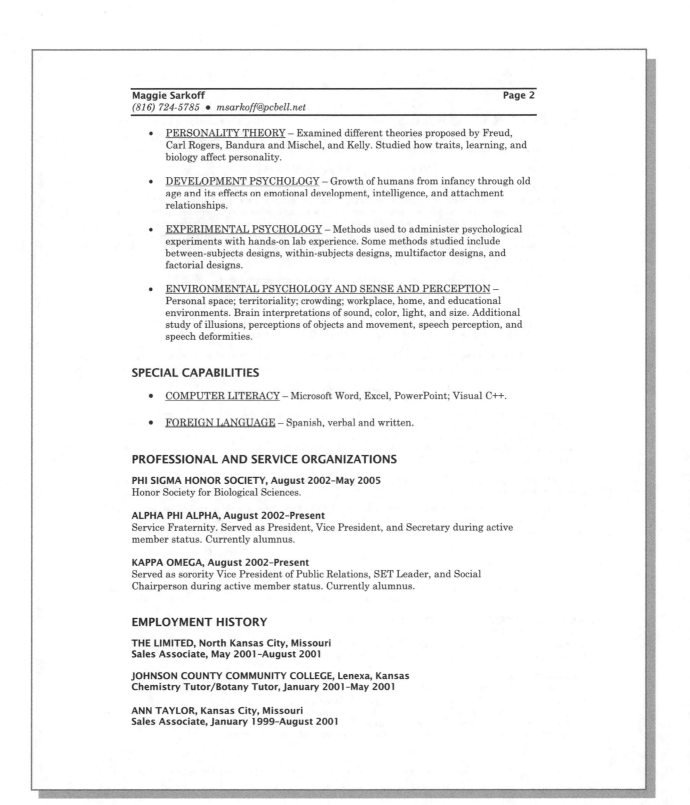

Maggie Sarkoff   Page 2
(816) 724-5785 ● *msarkoff@pcbell.net*

- PERSONALITY THEORY – Examined different theories proposed by Freud, Carl Rogers, Bandura and Mischel, and Kelly. Studied how traits, learning, and biology affect personality.

- DEVELOPMENT PSYCHOLOGY – Growth of humans from infancy through old age and its effects on emotional development, intelligence, and attachment relationships.

- EXPERIMENTAL PSYCHOLOGY – Methods used to administer psychological experiments with hands-on lab experience. Some methods studied include between-subjects designs, within-subjects designs, multifactor designs, and factorial designs.

- ENVIRONMENTAL PSYCHOLOGY AND SENSE AND PERCEPTION – Personal space; territoriality; crowding; workplace, home, and educational environments. Brain interpretations of sound, color, light, and size. Additional study of illusions, perceptions of objects and movement, speech perception, and speech deformities.

SPECIAL CAPABILITIES

- COMPUTER LITERACY – Microsoft Word, Excel, PowerPoint; Visual C++.

- FOREIGN LANGUAGE – Spanish, verbal and written.

PROFESSIONAL AND SERVICE ORGANIZATIONS

PHI SIGMA HONOR SOCIETY, August 2002–May 2005
Honor Society for Biological Sciences.

ALPHA PHI ALPHA, August 2002–Present
Service Fraternity. Served as President, Vice President, and Secretary during active member status. Currently alumnus.

KAPPA OMEGA, August 2002–Present
Served as sorority Vice President of Public Relations, SET Leader, and Social Chairperson during active member status. Currently alumnus.

EMPLOYMENT HISTORY

THE LIMITED, North Kansas City, Missouri
Sales Associate, May 2001–August 2001

JOHNSON COUNTY COMMUNITY COLLEGE, Lenexa, Kansas
Chemistry Tutor/Botany Tutor, January 2001–May 2001

ANN TAYLOR, Kansas City, Missouri
Sales Associate, January 1999–August 2001

Degree: BS, Pathologist's Assistant.
Job Target: Pathologist's assistant.
Strategy: Emphasized impressive experience gained through volunteer work—showing initiative and helping her stand out from other applicants.

JENNIFER J. JAMES

1010 Schreier Road • Rossford, Ohio 43460
419-666-4518 • E-mail: Jjames@juno.com

PATHOLOGIST ASSISTANT

Candidate for Bachelor of Science in Pathologist's Assistant program combined with numerous hours volunteering in career-related positions. Organized, detail oriented, resourceful, and responsible, with exceptional follow-through abilities. Excellent communicator capable of working effectively with a diverse group of individuals from all levels, maintaining an excellent rapport with peers and interdisciplinary staff. Perform extremely well under pressure; enjoy tackling new challenges and learning new concepts. Honest, confident, and hardworking with keen judgement and record of integrity and dependability. Adhere to high ethical and professional standards.

Bachelor of Science in Pathologist's Assistant—Scheduled graduation July 2005
Wayne State University, Detroit, Michigan
Scheduled for Fellowship Examination in September 2005

Clinical rotations: Sinai Grace, Huron Valley Hospital, Histopathology Associations, Hutzel Hospital, Harper Hospital, Botsford Hospital, and Wayne County Medical Examiner's Office

Member of the American Association of Pathologists' Assistants • 2004–Present

WORK EXPERIENCE AND VOLUNTEER PROFILE

WAYNE STATE UNIVERSITY ATHLETIC OFFICE—Ticket Sales / Hostess / Monitor	2001–Present
TENNIS & GOLF COMPANY, Southfield, MI—Sales Cashier	2001
CROY'S RESTAURANT, Dearborn, MI—Waitress	2000
MANOR HOUSE NURSING HOME, Novi, MI—Activities Coordinator	1999
BELMONT HEALTH CARE CENTER, Farmington Hills, MI—Business Office Assistant	1999

HENRY FORD HOSPITAL—PATHOLOGY DEPARTMENT, Detroit, MI	2001–2003

Lab Assistant—STAT Core Lab

Recorded 300 hours as a volunteer working in the STAT Core Lab. Offered paid part-time lab assistant's position handling the receiving and ordering of tests for specimens and delivering STAT and routine specimens per physician's orders. Prepared blood slides and filed specimen tags.

DR. GONZALES, WAYNE STATE UNIVERSITY BIOENGINEERING CENTER, Detroit, MI	2001–2003

Volunteer—150 hours

Observed bioengineering tests performed on cadavers and assisted in the removal of biohazardous waste. Entered cadaver measurements into database. Maintained inventory, processed orders, and contained costs thorough cost analysis that enabled efficient procurement of supplies.

JOHN HELTON, CERTIFIED PATHOLOGIST'S ASSISTANT, Detroit, MI	2001–2003

Volunteer—80 hours

Gained valuable experience working closely with this certified Pathologist's Assistant observing grossing and dictating as well as autopsies. Processed specimen information on cassettes.

OBSERVATIONS	1998–1999

Arranged for visitations to gain hands-on experience in the role of a Pathologist's Assistant.

- Wood County Medical Examiner's Office—observed autopsies.
- Pathologist—Medical College of Ohio —grossing and dictating.
- Pathologist—The Toledo Hospital & Children's Hospital—mini-internship observing first autopsy; noted appropriate measurements and witnessed microscopic analysis of slides.

Degree: BS, Agricultural Studies.
Job Target: A position in agribusiness.
Strategy: Created an interesting format to grab attention at college job fairs.

James L. Rasmusson

301 North 8th Street #1
Boone, IA 50010
Home: (515) 233-3333
Cell: (515) 231-3333
jrasmuss@aol.com

Work History

Ag Leader Technology, Inc., Boone, IA
SHIPPING AND RECEIVING (6/04–PRESENT)

- Member of four-person shipping and receiving team for global leader of precision farming electronics. Work with efficiency and timeliness to meet customers' needs during critical seasonal periods.

- Enter received parts and equipment into computer-inventory system for warehousing. Manage shipping duties for customer orders of 10 major products that support precision farming practices, including electronic yield monitors, global positioning satellite systems (GPS), and other precision equipment.

- Record returned parts, GPS, and electronic monitors into computer database for tracking repairs and maintaining customer accounts. Ship repaired products back to customer.

Ames Youth Sports Complex, Ames, IA
GROUNDSKEEPER (6/04–8/04)

- Spread fertilizer, applied chemicals, and prepared irrigation on soccer, baseball, and softball fields. Chalked and dragged softball and baseball diamonds, and painted lines on soccer fields as preparation for activities.

- Aerated, mowed, and seeded grass when needed throughout season to keep complex looking respectable for public use. Cleaned up trash, operated trimmer, and graded driveways.

TJ Ag Service, Inc., Cambridge, IA
Heart of Iowa Co-op, Roland, McCallsburg, IA
INTERNSHIPS—TRUCK DRIVER (4/03–6/03) / LABORER (4/01–6/01)

- Managed chemical building for TJ during post-chemical-application season. Prepared chemical and dry fertilizer orders for customer and company use; filled, weighed, and calibrated chemical bulk tanks; filled trucks with water or liquid nitrogen.

- Drove liquid- and dry-fertilizer tender truck during both internships; filled anhydrous ammonia tanks and delivered to customers; set up unloading process for liquid nitrogen and dry fertilizer from railroad car to company storage.

- Performed maintenance on equipment and buildings for storage and display. Used excellent customer-service skills while delivering seed and filling customers' orders from warehouse.

Profile

Lifelong interest in agriculture showcased by education, internships, and work experience in ag-related environments in crop management, production sales, customer relations, and systems technology.

Strong work ethic, dependability, and ability to perform independently or as part of a team.

Education

BS, Iowa State University
Ames, IA (May 2005)
AGRICULTURAL STUDIES

TEAM PROJECTS:
Nutrient Management

Fly-Ash Environmental Soil Management

AAS, Des Moines Area Community College
Ankeny, IA 2002
AGRICULTURAL BUSINESS

Computer Skills

*Microsoft Office
(Word, Excel, Access, PowerPoint)*

GIS / ArcView

Degree: BS, Biology.
Job Target: Professional biology career.
Strategy: Emphasized unique work experiences associated with degree and excellent college record.

WILLIAM M. WOOD

402 Pine Lake Lane • Melbourne, FL 32919
Phone 321-322-4512 • E-mail Wmwood@aol.com

OBJECTIVE

A Professional Biological Career

EDUCATION

2003–2005   University of South Florida   Tampa, FL
B.S. Biology
- Graduated Summa Cum Laude; President's List: Fall '99–Fall '01
- Member of National Society of Collegiate Scholars

2000–2002   Brevard Community College   Cocoa, FL
A.A. General
- Honor Graduate; GPA: 3.9
- Member of Phi Theta Kappa Honor Society

WORK EXPERIENCE

2004 (Fall)   University of South Florida   Tampa, FL
Volunteer Student Research Assistant
- Project: Effect of Elevated CO_2 Levels on Food Webs
- Project Lead: Peter Burris, Ph.D.
- Research Site: John. F. Kennedy Space Center, FL
- Examined leaf specimens on site, counted leaf specimens on site, and collected leaf specimens for microscope study.

2004 (Spring)   University of South Florida   Tampa, FL
Volunteer Student Research Assistant
- Project: Effect of Reclaimed Phosphate Mines on Small Vertebrate Populations
- Project Lead: Henry Mushinsky, Ph.D.
- Research Site: Phosphate mines of West / Central Florida
- Collected (and released) small vertebrates for population studies within reclaimed and non-reclaimed phosphate mines.

(continued)

60 *(continued)*

WILLIAM M. WOOD

2004   Busch Entertainment Corporation   Tampa, FL
Guest Relations Supervisor / Representative
- Assisted guests via problem solving.
- Processed ticket / group sales and foreign currency exchanges.
- Supervised special projects, e.g., American Heroes Promotion.

2003 (Summer)   S.A.I.C.   Cape Canaveral AFB, FL
Database Analyst Assistant
- Researched / corrected problems with a large database.
- Acquisitioned technical manuals and schematic diagrams for existing equipment.

2002 (Summer)   Sverdrup Technologies, Inc. Cape Canaveral AFB, FL
Structural Engineering Baselining Assistant
- Revised / redrew schematics diagrams.
- Revised / edited technical documents.

2000–2001   Brevard Community College   Cocoa, FL
Math & Science Tutor
- Worked for Student Support Services, designed to assist students with learning disabilities or financial hardship.
- Received position based on academic standing.
- Initially hired as a volunteer; later was offered a paid position.

1999–2001   Merritt Island Public Library   Merritt Island, FL
Library Clerk
- Completed circulation functions.
- Acquisitioned items requested by patrons.
- Researched information for patrons.

Degree: BS, Civil Engineering.

Job Target: Wastewater civil engineer.

Strategy: Emphasized problems solved in class because he hadn't been able to obtain a summer job or an apprenticeship in engineering.

Charles W. Morgan

861 Lem Morrison Drive ⊕ Auburn, Alabama 36830 ⊕ ☎ [334] 555-5555

What I bring to the Wastewater Department as an Entry-Level Civil Engineer:

⊕ **Drive** to solve difficult problems — for the fun of doing it.

⊕ **Discipline** to handle complex challenges well.

⊕ Natural **aptitude** for advanced mathematics.

Education:

⊕ B.S., **Civil Engineering,** Auburn University, Auburn, Alabama — 2005

Worked up to 20 hours a week for six semesters while carrying 15 credit hours. Athlete of the year every year from 2001 to 2005.

Selected coursework:

⊕ Pipe and channel flow
⊕ Soils engineering
⊕ AutoCAD
⊕ Wastewater treatment

⊕ Open channel flow
⊕ Statistics
⊕ Water treatment
⊕ Technical and blueprint drawing

⊕ Environmental design
⊕ Engineering materials
⊕ Stormwater drainage design

Selected Examples of Problems Solved in Civil-Engineering Classes:

⊕ Helped design town's entire drinking and wastewater plant. Contributed to 30-page report. Presented oral report before civil engineer with years of on-the-job experience. Got good grade — even though I hadn't taken a prerequisite course.

⊕ Did extensive work to find the best site for a county landfill. Factored in major variables from elevation to soil type to climate. My written report well received.

⊕ Reviewed hundreds of pages of stringent regulations to help design airport. Laid out three runways that met tough operational requirements.

⊕ Analyzed three major engineering projects, parts of Denver International Airport. Demonstrated understanding of how engineering disciplines are integrated in the most challenging situations.

Basic Computer Literacy:

⊕ AutoCAD; MS Windows, Excel, Word, and PowerPoint; Internet search tools

Relevant Work Experience:

⊕ Summer jobs, including work as a **construction assistant** for W.K. Charning Construction, Montgomery, Alabama

Degree: BS, Chemical Engineering.
Job Target: Entry-level chemical engineering position.
Strategy: Highlighted numerous technical skills and experiences, including engineering class projects, as well as technical employment and internship. Included relevant keywords in course titles as well as work experiences.

SIMON R. PEREZ
2523 Pioneer Road, Hillsborough, NJ 08844
908-281-5555 Home ▪ srperez@juno.com

OBJECTIVE
Entry-level Chemical Engineering position utilizing my experience and knowledge in process improvement as well as technical support.

PROFILE
- ☑ Recent college graduate with proven technical and analytical abilities.
- ☑ Demonstrated track record of achieving goals in a team environment.
- ☑ **Computer Skills:** MS Windows, Word, Excel, PowerPoint, and IE; RS3Excel; ChemDraw; Hysys; ProII; Visio 2000; and Netscape Navigator.
- ☑ **Technical Equipment and Skills:** Instron tensile tester, Brabender torque rheometer, Brookfield viscomenter, and particle size analysis.

EDUCATION
Bachelor of Science, Chemical Engineering (GPA 3.0)   May 2005
Rutgers State University, New Brunswick, NJ
Specific coursework topics included Process Control, Chemical Plant Design, Polymer Processing, and Engineering Materials.

Engineering Class Projects (one per semester):
- ✓ Electrodialysis Membrane: Participated in 3-person team that increased the efficiency of a precious-metals refinery operation (Diamond Corporation) by introducing ionic separation of components to the refinery process.
- ✓ Biomedical Research: Conducted experiments in chemical engineering of the human body, particularly kidney dialysis and IV drug dosage.
- ✓ Thermal Crosslinking of Kevlar Fiber: Team project to perform tensile testing on heated Kevlar fiber and statistical data analysis.

EMPLOYMENT
Technical Assistant   November 2004–May 2005
Johnson Chemicals Research, Chemistry Division—Skillman, NJ

- ▪ Edited confidential documentation for 60 clinical trial projects in preparation for the development of drug-simulation software by an outside company. Assured accuracy of technical content, and eliminated and/or disguised proprietary information.
- ▪ Contributed to quality control of pharmaceutical research database, increasing the efficiency of data queries by editing data for uniformity. Utilized RS3Excel to extract research data in editing process.

Chemical Engineering Internship   May 2003–August 2003
Chemical Resins, Inc., Technical Service Division—Princeton, NJ

- ▪ Tested properties of Polyvinyl Chloride (PVC) resin (particle size, heat stability, and viscosity testing) for this specialty chemicals manufacturer.
- ▪ Provided technical support to three staff chemists in participatory team approach to testing and development of new PVC resin types.

ACTIVITIES
American Institute of Chemical Engineers, College Chapter   2001–2005
✓ Charter Member and Newsletter Editor (4 years)
Habitat for Humanity, Mountain Park Clean-up, Princeton, NJ   2005
✓ Volunteer
Willing to relocate within the tri-state area.

63

Degree: BS, Technology, major in Mechanical Design Technology.
Job Target: Mechanical design in the automotive industry.
Strategy: Presented a well-rounded and prepared professional-to-be by showcasing internship experience at a major automotive corporation and background as captain of her high school golf team.

Jenna L. Sweeney

JLSengineer@yahoo.com

8405 Meadowbrook Lane • Novi, Michigan 48377 • 248.555.6101

CAREER FOCUS

Mechanical Design in the Automotive Industry

EDUCATION & TRAINING

Arizona State University—West; Phoenix, AZ
Bachelor of Science in Technology, May 2005
Major: Mechanical Design Technology (GPA in Major: 3.7)
Recipient of Society of Manufacturing Engineering (SME) Scholarship—2004
Recipient of Educational Association Merit Scholarship—2001

Technical Skills:
Manual Drafting, AutoCAD, Mechanical Desktop, Unigraphics

Computer Applications:
Microsoft Word, PowerPoint, and Excel; Adobe PageMaker and Photoshop

RELATED EXPERIENCE

DaimlerChrysler Corporation, Fuel Delivery Systems (2002–2004)
PAD Room Intern—Technical Center; Auburn Hills, MI; Summer 2004
Member of Product Assembly Drawings team to explode and analyze assemblies of fuel lines. Attended slow-build production processes at other plants.
- Assisted with developing design drawings and specifications for the diesel high-pressure pump; drafted multiple views of assemblies.
- Participated in Design for Manufacturing meetings and biweekly mockup and design review meetings for information sharing and collaboration.
- Presented a PowerPoint presentation of overall accomplishments at conclusion of Internship.

Design Room Intern—Brighton Engineering Center; Brighton, MI; Summer 2003
Developed technical skills that benefited overall performance and expanded knowledge of detail and accuracy. Attended meetings to update group members on projects and programs.
- Modified drawings of air control values and production actuators.
- Created retainer application specifications.

Design Room Intern—Brighton Engineering Center; Brighton, MI; Summer 2001
Created detailed spreadsheets for parts included in fuel system projects. Developed technical skills as well as teamwork and communication skills while focusing on details and accuracy.
- Adapted existing drawings of in-tank reservoirs, single-phase torque motor to support a throttle body, and development of high-temperature actuators.
- Produced engineering work order for electromechanical fuel alternatives.
- Presented a PowerPoint presentation of overall accomplishments.

---

63 *(continued)*

OTHER EXPERIENCE

ARIZONA STATE RECREATION CENTER; Phoenix, AZ
Certified Aerobic Instructor, 2003–present
Teach all levels of aerobic sports at the university recreation center.

THE GAP; Bloomfield, MI & Scottsdale, AZ
Sales Representative, Summers/Part-time; 1999–2003
Provided customer assistance with merchandise selection and returns. Handled financial transactions (charge/credit and currency); worked on the computerized register. Worked with customers to identify and resolve problems.

PRECISION METAL INDUSTRIES; Trenton, MI
Lab Technician, 1999
Tested aluminum oxide and steel to ensure quality-control specifications were met. Worked independently toward problem identification and resolution.

ORGANIZATIONS & ACTIVITIES

College Of Technology Organization (COTO)—Chair, 2004–present

Society of Manufacturing Engineers (SME)—Chair, Student Chapter, 2003–present

Beta Mu Chapter of Delta Gamma Fraternity—Director of Activities, 2004–present; VP of New Member Education, 2003; Social Chair, 2002

HIGH SCHOOL
Senior Captain of Varsity Golf Team—Earned All-Area and All-Conference Honors

First female in the history of the high school to complete Computer-Aided Design Education Program.

— Excellent references available —

Jenna L. Sweeney
JLSengineer@yahoo.com
8405 Meadowbrook Lane • Novi, Michigan 48377 • 248.555.6101

Degree: BS, Management Computer Information Systems.
Job Target: Help desk position.
Strategy: Showed intern and work-study experience combined with education. It was important to demonstrate employability for this individual, who is a quadriplegic and has no paid experience.

MICHAEL R. PATEL

94 Dover Parkway   Albany, New York 12211   (518) 682-8810   mpatel94@hotmail.com

OBJECTIVE: Position utilizing training and hands-on experience in MIS, help-desk services, technical support, and customer service.

SUMMARY:
- Provide technical assistance and training to computer users, including Microsoft Office Suite, Microsoft FrontPage, Borland C++, and Internet browsers.
- Assist users in upgrading from Windows 98 and Me to Windows 2000 and XP.
- Direct students and staff members in the operation of peripheral equipment.
- Help PC users to improve ease of use, increase productivity, access Internet resources, utilize e-mail, and enhance efficiency.
- Utilize strong communication and interpersonal skills to assist students from diverse backgrounds and with varied knowledge base.

COMPUTERS:
Operating Systems: Windows 98, Me, 2000, and XP; Mac OS
Software: Microsoft Office Suite XP (Word, Access, Excel, and PowerPoint), Microsoft FrontPage, Norton Internet Security/Norton Antivirus, McAfee VirusScan, Corel Office, Adobe Photoshop
Hardware: X86, Pentium and equivalent systems, Macintosh, scanners, CD writers, Hewlett-Packard and Lexmark printers, Zip drives

EDUCATION:
Siena College, Richard R. Smith School of Business, Loudonville, New York
Bachelor of Science—Management Computer Information Systems, 12/05
<u>Relevant Courses</u>: Program Concepts for Business I and II (C++), Database Management Systems, Data Communications and Network, Business Computing Environment, Systems Analysis and Design

EXPERIENCE:
Siena College, Loudonville, New York   9/03–11/04
ITS Computer Consultant
Offered technical assistance to the 4,000 students and faculty using the systems and programs in the computer labs.
- Fielded questions about Microsoft Office productivity software, e-mail applications, and Internet browsers.
- Aided students and faculty in using peripheral equipment, such as scanners, modems, and printers.

NationsBanc Mortgage Corp., Albany, New York   5/02–12/02
Programming Intern
Created documentation for various system applications, including macros used to manipulate loan information. Utilized Visual Basic.

Phillips, Lytle, Hitchcock, Blaine & Huber, Albany, New York   6/99–8/99
MIS Intern
Collaborated with the law firm's Information Services staff in Y2K Discovery.
- Tested computer systems with both Clicknet and NSTL Y2K software, performing simulations to determine whether each system would roll over successfully.
- Installed software upgrades to ensure Y2K compliance.
- Performed troubleshooting of network card problems on individual systems and identified solutions.
- Installed and upgraded Windows operating system.

65

Degree: BS, Applied Science.
Job Target: Systems analyst.
Strategy: Dressed up a no-frills presentation with a unique logo and plenty of black-and-white facts that support his job target.

Bryce Williams

Permanent Address
1976 Paramont Way
Findlay, OH 45840
(419) 422-1258

Campus Address
516 Churchill Lane
Athens, OH 45701
(740) 589-0215
bdwilliams@yahoo.com

OBJECTIVE	SYSTEMS ANALYST
EDUCATION	OHIO UNIVERSITY, Athens, OH

Bachelor of Science in Applied Science
Major: Systems Analysis
Graduation: May 2005   GPA: 3.5 *Cum Laude*

Formal Methods Program (1 of 8 graduates), 2001–2005
An experimental curriculum funded by the National Science Foundation designed to teach students how to create software specifications using first-order logic and to use these specifications in the development of software systems.
See www.sas.ohiou.edu/san/formal/.

COMPUTER TECHNOLOGIES

Languages: C and C++, Visual Basic, Pascal, COBOL, SQL, HTML
Environments: MS-DOS, Microsoft Windows 95/98/NT/2000/XP, Linux, UNIX
PC Software: Microsoft Office XP Professional Series; Corel WordPerfect, Quattro Pro; Lotus 1-2-3, SmartSuite; Quicken; Adobe Photoshop 6.0; Macromedia Flash 5.0, Director 8.0, Dreamweaver 3.0

WORK HISTORY

8/03–PRESENT

OHIO UNIVERSITY SCHOOL of APPLIED SCIENCE   Athens, OH
Student Support Staff. Provide technical support to Engineering Computer Lab for software, hardware, and network problems. Facilitate installation of Windows NT and SmartCam.

8/01–5/03

OHIO UNIVERSITY LEARNING TECHNOLOGY CENTER   Athens, OH
Lab Consultant. Provided technical support to end users with software/hardware questions, assisted in troubleshooting software/hardware difficulties, monitored usage of computer lab, and maintained facilities.

SUMMER 2004
INTERNSHIP

HERCULES TIRE & RUBBER COMPANY   Findlay, OH
Financial Programming Intern. Analyzed synchronization of new receiving-system program with factory maintenance system, coordinated integration of program, and updated and created final report documentation. Reviewed existing programs to determine compliance and changed code when necessary. Performed analysis on purchasing reports to correct inaccurate totals.

SUMMER 2003
INTERNSHIP

HERCULES TIRE & RUBBER COMPANY   Findlay, OH
Client Services Intern. Served as troubleshooter for software, hardware, and network problems. Installed PC Ethernet network cards, loaded and tested network card drivers, and configured PCs for client use.

ACTIVITIES

Ohio University Collegiate Chorale, **Treasurer,** 2000; **President,** 2004–2005
Intramural Broomball, 2003–2004
Ohio University Musical Theatre, *West Side Story,* Part: Big Deal, 2002

66

Degree: BS, Computer Science.
Job Target: Systems analyst/programmer.
Strategy: Used challenge/action/results format to really get across abilities as a problem-solver and troubleshooter.

SUMAN TOMAN

128 Nelson Road
Rocklin, CA 95677

E-mail: stoman@bigpool.com

Residence: (916) 239-4044
Mobile: (510) 505-3432

SYSTEMS ANALYST • PROGRAMMER
NETWORKING • DATABASE DESIGN • SYSTEMS ANALYSIS • PROGRAMMING

IT graduate committed to delivering high-quality, responsive services. Practical projects and teamwork experiences during degree studies have revealed exceptional strengths in critical problem solving, analysis, project leadership, and technical troubleshooting. Easily adapt to change, with eagerness toward learning and expanding capabilities. Solid background in customer-centered work environments underscores commitment to high-quality service delivery and rapid response. **Acknowledged for**

- Consistently working as a contributing team member while achieving critical deadlines for project completion.
- Capacity to interpret and communicate technical concepts to non-technical users.
- Outstanding program debugging and problem-analysis expertise; proven ability to assess and hurdle obstacles; viewed as an exceptional troubleshooter.

EDUCATION

BACHELOR OF COMPUTER SCIENCE, University of California at Berkeley (2005)

TECHNOLOGY SKILLSET
Operating Systems: UNIX, Windows, DOS
Languages: Java, C, Oracle, SQL, UML, XML, Visual Basic, Perl, HTML
Applications: SQL Server, Microsoft Office, WinZip, CuteFTP

PROJECT & TEAMWORK EXAMPLES

CHALLENGE	Stimulate effective client-server communication on an unreliable network that loses connectivity after a series of drops, duplicates, delays, and bit errors within packets.
ACTION & RESULTS	Programmed system to utilize stop-and-wait protocol. **Client received complete error-free files from file server, directory server, POP server, and HTTP server.**
CHALLENGE	Provide user interactivity with racing-car environment defined by Bezier curve, and later extend solution to 3D, introducing car movement/control, night/day environments, scenic backgrounds, and driving hazards.
ACTION & RESULTS	Exploited TED (track editor), implementing rotate, scale, select, and reshape tools. **Successfully completed project on time to specification with full user interactivity.**
CHALLENGE	Design relational database for insurance company.
ACTION & RESULTS	Designed database implementing entity-relationship schema, relational schema, SQL queries, and updates; HTML/PHP web interface, **on time, to specification.**
CHALLENGE	Design simplified Ticketek system using B-Toolkit.
ACTION & RESULTS	Analyzed and designed system functionalities using DFDs, ER, and diagrams. Produced written report, including detailed analysis and design processes, and presented findings on software engineering challenges faced with creating new accounts and login facilities, ticket booking and payment procedures, price and event updates, event browsing, and credit-card validation.
CHALLENGE	Feasibility study of automated supermarket stock-control system using SDLC lifecycle.
ACTION & RESULTS	Defined problem, recommended solutions, and conducted feasibility assessment. **Produced detailed feasibility report** and oral presentation of proposal.

EMPLOYMENT EXPERIENCES

MYER GRACE BROTHERS, Rocklin, CA, **Sales Assistant** .... May 02–Present

BURGER BARNY, **Customer Service Crew Member** .... Jul 01–Apr 02

SEMINAR MARKETERS, Berkeley, CA, **Telesales Representative** .... Sep 00–Apr 01

REFERENCES UPON REQUEST

67

Degree: BS, Accounting.
Job Target: Entry-level accounting position.
Strategy: Equally emphasized strong education, activity, and employment experiences to present the picture of a multitalented, well-balanced individual.

RUTH KERZNER

67 Yorkshire Drive, Freehold, New Jersey 07728   (732) 345-5432   rkerz@aol.com

> Seeking Entry-level Position as…
> ### STAFF ACCOUNTANT
> **Utilizing Outstanding Analytical, Accounting, and Leadership Skills**
> **A Team Player with Excellent Communication and Interpersonal Skills**

A highly astute, energetic, and team-spirited 2005 graduate with impressive academic and employment performance **seeking opportunity to contribute to corporate goals and objectives.** Accurate, precise, and highly ethical in all work-related assignments. Employment history features personal income tax preparation, office management, employee supervision, and customer relations.

Computer Skills: Excel, Publisher, Word, Access, PowerPoint, and Internet applications

EDUCATION

GEORGIAN COURT COLLEGE, Lakewood, NJ
Bachelor of Science, Accounting, May 2005 (Dean's Scholar; Present GPA: 3.7)
* Annual Merit Scholarship Award recipient
* Delta Mu Delta Honor Award recipient, 2004 / 2005
* Delta Mu Delta Honor Society (Business Honor Society) member
* Business Club President, 2004 / 2005
* Festival of Life Chairwoman Award recipient, May 2004
* Township of Lakewood Proclamation Award recipient, May 2004
* Student Business Department Chair, 2003 / 2004
* Sensitivity Workshop Leader, 2003 / 2004

BROOKDALE COMMUNITY COLLEGE, West Lincroft, NJ
Associate of Applied Sciences, May 2003 (GPA: 3.6)
* Dean's List student, 2001–2003
* Service-Learning Program Certification of Recognition Award recipient, December 2001

EMPLOYMENT HIGHLIGHTS

Tax Assistant, ANTHONY PETROSINO AND ASSOCIATES P.C., Brooklyn, NY (8+ hours weekly during tax season, 2002–Present)
Input tax data into tax software program, collate and check tax returns for accuracy, reconcile cash receipts, record cash-disbursement journals, and gain valuable insight into chosen field as an employee of this small but thriving firm.

Office Manager, PACENT ENGINEERING, Matawan, NJ (20+ hours weekly, 2002–2003)
Provided high-level administrative support for this company that represented engineering firms, with added responsibility for managing catalog inventories, compiling monthly computer-sales reports, performing bank deposits, and making lead calls to prospective clients.

Assistant Manager, ESSENTIALS, Freehold Mall, Freehold, NJ (20+ hours weekly, 1999–2001)
Performed a host of responsibilities within this discount cosmetics chain, including employee supervision, inventory control and product ordering, high-quality customer service, problem solving, and reconciliation and proving of daily receipts against cash register tapes.

PROFESSIONAL MEMBERSHIPS

AICPA Student Member, NJSCPA Student Member

VOLUNTEER ACTIVITIES

Service-Learning Volunteer, CPC Behavioral Health, Morganville, NJ

Degree: BS, Management Information Systems.

Job Target: MIS position.

Strategy: Emphasized school project information and other specialized training because actual work experience is limited. Included summer work experience to make the point that he is mature, responsible, and not afraid to get his hands dirty (literally).

JOHN R. STROUT

26 Hamilton Street
Lewiston, Maine 04240

Telephone: (207) 595-2581   E-mail: jrstrout123@hotmail.com

CAREER PROFILE:

(MIS) Management Information Systems Candidate—with an excellent balance of project experience and training in varied technical system applications, hardware, and software—in addition to hands-on business and financial management skills and training. Ability to interact effectively on all levels in business while embracing diversity in technology in various environments and industries. Comfortable working in situations requiring leadership and management (on all levels) as well as with responsibilities requiring individual team participation. Ability to see the larger picture and to lead within assigned tasks to accomplish goals. Eager to put to use specialized training, education, and project experience in a growth-oriented environment in any geographic area.

EDUCATION:

B.S., Management Information Systems   **May 2005**
Clarkson University (Potsdam, NY)   Dean's List Student—Current GPA 3.7
Current President, MIS Leaders of Tomorrow (Clarkson Chapter)
Current President & Technical Advisor, Beta Tau Fraternity

Business Experience/Training Focus:

– Operations & Production Management   – Economics
– Organizational Policy, Strategy & Behavior   – Human Resources
– Accounting (Financial, Managerial & Systems)   – Marketing
– Microsoft Excel Accounting Applications

Technical Experience/Training Focus:

– Computer Networking   – Object-Oriented Programming
– Windows NT 4.0 Administration   – Human Resource Management
– HTML   – Web Design

M.C.S.E.   **Self Study, Anticipated Completion 2006**
Microsoft Certified Systems Engineer

QUALIFICATIONS:

Varied Projects Completed:

– Independent PC Building
Built personal PC using the following parts and components: AMD Athlon processor, 3 Western Digital hard drives, Panasonic CD-ROM drive, GE Force graphics chip, and Kingston 10/100 MB switchable Internet card (including numerous peripherals to complete the system).

– Software Design & Development
Was selected as a member of a 4-person group assigned the task of conceiving a specific project idea (grading software and database for the university); consulted with university officials to design system; made group presentations to the class upon completion of each phase of the project. Worked extensively with Microsoft Visual Basic and Microsoft Access applications to successfully complete the project.

– World Wide Web
Worked with a small team to create Web pages to illustrate how to install a hard drive into a PC; used HTML, JavaScript, and a digital camera; participated in presentation upon completion.

Page 1 of 2

68 *(continued)*

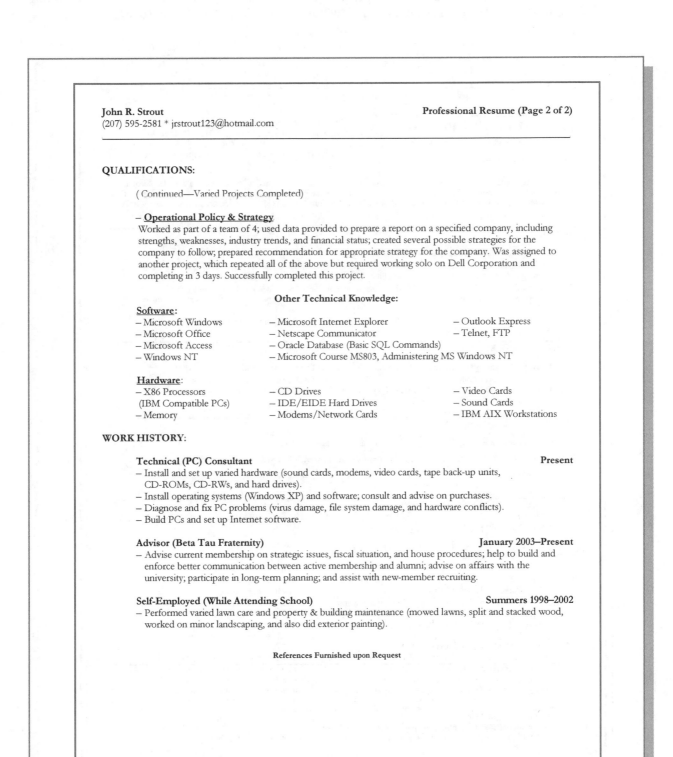

John R. Strout
(207) 595-2581 * jrstrout123@hotmail.com

Professional Resume (Page 2 of 2)

QUALIFICATIONS:

(Continued—Varied Projects Completed)

– Operational Policy & Strategy
Worked as part of a team of 4; used data provided to prepare a report on a specified company, including strengths, weaknesses, industry trends, and financial status; created several possible strategies for the company to follow; prepared recommendation for appropriate strategy for the company. Was assigned to another project, which repeated all of the above but required working solo on Dell Corporation and completing in 3 days. Successfully completed this project.

Other Technical Knowledge:

Software:
– Microsoft Windows
– Microsoft Office
– Microsoft Access
– Windows NT

– Microsoft Internet Explorer
– Netscape Communicator
– Oracle Database (Basic SQL Commands)
– Microsoft Course MS803, Administering MS Windows NT

– Outlook Express
– Telnet, FTP

Hardware:
– X86 Processors
  (IBM Compatible PCs)
– Memory

– CD Drives
– IDE/EIDE Hard Drives
– Modems/Network Cards

– Video Cards
– Sound Cards
– IBM AIX Workstations

WORK HISTORY:

Technical (PC) Consultant   **Present**
– Install and set up varied hardware (sound cards, modems, video cards, tape back-up units, CD-ROMs, CD-RWs, and hard drives).
– Install operating systems (Windows XP) and software; consult and advise on purchases.
– Diagnose and fix PC problems (virus damage, file system damage, and hardware conflicts).
– Build PCs and set up Internet software.

Advisor (Beta Tau Fraternity)   **January 2003–Present**
– Advise current membership on strategic issues, fiscal situation, and house procedures; help to build and enforce better communication between active membership and alumni; advise on affairs with the university; participate in long-term planning; and assist with new-member recruiting.

Self-Employed (While Attending School)   **Summers 1998–2002**
– Performed varied lawn care and property & building maintenance (mowed lawns, split and stacked wood, worked on minor landscaping, and also did exterior painting).

References Furnished upon Request

69

Degree: Bachelor of Commerce.

Job Target: Corporate accounting position.

Strategy: For this individual with no paid work experience, played up academic strengths and ended on a high note with a significant academic project. Note in the summary of professional expertise, the qualifying words "comprehensively trained in" instead of "skilled in," which would imply real-world experience.

GAYATHRI MUHINDARI

1 Drysdale Road, Rocklin, California 95677
Telephone: (916) 214-4590
gayathmuh@bigpool.com

Graduate Accountant/Accounting Intern
Computerized Accounting ~ MYOB, Quicken
Team Player
Highly Motivated ~ Strong Communicator

Commerce/Accounting graduate expertly trained in simulated corporate scenarios requiring solutions to complex accounting, business, and finance issues. "Real world" experience managing and tracking own financial planning, budgeting, and cash-flow requirements. Impressive academic record earning first-class distinctions in tough elective subjects.

PROFILE

- Commended by accounting teacher as *"Best Accounting Student."*
- Personally selected difficult electives (Business Statistics and Operations Research & Marketing) to provide a strong foundation for future corporate career. Passed First Class with Distinction in complex subjects.
- Elected by peers to hold class leadership role. Managed school team of 50 students and collaborated with teachers/parents to facilitate strong sense of community, improved relationships, and diversity of extracurricular activities.
- Appointed School Representative at Inter-School Commerce Festival and Commerce Quiz.

INFORMATION TECHNOLOGY

APPLICATIONS: Microsoft Word, Excel, PowerPoint, Access, Outlook	**PLATFORM:** Windows
	LANGUAGES: BASIC, Database
ACCOUNTING: MYOB, Quicken	**INTERNET:** Internet Explorer, e-mail

EDUCATION

Bachelor of Commerce, *Anna University*, Madras, India. First Class	2005
Higher Secondary (+2), *Matriculation Higher Secondary School*, Bangalore, India. First Class with Distinction	2002
All-India Secondary School Examination, *Senior Secondary School*, Bangalore, India. First Class	2000

SUMMARY OF PROFESSIONAL EXPERTISE

Comprehensively trained in

- Absorbing increased costs while maintaining gross margins
- Balancing bank statements
- Averting tax liabilities
- Budgeting for labor, capital expenses, and business expansion
- Collecting overdue accounts
- Analyzing cost variances; recommending appropriate action
- Comparing historical data with current accounts
- Adjusting general ledgers to comply with changes to taxation
- Eliminating variances via accounting system redesign

- Budget forecasting
- Making journal entries
- Minimizing risk and exposure
- Calculating depreciation schedules
- Preparing operating and capital budgets
- Reconciling discrepancies in accounting records
- Managing accounts payable and accounts receivable functions
- Collecting outstanding accounts

ACADEMIC PROJECTS

Accounting Practices Training Project: Engaged by university to explore different organizations and report on the diversity of office environments and accounting practices utilized. Communicated extensively with business leaders, quizzed staff on daily procedures, and gained "real world" knowledge of accountancy. Areas of investigation included bookkeeping, accounting software, scope and size of accounting sections (organizational behaviors), accounts closing, cost accounting, material cost accounting, and payroll systems.

REFERENCES AND TRANSCRIPTS OF RESULTS AVAILABLE UPON REQUEST

70

Degree: BS, Marine Business.
Job Target: Primarily marine business, but also interested in investment/financial analysis or market research.
Strategy: Because experience in chosen field is nonexistent, the resume emphasizes courses relevant to his career interests as well as skills applied and contributions made in employment and internship.

JOHN DENNISON

Email: jden45@aol.com   56 Main Street • Newport Beach, CA 89970   (978) 466-8866

PROFILE

Marine Business ... Investment/Financial Analysis ... Market Research

Talented professional with a solid academic foundation and cross-functional training in **business and marine management.** Demonstrated analytical, research, quantitative, and problem-solving skills. Excellent communications, detail/follow-through, and organizational skills; excel in fast-paced, demanding environments. Customer-service and team oriented. Recognized for productivity and dependability. Advanced computer skills; adept in quickly learning new technologies and applications. Fluent in Spanish and German.

Computer Capabilities—Operating Systems: Windows 2000/XP/NT. **Applications:** Microsoft Word, Excel, Access, PowerPoint, FrontPage, Photoshop, Dreamweaver, Lotus Notes, C-PAS, and various financial applications. **Programming:** Knowledge of JavaScript, HTML, Visual Basic, website design/maintenance.

EDUCATION

UNIVERSITY OF CALIFORNIA, Irvine, CA, May 2005
Bachelor of Science in Marine Business with minor in **Resource Economics**
- Magna cum laude, 3.9 GPA.
- Financed college tuition and expenses through various employment.

Relevant courses: Personal Finance Applications, Shipping & Port Management, Marine Resource Management, Human Use & Management, Economics of Resource Management, Economics & Politics, International Trade in Economics.

Activities: One of only 4 students chosen out of 230 applicants by the Alumni Relations Council to attend the Leadership Academy Training Program, a weeklong seminar held at Purdue University.

EXPERIENCE

Market Research Intern—PETERSON TECHNOLOGIES, Orange, CA (6/03–12/04)

Acquired market-research experience and contributed to business-development efforts at one of the nation's top 15 Internet technology consulting firms. Researched and generated sales lead contacts, as well as company and industry data. Updated and maintained an extensive client database. *Accomplishments:*
- Established more than 2,000 new client leads, boosting sales during the summer months.
- Co-authored training manual for new interns using both print and multimedia applications.

Administrative Support—UNIVERSITY OF CALIFORNIA — ALUMNI RELATIONS, Irvine, CA (9/02–5/03)

Initially hired as part of work-study program in Alumni Relations Office and quickly offered salaried position based on demonstrated skill set. Performed general office and technical support assignments, including creating several new databases that streamlined and enhanced information access.

Dock Manager—NEWPORT MARINA, Newport Beach, CA (9/00–9/02)

Promoted within first month of employment to co-manage dock area, seafood market, and lobster pound at one of the busiest marinas on the West Coast serving recreational and commercial fishing fleets. Key role in managing major fishing tournaments with nationwide competitors. Liaison between commercial fishermen and area fish brokers. *Accomplishments:*
- Achieved record sales, resulting in one of the most financially successful years to date.
- Instilled teamwork; supervised and trained 8 employees in all aspects of marina operations.
- Initiated conversion to a computerized accounting system (QuickBooks), increasing efficiency.

Additional: Established seasonal landscaping service and grew business to 50 accounts with 50% repeat/referral clientele based on consistent service quality and excellent customer relations (6/99–9/01).

71

Degree: BA, Political Science.

Job Target: Investment banking/financial services.

Strategy: Although his major, Political Science, isn't exactly on target with his career goal, he has significant coursework in economics and an internship with a Wall Street firm. Summer in England and extracurricular activities are pluses.

TOBIAS JACOBS

E-mail: TobiasJay@worldnet.att.net

42 East 65th Street, Apartment G • New York, New York 10019

212-307-9476 (Home)
917-653-0439 (Cell)

OBJECTIVE

An entry-level position in investment banking or financial services that will capitalize on education, strong interpersonal skills, and excellent organizational capabilities.

EDUCATION

Notre Dame University, South Bend, Indiana
Bachelor of Arts, Political Science, 2005
Concentration in International Politics & Economics / Minor in Economics
GPA: 3.3/4.0 (in major); Dean's List; Scholarship Athlete – Division I Lacrosse

Significant Coursework

International Relations	Micro Economics
International Conflict & Solutions	Macro Economics
International Politics & Economics in Developing Areas	Money & Banking

Cambridge University, Cambridge, England
Lord Rothemore Scholar, Summer 2004
Selected to participate in this exclusive program. Studied Modern British Social & Economic Policies under Cambridge University professor.

EXTRACURRICULAR ACTIVITIES

Phi Delta Upsilon Fraternity
Served as Director of Campus Affairs and Sergeant-at-Arms. Coordinated campus-wide events, including faculty programming, social events, and charity fund-raisers.

Digger Phelps Celebrity Auction & Fund-Raiser
Played a key role in organizing this charity event that raised more than $140,000 for cancer research at South Bend Medical Center Hospital.

WORK EXPERIENCE

Marketing Consultant, MatTran, Inc.; Penfield, New York   **Feb. 2004–May 2005**
Assisted this manufacturer and distributor of industrial materials-handling equipment to develop and refine Web site.
— Evaluated existing Web site to identify potential improvements.
— Made recommendations to improve site navigation and increase repeat traffic.
— Worked closely with Web developer to create interactive features for online parts ordering, online quoting, and real-time interaction with engineers and customer service.
— Doubled size of Web site and included information on various case studies, which enhanced firm's credibility with prospective customers.

Intern, Wall Street Investments; New York, New York   **Summer 2003**
— Gained knowledge of equity trading as it relates to hedge funds.
— Observed New York Stock Exchange trading practices and procedures at J & K Securities and on Merrill Lynch trading floor.
— Assisted stock analyst with various research activities and special projects.

Camp Counselor / Coach, College Lacrosse Camps   **Summer 2002**
— Taught basic lacrosse skills at camps held at Nazareth College, Notre Dame, and Hobart College.
— Worked with middle-school and high-school students to develop leadership and teamwork skills.

COMPUTER SKILLS

Microsoft Word, Excel, Outlook; HTML/XML programming

72

Degree: BS, Business Administration.
Job Target: A position in finance.
Strategy: With no work experience to highlight, the resume for this individual sells the excellent skills, education, and experience he gained in school (the functional skills listing is all from class projects). Job readiness is shown through academic achievements and projects.

Rudy Mendoza
4690 Kelly Road
New Brunswick, New Jersey 08903
(908) 941-9180
RudyMen@cs.com

OBJECTIVE: Entry-level position utilizing training and skills in financial research, strategic planning, investing, and financial analysis.

SKILLS:
- Utilized computer skills in Microsoft Office for word processing, database management, spreadsheet preparation, and slide presentation creation.
- Gained skills vital to increasing profits, enhancing productivity, improving customer satisfaction, and forecasting income/expense.
- Participated as member of reengineering team that developed budget that included projected costs, sales, cash flow, and overhead cost allocation.
- Prepared balance sheets, income and cash-flow statements, and annual reports for simulated business.
- Performed business/industry analysis, accounting analysis, financial analysis, forecasting of free cash flow, and forecasting of MVE to determine financial strength based on annual report.
- Studied Efficient Market Theory, Security Market Line, Cash Flow Analysis, Discounting, and the use of Derivatives.
- Evaluated NPV, IRR, capital budgeting, stock and bond valuation, and risk and portfolio diversification to help increase stockholder wealth.
- Presented findings and analysis results to group members.
- Demonstrated superior skills in creative and business writing as well as oral communication.

EDUCATION: Rutgers, The State University of New Jersey, Livingston College
Bachelor of Science—Business Administration, 6/2005
 Concentration: **Financial Analysis**

 Courses include
Management Accounting	Advanced Corporate Finance
Financial Reporting and Analysis	Strategic Management
Applied Economics	Total Quality Management
Integrated Planning and Control	Quantitative Business Methods
Production and Operations Management	Financial Institutions
Computers and Statistical Decisions	Public Speaking

COMPUTERS: Microsoft Office (Word, Access, Excel, and PowerPoint); Windows; e-mail and Internet applications

EXPERIENCE: New Brunswick Police Department, New Brunswick, New Jersey
Summer Intern — Office Clerk

REFERENCES: Furnished upon request.

Degree: BS, Business Management.
Job Target: A position in finance.
Strategy: Concentrated on solid academics, including leadership training and a broad range of business courses. Highlighted skills and potential.

BRIAN ROBERTS

Temporary Address:
505 Buffalo Avenue, #128
Cleveland, Ohio 44115

(216) 515-1408
brian505@hotmail.com

BUSINESS GRADUATE
Management Trainee / Financial Services / Investing

Professional Profile:

Proactive business graduate with training and hands-on experience in stock analysis, customer service, marketing, and account development. Extensive training in economics, statistics, and business management. Hands-on experience includes work in business services, individual investment, tutoring, and sales.

Core Skills:
Financial Research ... Customer Interface ... Solicitation / Marketing ... Written / Oral Communication ... Internet and Microsoft Office ... Marketplace Analysis ... Consumer Satisfaction ... Statistics

Indicators of Potential:
➤ Demonstrated versatility by successfully handling varied and diverse work experiences, including customer service, research, office administration, and sales / marketing activities.
➤ Performed damage control and problem avoidance by interacting extensively with all parties to gather information, solicit feedback, and listen carefully to concerns and suggestions.
➤ Energized by challenges and described as "intellectually curious and critical with an inner strength and discipline."
➤ Planned and presented lectures, seminars, and presentations, utilizing superior organizational, communication, and interpersonal skills.

Education:

John Carroll University, University Heights, Ohio
Bachelor of Science — Business Management   May 2005
GPA 3.2, Dean's List, Outstanding Student Award

Courses included

Applied Statistics	Business Ethics	International Business
Decision Making	Organizational Behavior	Business Law I and II
Supervision / Management	Communication in Organizations	Human Resources Management
Entrepreneurship	Management Information Systems	Microeconomics
Macroeconomics	Advanced French	Financial Management
PCs for Managers	Business Policy	Principles of Marketing

John Carroll University, Leadership Development Institute, University Heights, Ohio
Completed 8-week Leadership Training Program   2004

Topics included

Team Building	Effective Communication	Conflict Resolution
Proactive Problem Solving	Diversity Education	Organizational Development

Computer:

Microsoft Word, Excel, and PowerPoint
Internet Explorer

(continued)

73 *(continued)*

BRIAN ROBERTS   Page Two
(216) 515-1408 • brian505@hotmail.com

Experience:

Career Services Center, John Carroll University, University Heights, Ohio   2002–Present
Student Assistant
Assist students with job search and placement activities.
- Answer telephones, schedule appointments, and research job search resources.
- Prepare brochures, workshop flyers, and campus literature for bulk mailings.

Portfolio Management, Cleveland, Ohio   2001–Present
Individual Investor
Develop and manage a portfolio of six stocks with a 6% average rate of return.
- Research and analyze individual company performance with a focused interest in positive marketplace events.
- Analyze long-range growth and performance and invest with long-term goals in mind.
- Utilize such investment tools as *Wall Street Journal*, *Barron's*, *Morningstar*, Sharebuilder.com, ChaseMellon.com, and NBR.com.

Better Business Bureau, Cleveland, Ohio   Summer 2004
Business Intern
Handled consumer complaints and assisted with agency marketing.
- Processed complaints and forwarded them to companies.
- Documented companies' responses for internal records.
- Compiled business profiles for the general public.
- Revised consumer pamphlets and condensed contents into a more concise format.
- Filed consumer complaints, answered telephones, and prepared bulk mailings.

American Red Cross, Cleveland, Ohio   Summer 2004
Telerecruiter
Performed a variety of marketing and administrative tasks.
- Solicited donors by telephone.
- Managed donor files and updated database.

Total Relaxed Learning Day Camp, John Carroll University, University Heights, Ohio   Summer 2003
Counselor
Taught study skills to college students at academic risk.
- Utilized study techniques such as Pegging, Venn Diagram, Chunking, and Mind Maps.
- Supervised, encouraged, and disciplined program participants.
- Engaged in regular planning and strategy sessions with instructors.

Volunteer:

John Carroll University Residence Council
Multicultural Affairs Coalition

Interests:

Jazz, reading, and foreign films

References:

Furnished upon request.

74

Degree: BS, Economics.
Job Target: Retail management.
Strategy: Highlighted his eagerness to seize opportunities to learn more about his product and serve the customer better, in addition to his exposure to various areas of retail operations.

Joseph Plumb

Permanent address:
378 196th St.
Chicago, IL 60429
(780) 326-5214
joe445@yahoo.com

Current Address:
Saint Joseph's College
P.O. Box 8436
Rensselaer, IN 47978
(219) 866-6000

Profile

College senior possessing professional management internship and multiple retail work experiences seeking an opportunity in retail management. Prepared to "hit the ground running," drawing on customer service strengths, a desire to work with the public, and keen awareness of business-management principles. Bilingual in English and Spanish.

Education

Bachelor of Science, June 2005
Saint Joseph's College, Rensselaer, IN
Major: Economics **Minor:** Spanish

Experience

- Mozart's Music; Indianapolis, Indiana—August 2004–December 2004
  Management Intern; cross-trained in sales, credit, inventory management, repair department, and account management; learned key management aspects of operating a customer-focused business; offered an opportunity to return in a full-time position.

- Saint Joseph's College; Rensselaer, Indiana—August 2003–December 2004
  Resident Assistant; maintained a comfortable and safe student environment, organizing multifaceted activities and providing peer counseling for 60 residents.

- Olive Garden; Calumet City, Illinois—Summer 2003
  Customer Host; specifically trained for host-stand position after demonstrating superior customer-service skills; proved ability to handle multiple tasks and maintain composure during peak business.

- Kohl's Department Store; Calumet City, Illinois—Summer 2003
  Receiving associate; readily pitched in where needed to provide a seamless backroom operation for storefront efficiency; completed inventory-organization project.

- Home Depot; Glendale Heights, Illinois—Summer 2001
  Sales associate; took initiative in working with vendors to gain product knowledge in order to provide helpful information toward customer purchase decisions; maintained a clean and organized department in an effort to provide convenience to the customer.

- Chicago YMCA; Chicago, Illinois—Summer 2001
  Lifeguard; chosen to administer youth and adult aquatic instruction; CPR and first aid certified; maintained chlorine/ Ph balance of pools and provided security service; forklift trained and tested.

Extracurricular

Symphonic/Jazz/Concert Bands
Minority Student Union Board
Percussion Instructor—Kankakee, Beech Grove, Eastwood High Schools
NCAA Division II Basketball
Selected for Marine Officer Candidate School
Tutored peers in major and minor areas

75

Degree: BA, Human Resources.
Job Target: HR position.
Strategy: Focused on great background as an intern at NBC Studios.

Jeannie M. Adamson

Current Address	*E-mail: jadamson@juno.com*	*Permanent Address*
MS 222, 4381 S. Benton St.		546 Kouburn St.
Baltimore, MD 21210		Elmira, NY 14904
Phone: (410) 555-4009		Phone: (607) 712-7733

*Enthusiastic college graduate with outstanding work history
and experience in Human Resources.*

Education

LOYOLA COLLEGE, Baltimore, MD, May 2005
Bachelor of Arts, Human Resources

Related Professional Experience

NATIONAL BROADCAST COMPANY (NBC), New York, NY   Summer 2004
Human Resources Intern
- Researched and developed plan for first comprehensive intern program.
- Designed, planned, and facilitated business workshops and seminars for more than 120 summer interns.
- Researched MSNBC and CNBC intern programs; compiled binder materials for intern orientation.
- Screened 273 applicant resumes, conducted 82 preliminary interviews, and made recommendations for the Fall 2004 internship placement.
- Drafted NBC Intern community service proposal for Summer 2005 implementation.
- Created intern flyers and presentations after extensive Internet research.
- Developed an evaluation instrument that assessed intern needs.

LOYOLA COLLEGE, Baltimore, MD   2003–present
Student Coordinator
- Recruit and select students to participate in weekly service program.
- Created student application to determine student interest and commitment to service program.
- Coordinate and plan program activities. Participate in weekly sessions.
- Collaborate with organizations to develop partnerships and meet identified needs.
- Founded and led Thanksgiving Food Drive, 2002–2004.

Professional Organizations

- Society for Human Resources Management, Chapter Vice President   Fall 2004
- Toastmasters International, VP Membership, Charter Member   Fall 2004

Activities & Awards

- Alpha Kappa Alpha Sorority, Chapter President   2003–present
- The Lawrenceville School, Class Secretary   2000–present
- Loyola College, Community Service Representative   2002–2004
- Multicultural Service Award   2002
- Green and Grey Society Award (given to 14 seniors nominated by faculty)   2004
- Who's Who Among Students in American Universities & Colleges   2004

Excellent letters of reference and transcripts are available upon request.

76

Degree: BS, Communications, emphasis in Human Relations.

Job Target: Specific position with a specific organization: graduate hall director at Northwestern University.

Strategy: Showcased a well-rounded student leader and capable residential-services individual with the requisite skills to fulfill the job target. The list of Qualifications is specifically aligned with the job target.

AIESHA CHAMIN ATLDORE

3351 Pasario Drive
Chicago, Illinois 60625
773.822.8097 Residence   214.332.1883 Cell
aiesha@aol.com

CAREER OBJECTIVE

Graduate Hall Director at Northwestern University

QUALIFICATIONS

- Three years of experience in residential services in a midsize private university.
- Outstanding organizational skills; excel in managing and coordinating programs and upholding policy.
- Well-liked and respected by students, faculty, parents, and immediate supervisors.
- Valued for strong listening skills, commitment, creativity, and motivation.
- Extensive training in objectivity, diversity, and cultural sensitivity.

EDUCATION

Bachelor of Science—Southern Methodist University (SMU), Dallas, Texas, May 2005
- Major: Communications with emphasis in Human Relations
- Minor: Criminal Justice and Sociology
- Cumulative G.P.A.: 3.87/4.0
- International Study: SMU London School for Scholars, Spring 2005
- Paying 75% of college expenses via scholarships and employment

RELEVANT EXPERIENCE

- Resident Assistant—Laudmore Hall, Southern Methodist University, Fall 2002–Present
  ~ Provide oversight to 45+ residents and staff collaboration to ensure quality and excellence.
- Internship with SMU's Sociology Department Human Relations Chair, Spring 2004.
  ~ Created departmental promotional pieces, delivered PowerPoint presentations, and facilitated alumni relations within the field to expand community-wide knowledge of the department's growth and course opportunities.
- SMU Admissions Department—Work Study Program, Fall 2001–Spring 2002
  ~ Supported efforts of Admissions staff by efficiently performing routine administrative activities.

CAMPUS LEADERSHIP/ACTIVITIES

- Student Foundation — Selected to top leadership organization by SMU Administration, Fall 2003–Present
- Leadership Institute, "The Way of Leadership," a student leadership development conference, Spring 2004
- Criminal Justice Society, Vice President, 2001–Present; Sociology Society, Secretary, 2002–Present
- Speech Communications Honor Society, Member, Spring 2004–Present
- Alpha Pi Tau Sorority, Ambassador, Fall 2001–Present
- Undergraduate Interfraternity Institute Leadership Conference at Pepperdine University, Summer 2003
- Fraternity and Sorority Ambassadors, Spring 2003–Present; *Female Greek of the Year* Award, 2004

Life Motto: "Doing what is popular is not always right; doing what is right is not always popular."

CHAPTER 8

Resumes for Graduates with Advanced Degrees

Resume Number	Degree	Job Target
77	MBA, Global Management	Management training program (in a major firm doing international business/finance)
78	MBA, Finance	Finance—analysis/management
79	MS, Geography	Resource/environmental analyst
80	MBA	Management consulting for an Asian company or an American company with business interests in the Asia-Pacific region
81	MS, Industrial Management	Computer systems integration or project management
82	MS, Printing Management	Sales/management training program
83	MS, Industrial and Organizational Psychology	OD/training position
84	Postgraduate Diploma in Social Science	Community aid/overseas aid, and PR for community aid awareness
85	MS, Occupational Ergonomics, and BS, Human Kinetics	A position studying manufacturing processes for the Ontario Worker's Compensation Board
86	MA, Special Education/California Teaching Credential	Counselor, teacher, or case manager for special-needs youth
87	Master of Public Health	Technical sales: medical/pharmaceutical industries
88	MS, Nursing, Family Nurse Practitioner	Family nurse practitioner
89	MA, Sociology	Career in foreign service
90	MA, Political Science	Position in counterintelligence with a federal agency
91	JD	Associate attorney in a private firm
92	JD	Associate position
93	JD	Position not practicing law but using skills identified in the keyword summary
94	DVM	Position with a modern animal clinic with special interest in cats and the possibility of being mentored toward an ABVP diploma
95	MD (completing residency program)	Urologist in private practice
96	MD	Physician

77

Degree: MBA, Global Management.

Job Target: Management training program (in a major firm doing international business/finance). Transitioning from a career in a collections department (at a small law office and credit card company) to international business upon completion of MBA.

Strategy: Career Focus statement indicates job target and provides a quick overview of suitability for management training program. Value Offered section highlights functional skills/job qualifications.

KEVIN T. FITZSIMMONS

1500 South 1214 East ▪ Salt Lake City, Utah 84105
Home (801) 582-9054 ▪ Work (801) 571-2244 ▪ fitzkiwi@aol.com

**CAREER
FOCUS**

MANAGEMENT TRAINING PROGRAM—MBA graduate with solid preparation in Global Management/International Business and 8+ years of experience in business management, collections, legal support, and banking. Native New Zealander, educated in U.S., seeking leadership role in international business/economics. U.S. citizen.

**VALUE
OFFERED**

☑ **BUSINESS/PROJECT MANAGEMENT**: Organized, take-charge professional with exceptional follow-through abilities and detail orientation; oversee projects from concept to successful conclusion. Effectively prioritize a broad range of responsibilities to consistently meet tight deadlines.

☑ **LEADERSHIP/TEAM BUILDING**: Demonstrated ability to provide vision and then translate that vision into productive action. Combine strong analysis, planning, organization, and consensus-building abilities with effective problem-resolution, negotiation, and relationship-management skills. Recognized as a resource person, problem solver, troubleshooter, and creative leader.

☑ **COMMUNICATION/INTERPERSONAL SKILLS**: Highly articulate and effective communicator. Possess strong interpersonal skills; work effectively with individuals on all levels. Respect cultural differences in business practices. Listen attentively, assess situations, question assumptions, and propose well-considered solutions.

☑ **PROBLEM-RESOLUTION/PERSUASIVE SKILLS**: Defuse tense situations by identifying and addressing core issues, mediating disputes, and resolving conflicts; maintain composure under stress.

☑ **ANALYTICAL SKILLS**: Review and evaluate financial/statistical data, identify inefficiencies, streamline processes, and drive performance improvements. Proficient in Microsoft Windows 98/NT, Word, Excel, and Internet applications.

**PROFESSIONAL
EXPERIENCE**

COLLECTION DEPARTMENT MANAGER
Law Office of Randolf M. Hutchinson, P.C., Salt Lake City, Utah   2003–Present

Direct office operations and debt-collections team for collections/bankruptcy law practice. Resolve account-delinquency problems (consumer and commercial debt) for clients such as attorneys, banks and credit unions, capital companies, automobile finance companies, and commercial businesses from small enterprises to major corporations.

Supervise 4 collectors; a legal secretary; and part-time accounting clerk, locator, and file clerk. Oversee all human-resource management functions, including performance evaluations, goal setting, hiring/firing, and employee scheduling.

- Further developed and implemented a comprehensive policies and procedures manual, resulting in increased productivity and streamlined processes.
- Led collections team to average liquidation increases of 199.28% in 2003, 131.32% in 2004, and 106.98% in 2005. Achieved personal portfolio liquidation increase of 162.57% in 2005.
- Oversaw company placement volume increase over previous years by 34% in 2003, 17% in 2003, and 37% in 2005.
- Helped increase firm's early liquidation results; shortened average time for filing suit from 90–120 days to 30–45 days. Accelerated initial payments from an average of 90 days to 30 days.

(continued on Page Two)

77 *(continued)*

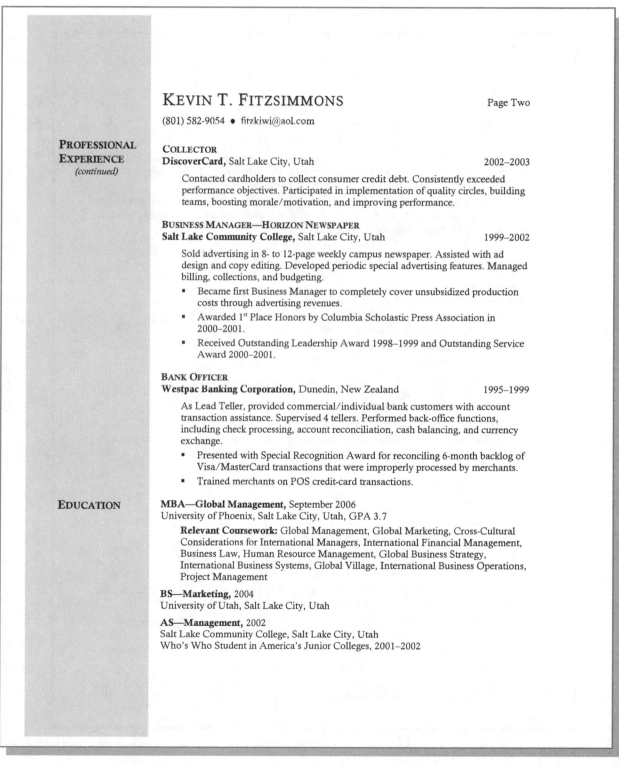

KEVIN T. FITZSIMMONS   Page Two

(801) 582-9054 ● fitzkiwi@aol.com

PROFESSIONAL
EXPERIENCE
(continued)

COLLECTOR
DiscoverCard, Salt Lake City, Utah   2002–2003

Contacted cardholders to collect consumer credit debt. Consistently exceeded performance objectives. Participated in implementation of quality circles, building teams, boosting morale/motivation, and improving performance.

BUSINESS MANAGER—HORIZON NEWSPAPER
Salt Lake Community College, Salt Lake City, Utah   1999–2002

Sold advertising in 8- to 12-page weekly campus newspaper. Assisted with ad design and copy editing. Developed periodic special advertising features. Managed billing, collections, and budgeting.

- Became first Business Manager to completely cover unsubsidized production costs through advertising revenues.
- Awarded 1st Place Honors by Columbia Scholastic Press Association in 2000–2001.
- Received Outstanding Leadership Award 1998–1999 and Outstanding Service Award 2000–2001.

BANK OFFICER
Westpac Banking Corporation, Dunedin, New Zealand   1995–1999

As Lead Teller, provided commercial/individual bank customers with account transaction assistance. Supervised 4 tellers. Performed back-office functions, including check processing, account reconciliation, cash balancing, and currency exchange.

- Presented with Special Recognition Award for reconciling 6-month backlog of Visa/MasterCard transactions that were improperly processed by merchants.
- Trained merchants on POS credit-card transactions.

EDUCATION

MBA—Global Management, September 2006
University of Phoenix, Salt Lake City, Utah, GPA 3.7

    Relevant Coursework: Global Management, Global Marketing, Cross-Cultural Considerations for International Managers, International Financial Management, Business Law, Human Resource Management, Global Business Strategy, International Business Systems, Global Village, International Business Operations, Project Management

BS—Marketing, 2004
University of Utah, Salt Lake City, Utah

AS—Management, 2002
Salt Lake Community College, Salt Lake City, Utah
Who's Who Student in America's Junior Colleges, 2001–2002

Degree: MBA, Finance.
Job Target: Finance—analysis/management.
Strategy: Used course projects, classes, and entrepreneurial experience to demonstrate strong qualifications despite limited job experience.

Meredith K. Holland

2345 NW 151st Street, Vancouver, WA 98685
mholland@yahoo.com
360-294-2570

SUMMARY

Economic Analyst with MA in Applied Economics and real-world research, analysis, and consulting experience—an effective combination of theoretical and practical knowledge and a solid understanding of how economic principles and policies affect business, social, and political programs.

Key strengths include communication skills, leadership, and the ability to complete projects and deliver results in both individual and team assignments. Proficient in business and statistical software, including MS Excel, SAS, SPSS, and Statistix.

EDUCATION

Master of Arts, Applied Economics   2005
UNIVERSITY OF WASHINGTON, Seattle, WA

- GPA: 3.7 / 4.0.
- University Graduate Scholarship and Assistantship.
- Relevant Coursework: Econometrics, Microeconomics, Macroeconomics, Regional Economics, Cost-Benefit Analysis, International Trade, Quantitative Analysis.

Bachelor of Arts, Economics   2003
SEATTLE PACIFIC UNIVERSITY, Seattle, WA

- GPA: 3.2 / 4.0.
- Selected by faculty committee to participate in SPU study-abroad program; spent four months in London attending Regents College and traveling extensively throughout Europe.
- Resident Advisor, Longworth Hall, 2002–2003.
- Varsity soccer player, 4 years.
- Volunteer Service Award, Washington Special Olympics, 2002.

RELEVANT EXPERIENCE

Co-founder and Principal Investigator: APPLIED ECONOMICS RESEARCH GROUP,
University of Washington Department of Economics   2003–2005

Played a key role in launching consulting practice providing economic analysis for local businesses and institutions. Group grew from initial four founders in 2000 to 10–15 investigators.

Developed consulting proposals and led teams in research, analysis, and report preparation; delivered presentations to client Board of Directors or management team.

- Completed economic analysis for major national retailer exploring entry into the Seattle market.
- Performed employment analysis for regional economic-development organization studying immigrant labor issues.
- Established scholarship fund to channel consulting proceeds to graduate-level economics students.

(continued)

78 *(continued)*

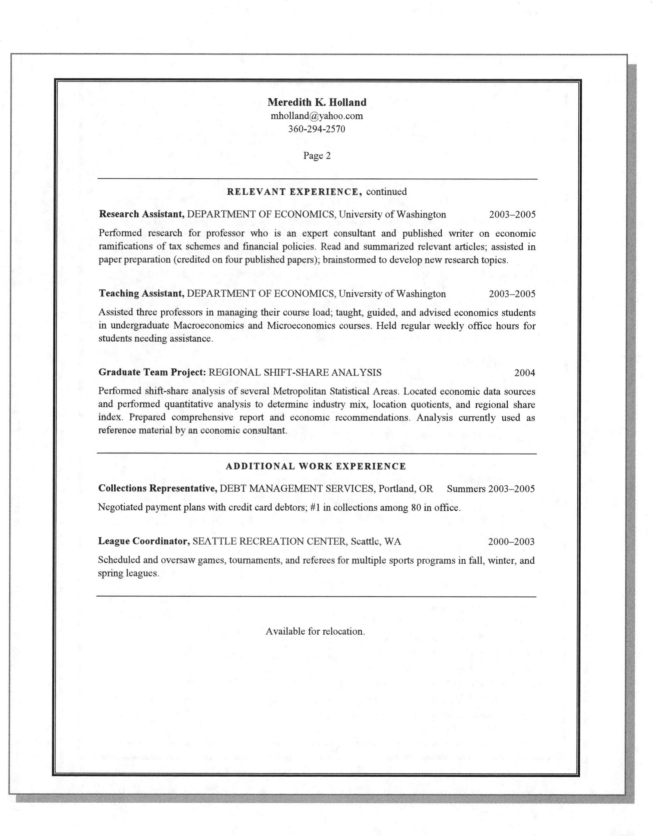

Meredith K. Holland
mholland@yahoo.com
360-294-2570

Page 2

RELEVANT EXPERIENCE, continued

Research Assistant, DEPARTMENT OF ECONOMICS, University of Washington   2003–2005

Performed research for professor who is an expert consultant and published writer on economic ramifications of tax schemes and financial policies. Read and summarized relevant articles; assisted in paper preparation (credited on four published papers); brainstormed to develop new research topics.

Teaching Assistant, DEPARTMENT OF ECONOMICS, University of Washington   2003–2005

Assisted three professors in managing their course load; taught, guided, and advised economics students in undergraduate Macroeconomics and Microeconomics courses. Held regular weekly office hours for students needing assistance.

Graduate Team Project: REGIONAL SHIFT-SHARE ANALYSIS   2004

Performed shift-share analysis of several Metropolitan Statistical Areas. Located economic data sources and performed quantitative analysis to determine industry mix, location quotients, and regional share index. Prepared comprehensive report and economic recommendations. Analysis currently used as reference material by an economic consultant.

ADDITIONAL WORK EXPERIENCE

Collections Representative, DEBT MANAGEMENT SERVICES, Portland, OR   Summers 2003–2005

Negotiated payment plans with credit card debtors; #1 in collections among 80 in office.

League Coordinator, SEATTLE RECREATION CENTER, Seattle, WA   2000–2003

Scheduled and oversaw games, tournaments, and referees for multiple sports programs in fall, winter, and spring leagues.

Available for relocation.

Degree: MS, Geography.

Job Target: Resource/environmental analyst.

Strategy: Highlighted functional skill areas in the Value Offered section. Check boxes encourage the reader to mentally check off the qualifications they are looking for. Packed lots of industry-specific keywords into the resume without harming readability; there is plenty of white space.

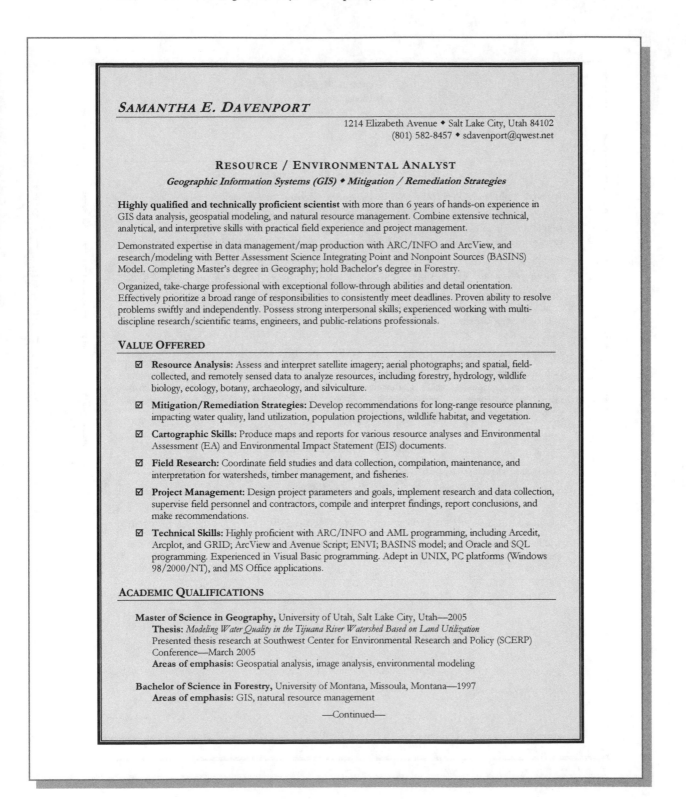

SAMANTHA E. DAVENPORT

1214 Elizabeth Avenue ◆ Salt Lake City, Utah 84102
(801) 582-8457 ◆ sdavenport@qwest.net

RESOURCE / ENVIRONMENTAL ANALYST
Geographic Information Systems (GIS) ◆ Mitigation / Remediation Strategies

Highly qualified and technically proficient scientist with more than 6 years of hands-on experience in GIS data analysis, geospatial modeling, and natural resource management. Combine extensive technical, analytical, and interpretive skills with practical field experience and project management.

Demonstrated expertise in data management/map production with ARC/INFO and ArcView, and research/modeling with Better Assessment Science Integrating Point and Nonpoint Sources (BASINS) Model. Completing Master's degree in Geography; hold Bachelor's degree in Forestry.

Organized, take-charge professional with exceptional follow-through abilities and detail orientation. Effectively prioritize a broad range of responsibilities to consistently meet deadlines. Proven ability to resolve problems swiftly and independently. Possess strong interpersonal skills; experienced working with multi-discipline research/scientific teams, engineers, and public-relations professionals.

VALUE OFFERED

☑ **Resource Analysis:** Assess and interpret satellite imagery; aerial photographs; and spatial, field-collected, and remotely sensed data to analyze resources, including forestry, hydrology, wildlife biology, ecology, botany, archaeology, and silviculture.

☑ **Mitigation/Remediation Strategies:** Develop recommendations for long-range resource planning, impacting water quality, land utilization, population projections, wildlife habitat, and vegetation.

☑ **Cartographic Skills:** Produce maps and reports for various resource analyses and Environmental Assessment (EA) and Environmental Impact Statement (EIS) documents.

☑ **Field Research:** Coordinate field studies and data collection, compilation, maintenance, and interpretation for watersheds, timber management, and fisheries.

☑ **Project Management:** Design project parameters and goals, implement research and data collection, supervise field personnel and contractors, compile and interpret findings, report conclusions, and make recommendations.

☑ **Technical Skills:** Highly proficient with ARC/INFO and AML programming, including Arcedit, Arcplot, and GRID; ArcView and Avenue Script; ENVI; BASINS model; and Oracle and SQL programming. Experienced in Visual Basic programming. Adept in UNIX, PC platforms (Windows 98/2000/NT), and MS Office applications.

ACADEMIC QUALIFICATIONS

Master of Science in Geography, University of Utah, Salt Lake City, Utah—2005
 Thesis: *Modeling Water Quality in the Tijuana River Watershed Based on Land Utilization*
 Presented thesis research at Southwest Center for Environmental Research and Policy (SCERP) Conference—March 2005
 Areas of emphasis: Geospatial analysis, image analysis, environmental modeling

Bachelor of Science in Forestry, University of Montana, Missoula, Montana—1997
 Areas of emphasis: GIS, natural resource management

—Continued—

79 *(continued)*

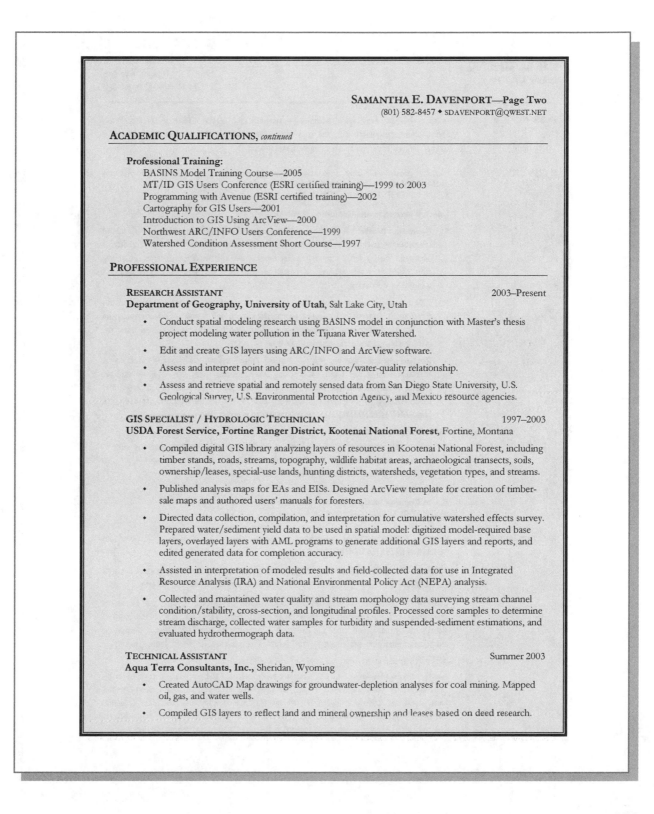

SAMANTHA E. DAVENPORT—Page Two
(801) 582-8457 ◆ SDAVENPORT@QWEST.NET

ACADEMIC QUALIFICATIONS, *continued*

Professional Training:
BASINS Model Training Course—2005
MT/ID GIS Users Conference (ESRI certified training)—1999 to 2003
Programming with Avenue (ESRI certified training)—2002
Cartography for GIS Users—2001
Introduction to GIS Using ArcView—2000
Northwest ARC/INFO Users Conference—1999
Watershed Condition Assessment Short Course—1997

PROFESSIONAL EXPERIENCE

RESEARCH ASSISTANT   2003–Present
Department of Geography, University of Utah, Salt Lake City, Utah

- Conduct spatial modeling research using BASINS model in conjunction with Master's thesis project modeling water pollution in the Tijuana River Watershed.

- Edit and create GIS layers using ARC/INFO and ArcView software.

- Assess and interpret point and non-point source/water-quality relationship.

- Assess and retrieve spatial and remotely sensed data from San Diego State University, U.S. Geological Survey, U.S. Environmental Protection Agency, and Mexico resource agencies.

GIS SPECIALIST / HYDROLOGIC TECHNICIAN   1997–2003
USDA Forest Service, Fortine Ranger District, Kootenai National Forest, Fortine, Montana

- Compiled digital GIS library analyzing layers of resources in Kootenai National Forest, including timber stands, roads, streams, topography, wildlife habitat areas, archaeological transects, soils, ownership/leases, special-use lands, hunting districts, watersheds, vegetation types, and streams.

- Published analysis maps for EAs and EISs. Designed ArcView template for creation of timber-sale maps and authored users' manuals for foresters.

- Directed data collection, compilation, and interpretation for cumulative watershed effects survey. Prepared water/sediment yield data to be used in spatial model: digitized model-required base layers, overlayed layers with AML programs to generate additional GIS layers and reports, and edited generated data for completion accuracy.

- Assisted in interpretation of modeled results and field-collected data for use in Integrated Resource Analysis (IRA) and National Environmental Policy Act (NEPA) analysis.

- Collected and maintained water quality and stream morphology data surveying stream channel condition/stability, cross-section, and longitudinal profiles. Processed core samples to determine stream discharge, collected water samples for turbidity and suspended-sediment estimations, and evaluated hydrothermograph data.

TECHNICAL ASSISTANT   Summer 2003
Aqua Terra Consultants, Inc., Sheridan, Wyoming

- Created AutoCAD Map drawings for groundwater-depletion analyses for coal mining. Mapped oil, gas, and water wells.

- Compiled GIS layers to reflect land and mineral ownership and leases based on deed research.

Degree: MBA.

Job Target: Management consulting for an Asian company or an American company with business interests in the Asia-Pacific region.

Strategy: Emphasized management-consulting work at the university and business internship experiences because she does not have paid experience in her field.

SUE L. CHENG
telephone: 3399-7744

6E Tower, Hillsdale Bay
Taipo, NT, Hong Kong
e-mail: slcheng@hongkong.net

■ OBJECTIVE

To apply skills and knowledge of e-business, e-government and telecom markets in the Asian-Pacific Region, project-management skills, and cross-cultural communications (Western and Asian) knowledge acquired through experience in diverse business environments.

■ EDUCATION

M.B.A. candidate with concentration in Management of Global Information Technology and e-Commerce Marketing, May 2006
BOSTON UNIVERSITY SCHOOL OF BUSINESS, Boston, MA

Selected Management-Consulting Projects:

- **Redman, Brotter & Williams Communications, Boston, MA** — Conducted comprehensive assessment of the business practices of public relations firm. Designed a detailed e-business plan for focusing on process improvement and communication strategies, integrating order fulfillment, service delivery, and customer relationship management, resulting in significant reduction in daily operating costs.

- **ADI Management Institute, Boston, MA** — Conducted an on-site analysis of the organization's management information systems requirements and designed a procurement system that integrated contracting, accounting, and receiving processes, resulting in a more responsive, user-friendly system with real-time trackable data.

- **PacSystems Inc., Boston, MA** — Analyzed existing business model and global expansion opportunities for a B2B e-marketplace serving the U.S. packaging industry. Conducted extensive research of major international packaging markets in Asia and Europe. Designed and presented to senior executives region-specific sales/marketing plan for effective market positioning and entry. Commended on research depth and dynamic presentation style.

Awards:

- Case competition winner out of 10 teams in the Managers in International Economy class on Steinway's entry strategy to the China market. Professor's comment: *"You made the best presentation on that case ever; no one else was even close."*

B.S. in Communications, graduated summa cum laude, 1999–2003
UNIVERSITY OF RICHMOND, Richmond, VA

■ INTERNSHIPS

CAPITAL CORPORATION, Boston, MA	2005
FORSTERI INTERNATIONAL, Boston, MA	2004

Intern — During the M.B.A. program, completed internships related to business outreach, e-commerce marketing, and e-business/e-government analysis. Engagement projects included the following:

Capital Corporation — Conducted market-risk analysis on telecom, Internet, and e-commerce development throughout the Greater China Region (China, Hong Kong, and Taiwan) and identified global market trends, growth areas, and investment opportunities for Aster Technologies, a client of the international investment and consulting firm. Results were published for senior decision makers on Aster's intranet.

Forsteri International — Assessed e-business policy/leadership and e-government readiness in the China market for global technology and policy consulting firm and clients, including Dunston-Patterson, Jones Smythe, and Hamden. Contributed research and analysis to company publication, *"Risk E-Business: Seizing the Opportunity of Global E-Readiness."* Utilized contacts in China and acted as liaison between firm and Chinese Ministry of Information Industry that regulates Internet and telecom development.

(continued)

80 *(continued)*

SUE L. CHENG
telephone: 3399-7744   Page 2

■ EMPLOYMENT

BOSTON UNIVERSITY, Boston, MA   2001–2003

Project Manager — Multicultural Affairs

Initiated, created, and marketed cultural training initiatives, special events, and educational programs; conducted workshops on cross-cultural issues. Designed department's website and served as webmaster. Coordinated, authored, and produced all office publications.

Accomplishments:

- Revamped, secured funding, and successfully promoted the academic training program. Results: increased participation rate 30% and achieved the highest retention rate organization-wide (34% above national average). Served as consultant to other organizations to establish similar programs.

- Appointed by President to direct the cross-functional strategic planning efforts that resulted in the development of the effective Leadership Training Institute.

- Chosen as internal consultant for the human resources practice in staff recruitment and retention to improve the university's diversity progress.

■ COMPUTER SKILLS

Microsoft Office Suite, Lotus Notes, SQL, HTML, SPSS, Datatel, Netscape Communicator, NJStar (Chinese Language Software), Compass Marketing Software, and Pagemaker.

■ LANGUAGES

Fluent in Chinese (Mandarin and Shanghai Dialects) and English.

■ REFERENCES

Available on request.

81

Degree: MS, Industrial Management.
Job Target: Computer systems integration or project management.
Strategy: Emphasized problem-solving skills, successful project-management experience, and work ethic (he is completely responsible for financing his education).

EDWARD A. STACKPOLE

313 Cherry Creek Road   864-326-0094
Clemson, SC 29631   edward@ureach.com

SYSTEMS INTEGRATION / PROJECT MANAGEMENT

Award-winning professional with excellent analytical, communication, and interpersonal skills. Diverse technical experience obtained through rapid learning and effective application of cutting-edge technologies. Team leader with fine-tuned multi-tasking capabilities. Accustomed to motivating, training, and mentoring others at all levels of technical expertise. Creative problem solver—accurately assess technical situational challenges and successfully transform ideas into appropriate workable solutions.

QUALIFICATION SUMMARY

- ❑ Keen observer—able to analyze current processes and develop new strategies and systems.
- ❑ Logical and practical in solving problems—systematic.
- ❑ Five years of experience with a variety of hardware platforms and software applications, including networking, peripherals, and database management.
- ❑ Five years of experience troubleshooting system problems, providing user training and help-desk support.
- ❑ Strong work ethic—personally responsible for 100% of living and educational expenses.
- ❑ Extensive hands-on, practical experience with technology, technical support, process improvement, logistics, and infrastructure management.
- ❑ Excellent communication abilities—able to convey complex technical information to non-technical individuals and groups.

EDUCATION

M.S., Industrial Management, 2005—Clemson University, Clemson, SC
B.S., Industrial Engineering, 2002—Clemson University, Clemson, SC

TECHNICAL EXPERTISE

- ❑ Design, testing, and assembly of computer systems
- ❑ System integration and installation
- ❑ Network design and implementation

PROJECT MANAGEMENT / COMMUNICATION

- ❑ Design and coordinate installation for inventory system of all equipment, software, and hardware and their location for Industrial Engineering Department.
- ❑ Design, fabricate, and/or procure all necessary equipment to complete all research projects for Department of Industrial Engineering, Clemson University. Coordinate and maintain support services for all departmental research projects.
- ❑ Implement and administer a fully functional Windows 2000 Workstation multimedia laboratory, which uses a client/server model for hands-on teaching and file distribution.
- ❑ Integrated multiple computer architectures to form network POS system using existing legacy equipment for Radio Shack.
- ❑ Trained and tutored students and employees in computer operation. Provided technical instruction to co-workers in a diversified computer environment.
- ❑ Provided technical support to customers of Radio Shack.

Page 1 of 2

---

81 *(continued)*

EDWARD A. STACKPOLE
864-326-0094

Page 2
edward@ureach.com

PROFESSIONAL EXPERIENCE

Department of Industrial Engineering, Clemson University, Clemson, SC
Director of Technical Operations, 1999–Present
❑ Coordinate location of equipment and administer resources for entire department. Instruct staff. Coordinate department security and building maintenance.
Accomplishments:
❑ Saved 40% in technology upgrades by using in-house expertise and eliminating outside technical assistance.
❑ Received Engineering Innovation Award, 2003.

Computer Specialist, Graduate School, 2000–2001
❑ Served as technical expert on the computer resources. Provided advice on technical issues.

Radio Shack, Greenville, SC
Computer Technician / Sales Associate, 1998–2001
❑ Handled customer technical support; managed/maintained POS system; repaired computer equipment and electronics.

NASA—Virginia Polytechnic Institute, Blacksburg, VA
Industrial and Systems Engineering Intern, 1997
❑ Assisted in the design of an experiment based on intelligent highway vehicular system (IVHS) and in the design and construction of a heads-up display model.

NASA—Clemson University, Greenville, SC
Computer Engineering Research Scholar, 1996
❑ Six-month project to provide technical drawings and documentation for a telemetry system.

Catawba Nuclear Station—Duke Power, York, SC
Information Systems Computer Technician, 1995
❑ Troubleshot, repaired, and configured PC and networking components.

ADDITIONAL EXPERIENCE

Engineering / Science Tutor—PEER Program, Clemson University, 1996–1999
Student Police Officer, CU Police Department, Clemson University, 1997–1998

ACADEMIC / COMMUNITY ACTIVITIES

Institute of Industrial Engineers (IIE)
National Society of Black Engineers (Communications Chairman, 1999)
AEL Graduate Honor Society (Membership Co-Chairman)
Beta Gamma Sigma Business Honor Society
Black Educational Support Team mentor
Classified Staff Awards Committee (Chairman, 2003–2004)
Kappa Alpha Psi Fraternity
Clemson University Traffic and Review Board
Tutor for Greenville's Littlejohn Community Center's homework center
City of Greenville Zoning and Review Board (Co-Chair)

82

Degree: MS, Printing Management.
Job Target: Sales/management training program.
Strategy: Emphasized graduate degree and involvement in a highly prestigious student organization. Work experience demonstrates sales capabilities and strong organizational skills. Additional experience as a graduate assistant and research fellow shows in-depth technical knowledge in leading-edge areas.

ALBERT DAVIDSON

92 Scottish Place, Apartment #3 ♦ Rochester, New York 14692 ♦ 585-731-9199 ♦ E-mail: aldav23@ur.edu

GRAPHIC ARTS SALES / MANAGEMENT ♦ MANAGEMENT-TRAINEE CANDIDATE

Disciplined and dynamic candidate with Master's degree in Printing Management and BFA in Photography. Exceptional academic record and practical experience in sales, project management, and team leadership. Seeking opportunity to join leading graphic arts firm in an entry-level sales or management-trainee position.

EDUCATION

UNIVERSITY OF ROCHESTER; Rochester, New York
Master of Science, Printing Management   **May 2006**
GPA: 4.0/4.0

Significant Courses:

- Database Marketing
- Operations Management
- Print Finishing Management

- Sales in the Graphic Arts
- Trends in Printing Technology
- Document Processing Languages

Special Projects:

Member of four-person team developing estimating software (using Excel) for Variable Data Printing.
Developing business plan and marketing plan for a digital print shop.
Part of two-person team that conducted study of image permanence, comparing liquid and dry toner technologies.

Extracurricular Activities:

*Served as **Vice President** of U of R Student Chapter of Association for Graphic Arts Technology (AGAT).*
- Functioned as Project Manager for 15-member student team charged with the concept, design, and production of publication for entry into annual competition. Delegated assignments, ensured equal participation among group members, and followed project from start to finish.
- Arranged seminars with corporate presenters on topics relevant to the graphic arts.

Bachelor of Fine Arts, Photography   **May 2004**
GPA: 3.44/4.0; Graduated with Honors.

Certificate in Business Management   **May 2004**
Three-course concentration in Management Process; GPA: 4.0/4.0.

PROFESSIONAL EXPERIENCE

WEBID.COM; New York, New York
Business Development Manager   **June 2003–Jan. 2004**
Served as outside sales representative for start-up website design firm catering to Fortune 1000 clients.
- Defined target markets and developed strategies for prospecting and qualifying leads.
- Cold-called major accounts and developed relationships with key corporate contacts.
- Established business relationships with blue-chip clientele, including Seagram's, MTV, the New York Jets, and major jewelry firms.
- On track to achieve multimillion-dollar sales goal for first 12 months.

CARL STEVENS; New York, New York
KEN MICHAELS; Brooklyn, New York
Photographer's Assistant (Co-op Assignments)   **2002–2003**
Supported professional photographers in arranging and executing photo shoots.
- Assisted advertising photographer with studio shoots in New York City:
    - Set up studio lighting for catalog shoots.
    - Worked with props and sets.
    - Loaded cameras and maintained equipment.
- Accompanied stock photographer on week-long remote shoot in The Bahamas:
    - Arranged locations and set up shoots.
    - Set up lighting, loaded cameras, and ensured that equipment was ready for shooting.
    - Coordinated scheduling of models.

82 *(continued)*

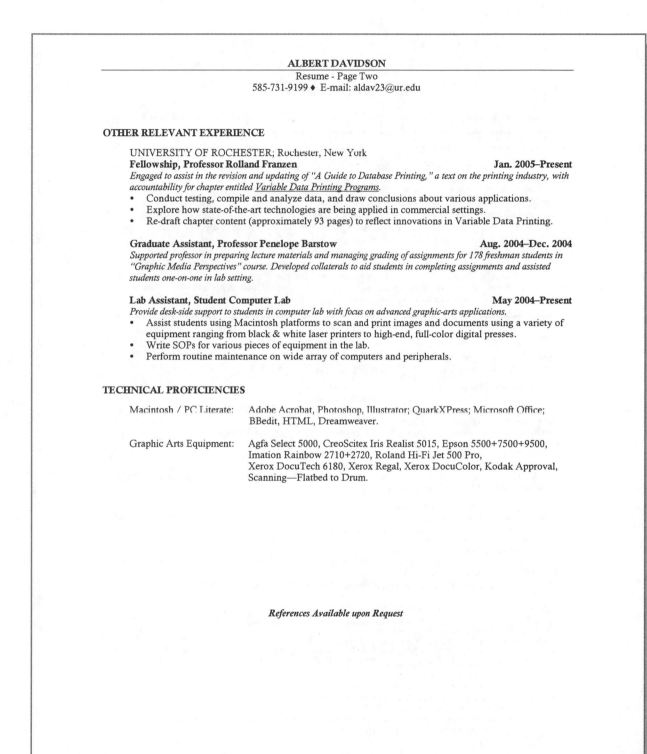

ALBERT DAVIDSON
Resume - Page Two
585-731-9199 ♦ E-mail: aldav23@ur.edu

OTHER RELEVANT EXPERIENCE

UNIVERSITY OF ROCHESTER; Rochester, New York
Fellowship, Professor Rolland Franzen   **Jan. 2005–Present**
Engaged to assist in the revision and updating of "A Guide to Database Printing," a text on the printing industry, with accountability for chapter entitled Variable Data Printing Programs.
- Conduct testing, compile and analyze data, and draw conclusions about various applications.
- Explore how state-of-the-art technologies are being applied in commercial settings.
- Re-draft chapter content (approximately 93 pages) to reflect innovations in Variable Data Printing.

Graduate Assistant, Professor Penelope Barstow   **Aug. 2004–Dec. 2004**
Supported professor in preparing lecture materials and managing grading of assignments for 178 freshman students in "Graphic Media Perspectives" course. Developed collaterals to aid students in completing assignments and assisted students one-on-one in lab setting.

Lab Assistant, Student Computer Lab   **May 2004–Present**
Provide desk-side support to students in computer lab with focus on advanced graphic-arts applications.
- Assist students using Macintosh platforms to scan and print images and documents using a variety of equipment ranging from black & white laser printers to high-end, full-color digital presses.
- Write SOPs for various pieces of equipment in the lab.
- Perform routine maintenance on wide array of computers and peripherals.

TECHNICAL PROFICIENCIES

Macintosh / PC Literate: Adobe Acrobat, Photoshop, Illustrator; QuarkXPress; Microsoft Office; BBedit, HTML, Dreamweaver.

Graphic Arts Equipment: Agfa Select 5000, CreoScitex Iris Realist 5015, Epson 5500+7500+9500, Imation Rainbow 2710+2720, Roland Hi-Fi Jet 500 Pro, Xerox DocuTech 6180, Xerox Regal, Xerox DocuColor, Kodak Approval, Scanning—Flatbed to Drum.

References Available upon Request

83
Degree: MS, Industrial and Organizational Psychology.
Job Target: OD/training position.
Strategy: With no prior business experience to include, this resume focuses on well-rounded internship experience in a corporate OD setting and includes a strong profile that captures his training, knowledge, and skills. The result: a very strong first page that has all the essential ingredients to position him for a training/OD role.

GREGORY MARTIN

67 Barkette Road   (914) 466-9901
Tarrytown, New York 10098   martin234@yahoo.com

PROFILE

Organizational Development/Change Management Professional with training and experience that provide a foundation for partnering human resources/OD initiatives with strategic business units to enhance productivity, performance, quality, and service. Core skills include the following:

Project/Program Management—Five years of project management experience that encompasses conceptualization, needs assessment, and planning through execution, post intervention assessment, feedback, and closure. Ability to integrate broader corporate values into functional project plans that yield deliverables aligned with enterprise objectives.

Training & Facilitation/Research—Versed in OD interventions: training, process improvement, team dynamics, meeting facilitation, performance assessment, 360° feedback instruments, coaching, change-management models, and human factors issues. Experience in researching, formulating, and conducting group training, including development of presentation materials. Competent researcher utilizing electronic databases (InfoTrac) and survey methods; trained in performing data analysis using SPSS, ANOVA, T Tests, and others.

EDUCATION

NEW YORK UNIVERSITY, New York, NY
Master of Science in Industrial and Organizational Psychology, May 2005

Selected Projects & Research:
* Transformational-leadership and change-management study.
* Peer-review and organizational-citizenship behavior in relationship to TQM, organizational satisfaction, and employee motivation.
* Study of lean manufacturing, participative management, cell concepts, and flexible structures.
* Onsite studies of workplace safety, human factors, and ergonomics issues.

Bachelor of Science in Psychology, *magna cum laude,* May 2002
Awards/Honors: Provost's Awards (2001, 2002); Outstanding Social Science Award; Psi Chi Honor Society (2002). Self-financed 100% of college tuition and expenses.

EXPERIENCE

KENWORTH CORPORATION, New York, NY
Organizational Development Consultant Intern (2003–2004)
Assisted the internal Senior Organizational Development Consultant in providing proactive OD consulting and interventions to enhance operational and human-resources effectiveness, efficiency, and quality in a Fortune 500 enterprise with 5,000 employees. Supported corporate training and development initiatives—including diversity training, Corporate University offerings, and customer-service training—in coordination with the Human Resources Service centers, Learning and Development Unit, Corporate Library, and Learning Centers.

Program Management, Training & Facilitation
* Planned, managed, and facilitated Manager Information Network, a management peer group from 5 business units sharing best practices and fostering company's commitment to excellence. Initiated group's intranet-based communication vehicle. Developed an organizational structure to allow group to become self-perpetuating.

Page 1 of 2

83 *(continued)*

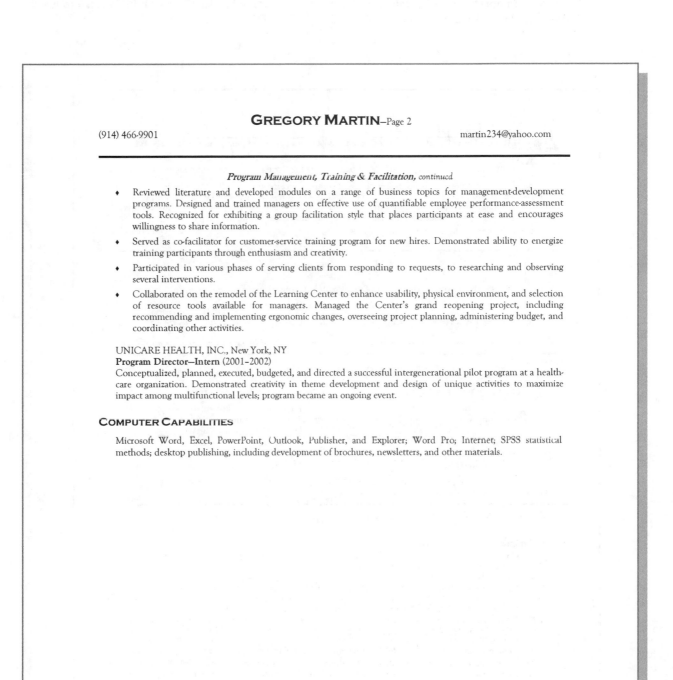

GREGORY MARTIN–Page 2

(914) 466-9901   martin234@yahoo.com

Program Management, Training & Facilitation, continued

♦ Reviewed literature and developed modules on a range of business topics for management-development programs. Designed and trained managers on effective use of quantifiable employee performance-assessment tools. Recognized for exhibiting a group facilitation style that places participants at ease and encourages willingness to share information.

♦ Served as co-facilitator for customer-service training program for new hires. Demonstrated ability to energize training participants through enthusiasm and creativity.

♦ Participated in various phases of serving clients from responding to requests, to researching and observing several interventions.

♦ Collaborated on the remodel of the Learning Center to enhance usability, physical environment, and selection of resource tools available for managers. Managed the Center's grand reopening project, including recommending and implementing ergonomic changes, overseeing project planning, administering budget, and coordinating other activities.

UNICARE HEALTH, INC., New York, NY
Program Director—Intern (2001–2002)
Conceptualized, planned, executed, budgeted, and directed a successful intergenerational pilot program at a health-care organization. Demonstrated creativity in theme development and design of unique activities to maximize impact among multifunctional levels; program became an ongoing event.

COMPUTER CAPABILITIES

Microsoft Word, Excel, PowerPoint, Outlook, Publisher, and Explorer; Word Pro; Internet; SPSS statistical methods; desktop publishing, including development of brochures, newsletters, and other materials.

Degree: Postgraduate diploma in Social Science.

Job Target: Community aid/overseas aid, and PR for community aid awareness.

Strategy: To support this job seeker's dual career targets, the resume emphasizes her background in both hands-on community aid and in raising public awareness of world hardships through PR/media/promotional work. Her work experience supports both targets as well.

ANGELIQUE KENNEDY

31 Johnson Street, Maiden, North Carolina 28650 • akennedy@bigpool.com • (916) 224-1111

FOCUS: OVERSEAS AID/COMMUNITY WORK • YOUTH & COMMUNITY CARE • PUBLIC RELATIONS

Globally focused graduate with strong awareness of complex socioeconomic, cultural, ecological, and resource-management issues. Successfully combine analytical and research expertise with flair for public speaking, presentation, writing, and communications. Keenly interested in developing a career in overseas aid, youth and community care, or global-aid marketing communications.

EDUCATION

POST-GRADUATE DIPLOMA IN SOCIAL SCIENCE, *University of Rocklin*, 2005

PSYCHOLOGY (BRIDGING COURSE), *University of Rocklin*, 2003

BACHELOR OF ARTS (**Social Science**); Major: Community Work, *University of Australia*, 2002

KEY CREDENTIALS

COMMUNITY/OVERSEAS AID

- Data Collection & Analysis
- Reporting & Funding Proposal Development
- Regulatory & Government Affairs
- Childhood Development Phases
- Issues Management
- Budget/Funds Analysis

PUBLIC RELATIONS/MARKETING

- Public Speaking/Presentations
- Teaching & Training
- Special-Event Coordination
- Program Development & Evaluation
- Media Communications
- Marketing & Promotions

Computer literate—Microsoft Office, Adobe Acrobat, Internet, e-mail.

EXPERIENCE SUMMARY

Communications, Research & Overseas Aid

- Conducted extensive interviews with people of drought-affected villages in northwest India; aided by an interpreter, researched, documented, and compiled the effects of a two-year drought.
- Composed a compelling case for food relief funding; produced and presented proposal to the National Dairy Development Board for distributing the nutritional dietary product "Khichidi."

Public Relations, Promotions & Media

- Propelled promotional ideas into definitive action plans, leading to highly profitable and successful special events. Driving force behind complete project coordination, including media communications, advertising design, venues, entertainment, outside broadcasts, and promotions.
- Generated impressive profits and record crowds to the *Miss Indy Competition*. Coordinated complete event from lighting and sound professionals to judges, contestants, patrons, and sponsors.
- Promoted radio events and competitions, conducted live broadcasts from outside vans, secured prizes from sponsors, and managed prize distribution at "live" locations.

Teaching & Organization

- Co-produced developmentally appropriate programs for children of varying ages, in conjunction with Child Care Director. Commended by parents and enjoyed by children, programs incorporated stimulating educational activities that were both safe and fun.

Angelique Kennedy   Page 1   Confidential

ANGELIQUE KENNEDY

akennedy@bigpool.com • (916) 224 1111

EMPLOYMENT SYNOPSIS

Field Worker/Researcher, *Self-Employed Women's Association*, India   2002–2004

Represented SEWA (Self-Employed Women's Association) in the State of Gujarat. Documented evidence of community hardship resulting from two years of drought. Assisted by an interpreter, interviewed villagers and produced a definitive proposal supporting the genuine need within the community for a supplementary dietary product chosen for its nutritional value and cost-effectiveness.

Promotions Coordinator, *Calm Waters Hotel*, Queensland, Australia   2002
Large hotel/motel catering primarily to tourist trade.

Strengthened business image and profits through increased promotional activities. Collaborated with management team to devise advertising campaigns and special events; followed through by supervising each project to completion. Communicated extensively with local businesses and sponsors to elicit participation in cooperative advertising.

Promotions Officer, *Sea FM Radio*, Miami, FL   2000–2002

Supported marketing and sales teams to brainstorm promotions and special events to drive revenue growth and boost listening audience. Includes paid promotions, competitions, and outside broadcasts.

Child Care Teacher Assistant, *Surfside Child Care Center*, Miami, FL   1996–1999

Privately owned and operated child-care center catering to more than 100 children from 15 months to school age.

Contributed toward the development of stimulating, age-appropriate activities meeting the needs of children at all levels. Supported the group leader in supervising games, rest periods, and children at play.

PERSONAL

Traveling and cultural experiences (26 countries visited to date); enjoy reading and surfing.

REFERENCES

Available upon request

Angelique Kennedy   Page 2   Confidential

85

Degree: MS, Occupational Ergonomics, and BS, Human Kinetics.
Job Target: A position studying manufacturing processes for the Ontario Worker's Compensation Board.
Strategy: Sold this individual primarily with his education and ancillary research and teaching work, with added value from his active participation in university athletics and community involvement. All of these items combined show a valuable, well-rounded individual with a unique background capable of teaching, further education, research, and, above all, communicating with people of all backgrounds.

| **MATTHEW R. JONES, BHK** | 22 Waverley Lane, Bedford, MA 02157
Home: 781.891.2345 E-mail: mattjones@yahoo.com |

OBJECTIVE | ERGONOMIST ▪ KINESIOLOGIST

PROFILE
- Energetic, motivated, and disciplined professional with an outstanding theoretical and practical background in performing physical-demands analysis, providing ergonomic assessments, and creating job modifications.
- Task oriented; work methodically to produce consistent quality work; meet objectives within strict time frames. Superior organizer; able to manage concurrent projects with attention to detail and accuracy.
- Articulate; build profitable rapport among clients, supervisors, peers, and other stakeholders.
- Analytical; able to extract pertinent information from a mass of data and produce quality reports for presentation.
- Effective problem solver; thrive in a fast-paced, dynamic, and challenging environment of ongoing change.
- Knowledge of government regulatory compliance relating to WSIB, Health & Safety Act, and other legislation.

EDUCATION

University of Massachusetts, Lowell, MA   June 2006
MASTER OF SCIENCE—Occupational Ergonomics
- 3.8 GPA.
Course modules include

Field Evaluations	Occupational Biomechanics
Physical Agents Evaluation	Advanced Biomechanics
Design for Injury Prevention	Toxicology & Health
Human Factors	Methods in Work Analysis
Workers Compensation (Ontario)	Industrial Hygiene & Ergonomics
Capstone Course	Bio Statistics & Epidemiology

University of Windsor, Windsor, ON   2003
BACHELOR OF HUMAN KINETICS—Movement Science
Course modules included

Human Physiology	Adolescent Psychology
Anthropology	Perceptual Motor Control
Research & Development	Physiology of Exercise
Anatomy	Human Performance

PROFESSIONAL EXPERIENCE

University of Massachusetts, Lowell, MA   2004–present
RESEARCH ASSISTANT
- Play a pivotal role in a unique case study involving the compilation of data and analysis of multidisciplined health-care workers in four local hospitals. Process includes following workers throughout their daily routine; charting a detailed report every 45 seconds on person's movements; and tabulating daily results into a database.
- Designing a complex ergonomic chart focusing on movement charting for every 45 seconds during a 12-hour shift.

TEACHER ASSISTANT   2004–present
- Facilitate as assistant to Doctor Paul Hawkins, "Occupational Biomechanics" postgraduate module. Oversee the laboratory functions; grade papers and homework.

Page One of Two

85 *(continued)*

MATTHEW R. JONES, BHK	781.891.2345 ▪ MATTJONES@YAHOO.COM ▪ **PAGE TWO**	

PROFESSIONAL EXPERIENCE ...continued

Liberty Mutual Research Center, Hopkinton, MA   6/2004–8/2004
RESEARCH FELLOW
- Awarded the 2004 *"American Society of Safety Engineers"* (ASSE) Research Fellowship.
- Conducted an extensive research project into workers' ability to estimate their grip force, utilizing two common tools: screwdriver and ratchet. Report currently under review by *Professional Safety* magazine.

Doctor Nathan Hanna, University of Massachusetts, Lowell, MA   2/2004–5/2004
RESEARCH ASSISTANT
- Reviewed 68 papers in epidemiologic studies to abstract and tabulate information on ergonomic exposure assessment methods in health care for the head of the exposure and epidemiology assessment team.

Fizzles Night Club, London, ON   4/2003–8/2003
BARTENDER/WAITER

General Electric Locomotive, London, ON   10/2002
ERGONOMIC CONSULTANT—Health & Safety
- Conducted, as a volunteer, physical demand analyses for the Chassis Construction Division.

SGL Plastics Limited, Whitby, ON   1993–1997
MACHINE OPERATOR—Summer employment

SPECIALIZED TRAINING

Proactive Ergonomic Concepts, Inc., Windsor, ON   9/2002
Physical Demands Analysis Course
- Introduction to the skills and techniques involved in performing a physical demand analysis.

MEMBERSHIPS & AFFILIATIONS

Human Factors and Ergonomics Society   2004–present
STUDENT MEMBER

COMMUNITY INVOLVEMENT

University of Massachusetts, Lowell, MA   2003–present
MEN'S CLUB BASKETBALL TEAM MEMBER

University of Windsor, Windsor, ON   2002–2003
ATHLETE MENTOR
- Conducted presentations to elementary school students with the aim of motivating them to succeed and guiding them in their future choices.

MEN'S VARSITY BASKETBALL TEAM   2003
- Honored for being the *"Most Valuable Player as Team Captain."*
- Recipient of the *"Lancer Award,"* given to an athlete for being an exemplary role model.

Canadian Red Cross Society, Oakville, ON   1998–2000
YOUTH MEMBERSHIP COORDINATOR
- Acknowledged for actively addressing a shortage of youth members. Planned and organized many events; increased membership by 76%.

Big Brothers, Oakville, ON   1998
Big Brother—Appleby College School
- Active participant in the Big Brothers program.

LANGUAGES

Fluent: English, German, Spanish   Proficient: French, Italian

86 Degree: MA, Special Education/California Teaching Credential.
Job Target: Counselor, teacher, or case manager for special-needs youth.
Strategy: The reader's attention is drawn to the job seeker's impressive career through use of keywords in the opening and subsequent paragraphs. The graphic element emphasizes commitment to children.

MARIKO K. OZEKI
555 Alamo Court, Signal Hill, California 90806
(360) 278-9256—mozeki@juno.com

PROFESSIONAL QUALIFICATIONS

> ➤ **Counselor, Teacher, and Case Manager for Special-Needs Youth—7 years.**
> ➤ Specialist in diagnosis and treatment of developmental disabilities.
> ➤ Master of Arts in Special Education / California Teaching Credential expected in 2006.
> ➤ Bilingual teaching experience: Spanish / English.

EDUCATION

Master of Arts in Special Education / California Teaching Credential   Expected 2006
California State University, Dominguez Hills, California
Bachelor of Arts Degree in Community Service & Public Affairs   1997
University of California at Los Angeles

PROFESSIONAL EXPERIENCE

SPECIAL-NEEDS INSTRUCTOR   2001–Present
Outreach Training Center, Long Beach, California
Teach community living skills to developmentally disabled teenagers and adults. Prepare and present traditional and multimedia lessons, tailoring them to group and individual needs. Follow up with coaching and lesson assessment. Consult with senior instructors, clinicians, and parents to create comprehensive rehabilitation plans.
> ➤ The Center has placed roughly 80% of our special-needs clients into mainstream society during the past 2 years.

COUNSELOR   1998–2001
California Youth Authority, Corona, California
Counsel and instruct up to 800 juvenile offenders. Recommend youth placements in community jobs or in crisis-intervention or substance-abuse programs. Collaborate with interdisciplinary teams regarding case management of treatment-resistant individuals. Develop and coordinate recreational and social programs.

COMMUNITY SERVICE

BIG SISTER   2003–Present
Big Sisters of South Bay, Long Beach, California
Provide friendship and guidance to adolescents on weekends and on-call.

87

Degree: Master of Public Health.

Job Target: Technical sales: medical/pharmaceutical industries.

Strategy: The Summary of Qualifications is the key section in this resume. It highlights an advanced technical degree in the health-care field, sales experience, experience working in hospital/surgical settings, knowledge of pharmaceuticals, relationship-building skills (particularly with physicians and their staffs), communication skills, and the ability to set and achieve goals.

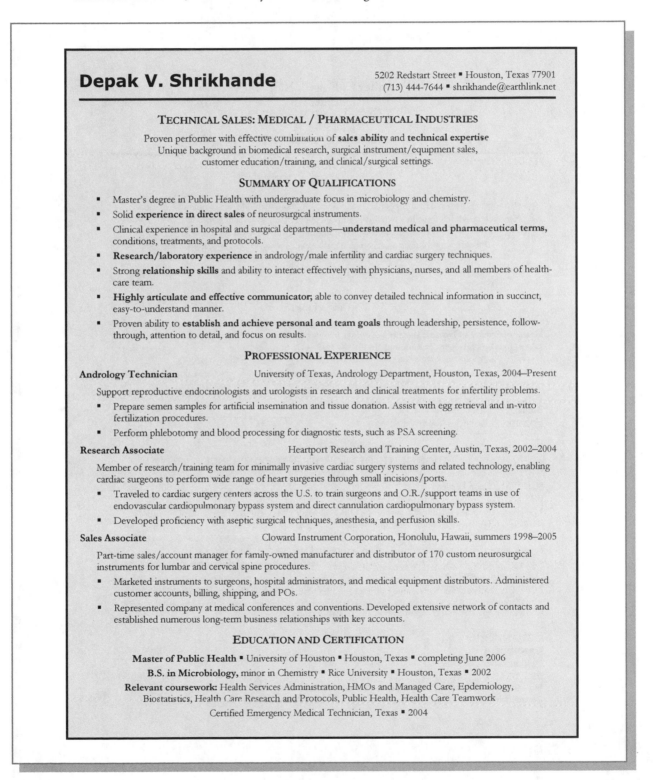

Depak V. Shrikhande

5202 Redstart Street ▪ Houston, Texas 77901
(713) 444-7644 ▪ shrikhande@earthlink.net

TECHNICAL SALES: MEDICAL / PHARMACEUTICAL INDUSTRIES

Proven performer with effective combination of **sales ability** and **technical expertise**
Unique background in biomedical research, surgical instrument/equipment sales,
customer education/training, and clinical/surgical settings.

SUMMARY OF QUALIFICATIONS

- Master's degree in Public Health with undergraduate focus in microbiology and chemistry.
- Solid **experience in direct sales** of neurosurgical instruments.
- Clinical experience in hospital and surgical departments—**understand medical and pharmaceutical terms,** conditions, treatments, and protocols.
- **Research/laboratory experience** in andrology/male infertility and cardiac surgery techniques.
- Strong **relationship skills** and ability to interact effectively with physicians, nurses, and all members of health-care team.
- **Highly articulate and effective communicator;** able to convey detailed technical information in succinct, easy-to-understand manner.
- Proven ability to **establish and achieve personal and team goals** through leadership, persistence, follow-through, attention to detail, and focus on results.

PROFESSIONAL EXPERIENCE

Andrology Technician   University of Texas, Andrology Department, Houston, Texas, 2004–Present

Support reproductive endocrinologists and urologists in research and clinical treatments for infertility problems.

- Prepare semen samples for artificial insemination and tissue donation. Assist with egg retrieval and in-vitro fertilization procedures.
- Perform phlebotomy and blood processing for diagnostic tests, such as PSA screening.

Research Associate   Heartport Research and Training Center, Austin, Texas, 2002–2004

Member of research/training team for minimally invasive cardiac surgery systems and related technology, enabling cardiac surgeons to perform wide range of heart surgeries through small incisions/ports.

- Traveled to cardiac surgery centers across the U.S. to train surgeons and O.R./support teams in use of endovascular cardiopulmonary bypass system and direct cannulation cardiopulmonary bypass system.
- Developed proficiency with aseptic surgical techniques, anesthesia, and perfusion skills.

Sales Associate   Cloward Instrument Corporation, Honolulu, Hawaii, summers 1998–2005

Part-time sales/account manager for family-owned manufacturer and distributor of 170 custom neurosurgical instruments for lumbar and cervical spine procedures.

- Marketed instruments to surgeons, hospital administrators, and medical equipment distributors. Administered customer accounts, billing, shipping, and POs.
- Represented company at medical conferences and conventions. Developed extensive network of contacts and established numerous long-term business relationships with key accounts.

EDUCATION AND CERTIFICATION

Master of Public Health ▪ University of Houston ▪ Houston, Texas ▪ completing June 2006
B.S. in Microbiology, minor in Chemistry ▪ Rice University ▪ Houston, Texas ▪ 2002
Relevant coursework: Health Services Administration, HMOs and Managed Care, Epdemiology, Biostatistics, Health Care Research and Protocols, Public Health, Health Care Teamwork
Certified Emergency Medical Technician, Texas ▪ 2004

88 **Degree:** MS, Nursing, Family Nurse Practitioner.
Job Target: Family nurse practitioner.
Strategy: To set this client apart from the average "new graduate," the resume highlights her extensive experience and strong accomplishments in implementing new programs, cutting costs, improving productivity, and developing new business. Condensed her 20+ years of work experience so that her most impressive contributions would not be obscured by ordinary responsibilities.

Jennifer C. Powell, RN, FNP
P.O. Box 5578
Towson, MD 21204
(410) 559-2211
E-mail: jennpowell@earthlink.net

KEY QUALIFICATIONS

▶ Innovative, dedicated Family Nurse Practitioner with more than 20 years of nursing experience.
▶ Strong interest in adolescent health issues. Ten years of experience conducting seminars on teen sexuality.
▶ Excellent problem-solving and organizational skills.
▶ Wide range of nursing experience: cardiac, emergency, critical care, home care,
long-term care, oncology, outpatient, and management.
▶ Demonstrated ability to communicate effectively with patients, families, medical staff, and the public.

EDUCATION

Master of Science in Nursing (Family Nurse Practitioner major)   May 2005
Johns Hopkins University, Baltimore, MD; GPA — 3.95

Consistently worked more than the minimum number of clinical practice hours. Clinical rotations provided experience in Women's Health, Pediatric Health, and Adult Health.

Bachelor of Science in Nursing   1983
University of Kentucky, Louisville, KY

HIGHLIGHTS OF PROFESSIONAL EXPERIENCE

Staff Nurse/Team Leader   2001 to present
Baltimore Cardiac Care Center, Baltimore, MD
▶ Serve as a resource on clinical issues for the Office Manager. Assist with the development of clinical policies and procedures. Make recommendations leading to cost savings, increased efficiency, and patient satisfaction.
▶ Assist physicians in understanding ancillary services and utilizing them appropriately.
▶ Helped institute a CHF Nursing Practice. Perform patient assessments and drug titrations under cardiologist supervision.
▶ Facilitate better patient well-being by educating patients and their families about medical conditions and procedures.
▶ Promote teamwork and communication among staff members.

Consultant   2000 to 2002
Johnson County Home Care, Lanham, MD

▶ Conducted Medicare audits and chart reviews that contributed to this agency receiving its first JCAHO accreditation.

(continued)

88 *(continued)*

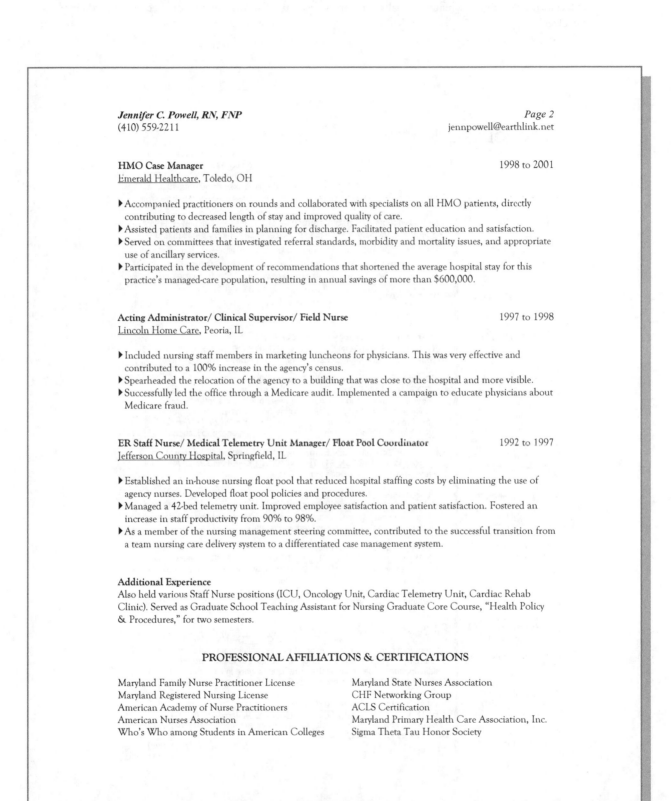

Jennifer C. Powell, RN, FNP   *Page 2*
(410) 559-2211   jennpowell@earthlink.net

HMO Case Manager   1998 to 2001
Emerald Healthcare, Toledo, OH

▶ Accompanied practitioners on rounds and collaborated with specialists on all HMO patients, directly
   contributing to decreased length of stay and improved quality of care.
▶ Assisted patients and families in planning for discharge. Facilitated patient education and satisfaction.
▶ Served on committees that investigated referral standards, morbidity and mortality issues, and appropriate
   use of ancillary services.
▶ Participated in the development of recommendations that shortened the average hospital stay for this
   practice's managed-care population, resulting in annual savings of more than $600,000.

Acting Administrator/ Clinical Supervisor/ Field Nurse   1997 to 1998
Lincoln Home Care, Peoria, IL

▶ Included nursing staff members in marketing luncheons for physicians. This was very effective and
   contributed to a 100% increase in the agency's census.
▶ Spearheaded the relocation of the agency to a building that was close to the hospital and more visible.
▶ Successfully led the office through a Medicare audit. Implemented a campaign to educate physicians about
   Medicare fraud.

ER Staff Nurse/ Medical Telemetry Unit Manager/ Float Pool Coordinator   1992 to 1997
Jefferson County Hospital, Springfield, IL

▶ Established an in-house nursing float pool that reduced hospital staffing costs by eliminating the use of
   agency nurses. Developed float pool policies and procedures.
▶ Managed a 42-bed telemetry unit. Improved employee satisfaction and patient satisfaction. Fostered an
   increase in staff productivity from 90% to 98%.
▶ As a member of the nursing management steering committee, contributed to the successful transition from
   a team nursing care delivery system to a differentiated case management system.

Additional Experience
Also held various Staff Nurse positions (ICU, Oncology Unit, Cardiac Telemetry Unit, Cardiac Rehab
Clinic). Served as Graduate School Teaching Assistant for Nursing Graduate Core Course, "Health Policy
& Procedures," for two semesters.

PROFESSIONAL AFFILIATIONS & CERTIFICATIONS

Maryland Family Nurse Practitioner License	Maryland State Nurses Association
Maryland Registered Nursing License	CHF Networking Group
American Academy of Nurse Practitioners	ACLS Certification
American Nurses Association	Maryland Primary Health Care Association, Inc.
Who's Who among Students in American Colleges	Sigma Theta Tau Honor Society

89 **Degree:** MA, Sociology.
Job Target: Career in foreign service.
Strategy: Targeted the resume to display education achievements and leadership/internship experience. Selected the indented format to visually categorize a variety of student educational activities as they occurred.

NICHOLAS C. KOSTAS

4122 Roosevelt Lane
Seattle, Washington 99231
Phone: (204) 611-1422
Email: nickkostas@hotmail.com

PROFILE

A dedicated professional with a strong record of academic achievements and professional leadership. Noted for excellence in highly detailed and demanding environments.

SOCIAL SERVICES ADVISOR	*AUDITING COMMUNICATIONS*	*MENTORING INITIATOR*

Language **Fluent in Greek**

EDUCATION

Master of Arts—Sociology (December 2005)
<u>CENTRAL WASHINGTON STATE UNIVERSITY</u>—Ellensburg, WA
Graduate Paper: College Students' Negative Attitudes Toward Police.

Social Service
Graduate Assistant—On-Air Talent—2002 to 2003
<u>CWS INFORMATION SERVICE</u>—On Campus
Prepared and voiced four hours of news and feature information daily (Monday–Friday) for airing to the blind. Edited tape, prepared features, and sourced wire services, the *Seattle Post Intelligencer,* the *Yakima Herald,* and major national and regional publications.

Bachelor of Science—Law Enforcement and Justice Administration
<u>CENTRAL WASHINGTON STATE UNIVERSITY</u>—Ellensburg, WA
Selected—Alpha Kappa Delta Honor Society

Legal Analysis
Legal Assistant—2001 to 2003
<u>CWU STUDENT LEGAL SERVICES</u>
Provided initial advice to students, primarily for alcohol-related offenses. Mediated landlord / tenant disputes.

Judicial Processes
Internship—2001 (Summer)
<u>YAKIMA COUNTY JUVENILE DETENTION CENTER</u>—Yakima, WA
Assisted with the intake and initial interview of juveniles in the court system, post-arrest onward. Gathered demographics, did group discussions, tutored with school homework, and facilitated educational discussions and training.

PROFESSIONAL
Leadership
Crime in a University Town—2003
<u>ASSOCIATION FOR HUMANIST SOCIOLOGISTS</u>—Memphis, TN
Presented a one-hour presentation at the Association's regular meeting concerning a study evaluating police arrest rates in Ellensburg. Found validity in student perceptions that arrest rates were in excess of the norm. The presentation was a forerunner of the Master's paper presented 2005.

Initiative
Public Relations—Founding Member
<u>WESTERN ANTHROPOLOGY / SOCIOLOGY CLUB</u>—On Campus
Responsible for creating publicity for professional panels, field trips, and conferences on a variety of social issues.

(Continued on page two)

89 *(continued)*

	Kostas — page two	*(204) 611-1422* ➢ *nickkostas@hotmail.com*

Leadership	**Secretary—Founding Member** GRADUATE SOCIOLOGY ORGANIZATION—On Campus Assisted sociology majors in developing study habits, provided tutoring, and arranged professional conferences on topics of interest.
Advisor	**Graduate Advisor** STUDENT TENANT UNION Selected to advise undergraduates on area real estate lease provisions and assist in dispute resolution. Advised undergraduates on rights and complaint procedures.
Leadership	**Philanthropic Chair / Public Relations Chair** SIGMA KAPPA FRATERNITY—On Campus Organized "Arrows for Alzheimer's," raising more than $1,000 for charity.

EMPLOYMENT Internet Based	2004 to Present	NETSAFE MORTGAGE COMPANY—Seattle, Washington **Mortgage Loan Auditor** Accountable for determining underwriting and processing documentation errors for up to 60 residential mortgages daily for one of the nation's first totally Web-based mortgage companies.

➢ Review the corporate auditors' results, reviewing approved documents (title policy audits, recording audits) for accuracy and conformity to state, federal, and investor underwriting parameters.
➢ Assure multi-state licensing conformity for company principals—resident and non-resident insurance—including renewals and new applications.
➢ Resolved accounting issues concerning problematic documentations—claims for property taxes, lost and misplaced financial instruments.

Contributions
➢ Saved the company more than $500,000 in charge-backs or non-funded loans nationwide by catching errors in underwriting or documentation.
➢ Developed proprietary MS Access programs (Audit and Quality Control department), giving instant access to interdepartmental files and streamlining the internal audit processes. Access restricted to Audit and senior executives.
➢ Commended on annual performance reviews for learning, taking direction, and accuracy.

Law Enforcement	2002 to 2004	LAWYERS PRIVATE SERVICE—Ellensburg, WA **Process Server** Served summonses on businesses and individuals in the area.

TECHNICAL	MS Office (all applications) WAV formatWordPerfect	Adobe Acrobat LANTech	Digital scanning

References upon Request

90 **Degree:** MA, Political Science.
Job Target: Position in counterintelligence with a federal agency.
Strategy: Positioned this student with no applicable work history in a favorable light with the CIA. Highlighted skills and experience known to be of value for her job target.

Amanda Hart Marston

200 Slocum Road ❖ Wetumpka, Alabama 36092 ❖ [334] 294-7076 ❖ ahm@juno.com

VALUE TO THE UNITED STATES

Help serve security interests by applying my Russian-language skills as an **all source analyst** with the Central Intelligence Agency.

CAPABILITIES YOU CAN USE NOW

❖ Mission-oriented team player ❖ Quick study ❖ Thrive on getting results ❖ Unflappable

EDUCATION

❖ Pursuing Master of **Political Science,** Auburn University, Montgomery, Alabama. Scheduled to graduate: Feb 2006. GPA **3.3+**
❖ B.A., **International Studies, Russian Language** (minor: Business), University of South Alabama, Mobile, Alabama, Jun 2004

    ❖ Research paper: "The Impact of Illegal Transfer of Nuclear Weapons by the Russian Mafia" (working title)
    ❖ Research paper on approaches to conflict resolution among Somali warlords
    ❖ Selected coursework of interest: Comparative Government and Politics; Applied Research and Program Evaluation Methods

SPECIALIZED EDUCATION

❖ **Full immersion Russian** language program, Norwich University, Northfield, Vermont, 2003, GPA **3.5**
❖ **Russian** language and culture program, St. Petersburg State University, St. Petersburg, **Russia,** Dec 2005, GPA **3.5**
❖ Pursued M.A., **Russian** Language, University of Arizona, Tucson, Sep 1999–Jun 2000

COMPUTER LITERACY

Capable in Lotus 1-2-3, proprietary statistical packages, Word for Windows and WordPerfect; familiar with composing in **Cyrillic alphabet**

WORK HISTORY

Sales Associate (Aug 2005–Present)   Right Tog, Montgomery, Alabama
           Part-time and summer jobs while pursuing degrees:
Part-Time Sales Associate   Tropics, Tucson, Arizona
(Jul 2002–May 2004)   Foxmoor, B & B Pets, Sears, Gayfers
                           (all in Mobile, Alabama)

Secretary (Jun 1998–Jul 2002)   Mailor Associates, Wetumpka, Alabama

CONTRIBUTIONS TO THE COMMUNITY

❖ President, International Studies Club, University of South Alabama, 2004
❖ As a staff member representing the **"Russian delegation,"** spoke before the Student United Nations, Auburn University, Auburn, Alabama, 2003

91

Degree: JD.
Job Target: Associate attorney in a private firm.
Strategy: Showed the unusual experience she has. Because of a rather obscure rule, she has been able to "practice law" under the supervision of an attorney. That's especially important because the law school from which she graduated isn't accredited.

Allison Bristow

323 Coldstone Court, Montgomery, AL 36100   [334] 207-1255 • allisonjd@juno.com

SITTING FOR BAR EXAM: July 06

CAPABILITIES DONNELLY & SHOREDITCH CAN USE NOW:
- **Communications skills** tested by uninformed clients
- **Research skills** tested by practicing attorneys
- **Presentation skills** tested in court

LAW-RELATED EXPERIENCE:
- **Law Clerk** *later* **Legal Intern**   Smith & Hawken, L.L.C., Wetumpka, AL
  Jan 03–Present

EXPERIENCE AS AN ADVOCATE FOR CLIENTS IN COURT

• Bond reduction hearings • Pendente lite hearings • Juvenile court hearings • Sentence reviews • Arraignments • Probation revocation hearings • Administrative hearings • District criminal, civil, and traffic courts • Dependency hearings • Sentencing hearings • Plea hearings

EXPERIENCE PREPARING FOR COURT

• Investigations • Drafting and filing motions • Writing briefs and memoranda • Negotiating plea bargains • Interviewing • Evaluating worth of civil cases • Legal research • Explaining legal rights and evidence

---

- Successfully defended client in suit against real-estate attorney with a decade of practice. Handled case after only four months of internship.
- Proved in court my juvenile client was not guilty in assault case, even though experienced law officers were witnesses for the prosecution.
- Carried the argument before a tough judge that my client's probation should not be revoked—even though he had tested positive for drugs. Had 15 minutes to prepare this case.

EDUCATION AND PROFESSIONAL DEVELOPMENT:
- J.D., Craft School of Law, Montgomery, Alabama, 02
  Pursued at night while working up to 45 hours a week.
- B.A., Broadcast Journalism, University of Southern Arkansas, Littleburg, Arkansas: 01
- B.S., Business Administration **(Industrial Management)**, University of Arkansas, Littleburg, Arkansas: 97
- "Alabama Mediation Training," Resolution Resources, Birmingham, Alabama: 04
  Self-funded, 21 CLE hours.

PROFESSIONAL ORGANIZATIONS: Future Trial Lawyers Association

OTHER EXPERIENCE:
- More than 13 years in various positions in sales, broadcasting, manufacturing, and public relations.

Degree: JD.
Job Target: Associate position.
Strategy: Focused on internships and scholarships, placing education up front.

LIZ D. ENGEL

5298 Crow Avenue   212.432.5551
New York, NY 10027   liz@hotmail.com

CAREER FOCUS

Entry-level, Full-time Law Associate
· Corporate · Labor · Civil ·

OVERVIEW

❑ Background in analyzing diversified corporate issues and drafting high-quality written documents.
❑ Superior interpersonal skills, able to build strong relationships and conduct liaison.
❑ Exposed to a variety of legal proceedings, research, and processes.
❑ Held several paid internship and clerk positions.

EDUCATION

▪ **Juris Doctor, May 2005**
  Corporate Counsel Certificate, May 2005
  New York University College of Law, New York, New York
  — Dean's List
  — Editor, *Journal of International Relations and Economics*
    Completed a note on the difficulties of prosecuting insider-trading violations

▪ **Bachelor of Arts in Economics and Finance, Minor in Psychology, May 2003**
  New Jersey State University, New Brunswick, New Jersey
  — Graduated with Honors (GPA: 3.8)
  — Dean's List, Golden Key National Honor Society, Summit Scholarship, Brenton
    Hospital Auxiliary Scholarship, Marcus Scholarship, College Club of Inglewood
    Scholarship, Athletic Achievement Award

PROFESSIONAL EXPERIENCE

Law Clerk
Michaels, Brenner, Schmidt & Associates, Fairfield, Connecticut   Summer 2005

  ▪ Analyzed diversified corporate issues involving labor, contract, environmental,
    bankruptcy, and real estate law, and drafted complaints, interrogatories, and
    legal memoranda for attorneys.
  ▪ Examined the legislative history of the statutes of limitations to clarify intent for
    specific cases. Thoroughly researched procedures required to commence
    actions and determined proper jurisdiction to file suits.
  ▪ Actively participated in case discussions, strategy conferences, and settlement
    negotiations.

Page 1 of 2

92 *(continued)*

Legal Intern
Law Office of Marsha Bender, Laurel, Maryland   **Summer 2004**

- Drafted complaints, interrogatory responses, and memoranda involving personal-injury claims. Served as an advocate to clients and negotiated settlements in insurance and elder law.
- Conducted legal research. Corresponded with clients and attorneys.
- Participated in real estate closings.

Legal Intern
Honorable Mark L. Williams
Assignment Judge, Criminal Division, Superior Court, Connecticut   **Summer 2003**

- Prepared pre-sentence investigation summaries for court proceedings.
- Worked directly with inmates to procure unawarded jail credit. Reconciled inmate appeals regarding issued bench warrants. Accessed the Promise Gavel Database for inmate verification and case status.
- Observed criminal and divorce trials, voir dire, and mediation proceedings.

Legal Intern
Howard County Probative Services Division, Columbia, Maryland   **Summer 2002**

- Observed child-support enforcement cases and managed pertinent recordkeeping of proceedings.
- Participated in case discussions and analysis with the attorneys and hearing officer.

MEMBERSHIP

American Bar Association, 2005 to Present

TECHNICAL PROFICIENCY

Lexis/Nexis ▪ Westlaw ▪ Library Legal Research ▪ Microsoft Office ▪ WordPerfect

Degree: JD.
Job Target: Position not practicing law but using skills identified in the keyword summary.
Strategy: Emphasized a broad range of skills and provided examples of how those were used both within and outside the legal area.

KEISHA CRAWLEY

4725 Montrose Court
Cincinnati, OH 45229
(513) 652-0907   E-mail: keishacrawley@hotmail.com

SUMMARY	Dedicated self-starter who enjoys managing projects from conception to completion. Excellent follow-up skills. Experienced in dealing with people on all levels.

Increasing interests and responsibilities in the following areas:

- Research/Writing
- Presentations
- Non-Profit Administration
- Interviewing/Counseling
- Public Relations and Marketing

- Program Development
- Business Administration
- Governmental Agencies
- Team Building
- Management/Leadership

RESEARCH/WRITING

Write persuasively and accurately with attention to detail and legal technicalities. As Law Clerk for Ohio Attorney General, Criminal Appellate Bureau, researched and wrote documentation involving various issues.

Gained knowledge and writing expertise in the areas concerning ineffective assistance of counsel, competency of witnesses, and excessive sentences.

While interning for Judge Ronald Petty in the Criminal Division, performed legal research and writing involving habeas petitions for post-conviction relief. Assisted Judge Petty at trial and worked on various trial motions. Outlined pre-trial programs concerning judicial issues and questions.

ADMINISTRATION

Recorded, assigned, and accepted out-of-county and out-of-state cases for Hamilton County Probation Department. Scheduled court dates for violation of probation cases. Investigated cases; determined eligibility and qualifications for acceptance by either state or county. Assigned cases to Senior Probation Officer.

Position with the Montgomery County Probation Department provided the opportunity to gain excellent supervisory and project-management skills.

PUBLIC RELATIONS

Performed extensive public relations duties working for the Cincinnati Art Museum. Answered inquiries and educated the public about museum programs. Wrote weekly reports regarding museum attendance and the public's satisfaction levels.

As a member of the American Friends Service Committee, assisted prisoners with contacting their attorneys and families. Helped inmates seeking bail reductions. Facilitated enrollment in vocational programs.

Performed community service at various Ohio shelters, providing homeless people with information regarding food and living arrangements.

EXPERIENCE

Summer 2004	■ Ohio Attorney General, Criminal Appellate Bureau	Law Clerk
Summer 2003	■ Judge Ronald Petty, Criminal Division, Columbus, OH	Summer Intern
2002	■ Hamilton County Probation Department, Cincinnati, OH	Clerk
1999–2001	■ American Friends Service Committee	Volunteer
1997–2000	■ Cincinnati Art Museum, Cincinnati, OH	Receptionist

EDUCATION

	The Ohio State University College of Law, Columbus, OH	JD, May 2005

University of Cincinnati, Cincinnati, OH   BS Criminal Justice, 2001
Honors: Dean's List
Activities: Anthropology Club, New Jersey Public Interest Research Group

Traveled extensively throughout Europe (France, Italy, and England). Enjoy foreign and independent films.

94

Degree: DVM.

Job Target: Position with a modern animal clinic with special interest in cats and the possibility of being mentored toward an ABVP diploma.

Strategy: Used quotes from clients to add value to this vet's resume and help sell her qualifications to a high-profile hospital in spite of limited experience in a small-town clinic.

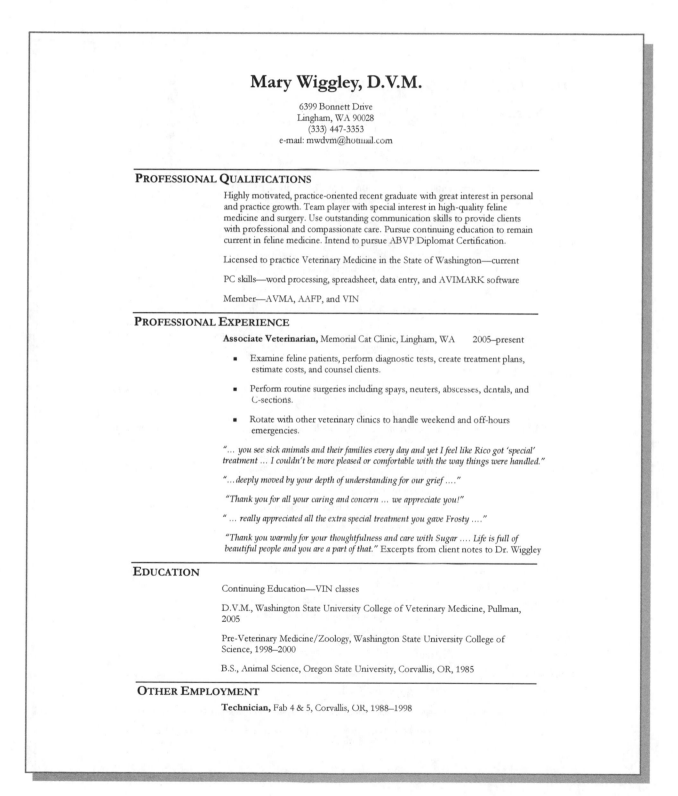

Mary Wiggley, D.V.M.

6399 Bonnett Drive
Lingham, WA 90028
(333) 447-3353
e-mail: mwdvm@hotmail.com

PROFESSIONAL QUALIFICATIONS

Highly motivated, practice-oriented recent graduate with great interest in personal and practice growth. Team player with special interest in high-quality feline medicine and surgery. Use outstanding communication skills to provide clients with professional and compassionate care. Pursue continuing education to remain current in feline medicine. Intend to pursue ABVP Diplomat Certification.

Licensed to practice Veterinary Medicine in the State of Washington—current

PC skills—word processing, spreadsheet, data entry, and AVIMARK software

Member—AVMA, AAFP, and VIN

PROFESSIONAL EXPERIENCE

Associate Veterinarian, Memorial Cat Clinic, Lingham, WA   2005–present

- Examine feline patients, perform diagnostic tests, create treatment plans, estimate costs, and counsel clients.

- Perform routine surgeries including spays, neuters, abscesses, dentals, and C-sections.

- Rotate with other veterinary clinics to handle weekend and off-hours emergencies.

"... you see sick animals and their families every day and yet I feel like Rico got 'special' treatment ... I couldn't be more pleased or comfortable with the way things were handled."

"...deeply moved by your depth of understanding for our grief ...."

"Thank you for all your caring and concern ... we appreciate you!"

" ... really appreciated all the extra special treatment you gave Frosty ...."

"Thank you warmly for your thoughtfulness and care with Sugar .... Life is full of beautiful people and you are a part of that." Excerpts from client notes to Dr. Wiggley

EDUCATION

Continuing Education—VIN classes

D.V.M., Washington State University College of Veterinary Medicine, Pullman, 2005

Pre-Veterinary Medicine/Zoology, Washington State University College of Science, 1998–2000

B.S., Animal Science, Oregon State University, Corvallis, OR, 1985

OTHER EMPLOYMENT

Technician, Fab 4 & 5, Corvallis, OR, 1988–1998

95

Degree: MD (completing residency program).

Job Target: Urologist in private practice.

Strategy: In this fairly straightforward CV presentation, used two strategies to set this candidate apart from others. His earlier career as a Naval officer is detailed at some length on page 2, and an eye-catching graphic is used as a visual attention-getter.

JOHN D. ANDENORO, M.D.

Curriculum Vitae

Residence:
1214 Fenway Avenue ▪ Salt Lake City, UT 84102
Phone/Fax: (801) 582-8862 ▪ jdande@qwest.net

Business:
University of Utah Medical Center ▪ 50 Medical Drive ▪ Salt Lake City, UT 84132
Phone: (801) 581-4703 ▪ Pager: (801) 339-3814 ▪ Cellular: (801) 891-1785

SPECIALTY

Urologic Surgery
Oncology, Stone Disease, Pediatric Urology, Laparoscopic Surgery, Incontinence, Female Urology and Infertility

EDUCATION

Medical	**Baylor College of Medicine,** Houston, TX **M.D.**	2000
Undergraduate	Washington & Jefferson College, Washington, PA B.A. Biology	1988

MEDICAL TRAINING

Chief Resident	University of Utah Health Science Center Salt Lake City, UT Urologic Surgery	2004–2005
Resident	University of Utah Health Science Center Salt Lake City, UT Urologic Surgery	2002–2004
Resident	University of Utah Health Science Center Salt Lake City, UT General Surgery	2001–2002
Intern	University of Utah Health Science Center Salt Lake City, UT General Surgery	2000–2001

LICENSURE AND CERTIFICATION

Physician & Surgeon	Utah License Number 348070-1205	2000–Present
Board Certification	Applicant to American Board of Urology	in process
Certified	Advanced Trauma Life Support	Current
	Basic & Advanced Cardiac Life Support	Current

PROFESSIONAL AFFILIATIONS

American Urological Association	2002–Present
American Medical Association, Resident Section	2000–Present
Utah Medical Association	2000–Present
American Medical Association, Medical Student Section	1996–2000
Texas Medical Association	1995–1999
Texas Medical Association, Legislation Committee, Medical Student Representative	1997–1999

Continued on Page Two

(continued)

JOHN D. ANDENORO, M.D.

(801) 582-8862 ▪ jdande@qwest.net

Curriculum Vitae
Page Two

PRESENTATIONS

Andenoro, J., Snow, B., Cartwright, P. "Serum Potassium and Creatinine Changes Following Unstented Bilateral Ureteral Reimplantation." Accepted for presentation at Western Section of the American Urologic Association. Palm Desert, CA. Nov 2005.

Andenoro, J., Snow, B., Hamilton, B., Cartwright, P. "Laparoscopic Renal Surgery in Infants: Is Age a Contraindication?" American Urological Association Annual Meeting. Atlanta, GA. Apr 2005.

Andenoro, J. "Tissue Engineering: Surgical Applications and Urologic Frontiers." University of Utah Division of Urology Grand Rounds. Salt Lake City, UT. Mar 2005.

Andenoro, J., Stephenson, R., Middleton, R. "Biochemical Failure After Radical Prostatectomy: The First 5 Years of the PSA Era." Western Section of the American Urologic Association. Monterey, CA. Oct 2003.

Andenoro, J. "Nephron Sparing Surgery: State of the Art in Open and Laparoscopic Partial Nephrectomy, Cryosurgery and Auto-Transplantation." University of Utah Division of Urology Grand Rounds. Salt Lake City, UT. Jun 2003.

Andenoro, J., Morton, R., Scardino, P. "Immunohisto-Chemical Analysis of E-Cadherin Expression in Prostate Cancer." American Urological Association Annual Meeting. Apr 2000.

RESEARCH PROJECTS

Randomized Survey of Prostate Cancer Screening in Utah	2000
Immunohisto-Chemistry of E-Cadherin Expression in Prostate Cancer	1999

MILITARY SERVICE

Physician	Utah Air National Guard, Rank: Major 151st Medical Squadron, Salt Lake City, UT	2002–Present
Medical Training	Flight Surgeon Training Courses Mass Casualty/Combat Medicine Course	2002 & 2003 2004
Intelligence Officer	United States Navy Reserve, Lieutenant Commander Mine Warfare Command, Corpus Christi, TX Naval Intelligence Service, Houston/Corpus Christi, TX Defense Intelligence Agency, Austin, TX	1995–2000
	United States Navy (Active Duty) Commander-in-Chief, U.S. Navy, Europe London, U.K.	1992–1995
	United States Navy (Active Duty) Fighter Squadron 102 Virginia Beach, VA USS *America,* USS *Theodore Roosevelt*	1989–1992

Degree: MD.

Job Target: Physician.

Strategy: This individual is a foreign medical graduate and therefore faces much competition. To strengthen his case, the resume highlights his top-of-class status in Egypt, his position as chief resident in the U.S., and teaching experience, all of which should help him stand out from the crowd.

Josef Rahman, M.D.
115 Abernathy Court
New York, NY 10023
(212) 861-2222
drrahman@mci.net

PROFILE

Compassionate, organized physician with well-rounded medical training and solid crisis-management skills. Available for employment in July 2006. Able to work effectively with people of various ages, ethnicities, and socioeconomic backgrounds. Confident and able to learn new skills quickly. Member of American College of Physicians—American Society of Internal Medicine. Special interest in cancer and AIDS.

CERTIFICATIONS & LICENSURE

New York medical license—pending
USMLE
ECFMG
ACLS

EDUCATION

Bachelor of Medicine/Bachelor of Surgery (equivalent to M.D. in the United States)   1998
Asif Medical College, Cairo, Egypt
- Ranked in top 2% of students taking the medical school entrance exam and top 5% of class at Asif Medical College.
- Awarded a full academic scholarship at this prestigious medical school.
- Received "Mr. Team Player" award for demonstrating excellent interpersonal skills.
- Completed internship at Cairo General Hospital. Rotations included pediatrics, surgery, cardiology, emergency medicine, and community health.

Pre-Medical Education
Cairo Junior College, Cairo, Egypt   1989–1991
First in a class of 100 students.

PROFESSIONAL EXPERIENCE

Medical Resident   2003–present
Mount Sinai Medical Center, New York, NY

- Completed clinical rotations in infectious diseases and neurology.
- Selected as Chief Resident.

Josef Rahman, M.D.   Page 2
(212) 861-2222 • drrahman@mci.net

Medical Resident   2001–2002
St. Luke's–Roosevelt Hospital, New York, NY

- Acquired experience in intensive care, coronary care, general medicine, ambulatory care, and emergency medicine.
- Completed clinical rotations in hematology, oncology, nephrology, and intensive care.
- Organized and set up a research project on diabetic ketoacidosis.

Telemetry Volunteer   2000–2001
Rochester Community Hospital, Rochester, NY

- Assisted with patient monitoring in the telemetry department.

Physician   1999
Private Practice, Cairo, Egypt

- Assisted attending physician in caring for patients in the office and hospital.

Senior Intern   1998
Institute of Mental Health, Alexandria, Egypt

- Acquired experience in psychiatric medicine from this 10-week specialty internship.

PRESENTATIONS & TEACHING EXPERIENCE

- Tuberculosis in Immunocompromised Patients, Columbia University conference
- Colon Cancer Screening inservice, Mount Sinai Hospital
- Pneumocystis Carinii Pneumonia inservice, St. Luke's–Roosevelt Hospital
- Diabetics and Genetics, St. Luke's–Roosevelt Hospital

Taught medical students at Mount Sinai School of Medicine:
- Introduction to Clinical Skills, Mount Sinai Hospital
- Preparation for Clinical Medicine, Mount Sinai Hospital
- Ambulatory Medicine, Mount Sinai Hospital
- Advanced Medicine, Mount Sinai Hospital

CHAPTER 9

Resumes for "Average" Students

If you've looked at all of the resumes in this book, you might think that all of them were written for "star performers"—above-average students with exceptional accomplishments. While it's true that many of these resumes represent students with outstanding qualifications, in other cases it's simply a matter of making the most of every activity and accomplishment and showing how these can be valuable to an employer.

To make my point, in this chapter I've selected resumes of "average" students. By this I mean students with GPAs below 3.0 (and thus not featured on their resumes, as recommended in chapter 2), students who have not been leaders of on-campus organizations, who have not held strong and relevant co-op or internship positions, and who might not have been involved in any campus activities or work experience whatsoever!

I realize that not everyone is an outstanding student in college. Perhaps you fit this category. For any number of reasons, you might have earned grades that are only fair or even poor. Perhaps you had to work to cover the cost of your education. Maybe you started out in the wrong major and either struggled or lost interest. You might have been unmotivated your first year or two and didn't really apply yourself. Similarly, you might have been caught up in the excitement of being away at school and devoted yourself to parties, fun, and friends rather than your studies or any meaningful on-campus involvement. But now you are about to finish school, need to find a job, and indeed do have lots to offer. The resumes in this chapter will show you how to make the most of your college experiences, no matter how "average" you might feel your experiences and qualifications are.

Resume Number	Degree	Job Target
97	BS, Business Administration	Executive assistant
98	BA, Business Studies	Sales
99	BS, Business Management, Private Recreation	Public relations, product promotion, sales, recreation
100	BA, Business Management	Sales and marketing position
101	BS, Biology	Medical/ pharmaceutical sales position
102	BS, Marketing	Marketing/ advertising position
103	BA, Political Science	International Business Development
104	BS, Finance	Financial services sales
105	BA, Architectural Studies	Architectural resource library manager
106	BS, Human Resource Management	Clerk/administrator position
107	BS, Recreation, Parks, and Tourism	Hospitality management position

Resume Number	Degree	Job Target
108	BA, Radio and Television	Television, film, or radio production position
109	AS, Recording Arts	Audio production position
110	BS, Biological Sciences	Laboratory technician
111	BS, Biology	Zookeeper
112	AS, Network Administration	Help desk position
113	BS, Business Administration	Position in marketing or economics
114	BA, Business Management	Management trainee
115	BS, Regional Development	Internship or entry-level position in commercial real-estate development

97

Degree: BS, Business Administration.
Job Target: Executive assistant.
Strategy: Described in detail two summer jobs, including a stint as a bartender/server that demonstrates customer-service skills and reliability. Highlighted relevant capabilities in the summary.

RACHEL A. WRIGHT

1234 10th Street   Phone (602) 555-1234
Phoenix, Arizona 85019   E-mail rawright@hotmail.com

CAREER TARGET: EXECUTIVE ASSISTANT

A reliable and dependable administrative professional with strong multi-tasking and time management capabilities. Mature and confident in business interactions, with proven communication, interpersonal, and negotiation skills. Demonstrated ability to prepare, analyze, and report data with exceptional attention to detail. Established a reputation for relating warmly to people of different personalities and cultures, generating trust and rapport. Fully proficient in the Microsoft Office Suite.

▶ Management Support   ▶ Client Correspondence   ▶ Telephone Support
▶ Office Administration   ▶ Customer Satisfaction   ▶ Workflow Prioritization
▶ Confidential Assistance   ▶ Teamwork & Training   ▶ Records & Data Management

EDUCATION

Arizona State University, Tempe, Arizona   **Expected Completion 2005**
◆ Bachelor of Science, Majoring in Business Administration
◆ Courses include Office Administration, Managerial Accounting, Effective Communications, Project Management, and Interpersonal Relations.

PROFESSIONAL EXPERIENCE

Private Medical Practice, Phoenix, Arizona   **Summer 2004**
Administrative Assistant
Reporting directly to the senior partner, responsible for organizing the doctor's office, classifying patient charts, handling phone calls, filing, and billing. Accountable to manage the Family Health Network program, patient roster, and materials.
◆ Categorized and compiled a comprehensive patient roster on disk. Successfully completed the entry of 750 patients in the practice within two months of hire.
◆ Designed the patient correspondence, procedures, and checklists on the Family Health Network Program. Trained and updated staff to ensure program effectiveness and consistency.
◆ Organized charts for up to 100 patients on a daily basis with virtually 100% accuracy.

Relax Hotel & Conference Centre, Phoenix, Arizona   **Summer 2003**
Bartender/Server
Interacted with customers in a professional manner. Responsibilities included greeting customers, taking reservations, serving, and bartending. Accountable for opening and closing the restaurant, training employees, and balancing cash.
◆ Commended on a regular basis from supervisors and customers for exceptional customer service and satisfaction skills.
◆ Assigned to work independently, handle large groups and banquets, and supervise functions due to maturity and reliability.

COMPUTER SKILLS

Proficient in a variety of computer technology and software, including
◆ Microsoft Outlook and Explorer
◆ Microsoft Office (Word, Excel, and PowerPoint)

◆◆◆ Outstanding References Available upon Request ◆◆◆

Degree: BA, Business Studies.
Job Target: Sales.
Strategy: Expanded a part-time job in sales to include both position duties and accomplishment statements. Added a strong third-party endorsement in the form of a supportive quote from the boss.

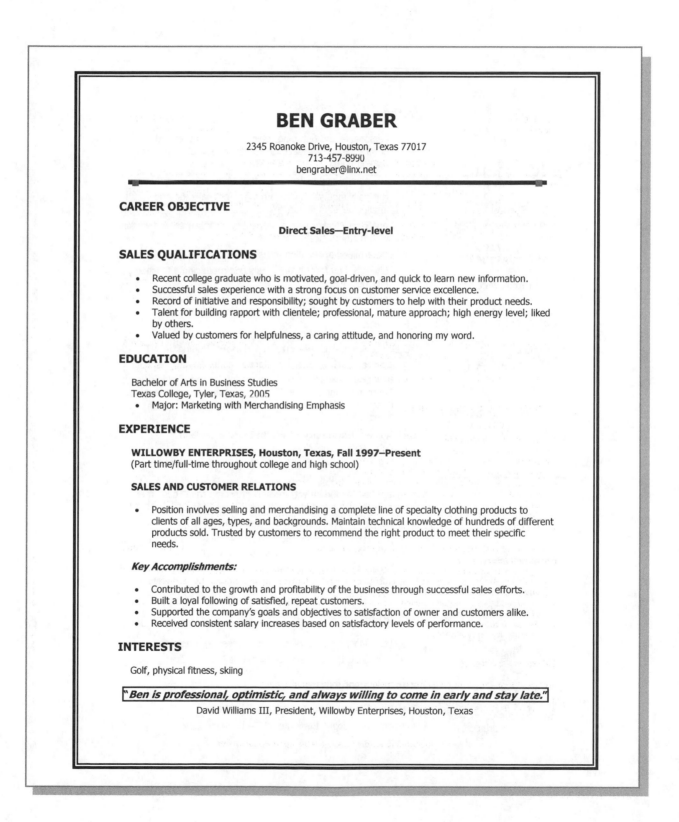

BEN GRABER

2345 Roanoke Drive, Houston, Texas 77017
713-457-8990
bengraber@linx.net

CAREER OBJECTIVE

Direct Sales—Entry-level

SALES QUALIFICATIONS

- Recent college graduate who is motivated, goal-driven, and quick to learn new information.
- Successful sales experience with a strong focus on customer service excellence.
- Record of initiative and responsibility; sought by customers to help with their product needs.
- Talent for building rapport with clientele; professional, mature approach; high energy level; liked by others.
- Valued by customers for helpfulness, a caring attitude, and honoring my word.

EDUCATION

Bachelor of Arts in Business Studies
Texas College, Tyler, Texas, 2005
- Major: Marketing with Merchandising Emphasis

EXPERIENCE

WILLOWBY ENTERPRISES, Houston, Texas, Fall 1997–Present
(Part time/full-time throughout college and high school)

SALES AND CUSTOMER RELATIONS

- Position involves selling and merchandising a complete line of specialty clothing products to clients of all ages, types, and backgrounds. Maintain technical knowledge of hundreds of different products sold. Trusted by customers to recommend the right product to meet their specific needs.

Key Accomplishments:

- Contributed to the growth and profitability of the business through successful sales efforts.
- Built a loyal following of satisfied, repeat customers.
- Supported the company's goals and objectives to satisfaction of owner and customers alike.
- Received consistent salary increases based on satisfactory levels of performance.

INTERESTS

Golf, physical fitness, skiing

"Ben is professional, optimistic, and always willing to come in early and stay late."

David Williams III, President, Willowby Enterprises, Houston, Texas

99

Degree: BS, Business Management, Private Recreation.
Job Target: Public relations, product promotion, sales, recreation.
Strategy: Used a "creative expression" section in the lower-left column to relate personal pursuits to current job interests. Included a short-term internship at a skate park.

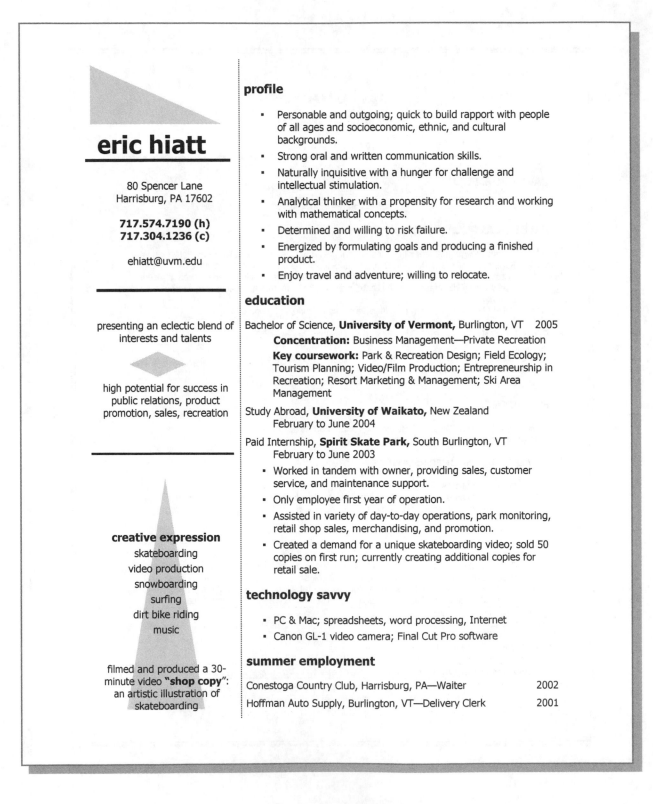

eric hiatt

80 Spencer Lane
Harrisburg, PA 17602

717.574.7190 (h)
717.304.1236 (c)

ehiatt@uvm.edu

presenting an eclectic blend of
interests and talents

high potential for success in
public relations, product
promotion, sales, recreation

creative expression
skateboarding
video production
snowboarding
surfing
dirt bike riding
music

filmed and produced a 30-
minute video **"shop copy"**:
an artistic illustration of
skateboarding

profile

- Personable and outgoing; quick to build rapport with people of all ages and socioeconomic, ethnic, and cultural backgrounds.
- Strong oral and written communication skills.
- Naturally inquisitive with a hunger for challenge and intellectual stimulation.
- Analytical thinker with a propensity for research and working with mathematical concepts.
- Determined and willing to risk failure.
- Energized by formulating goals and producing a finished product.
- Enjoy travel and adventure; willing to relocate.

education

Bachelor of Science, **University of Vermont,** Burlington, VT 2005
   Concentration: Business Management—Private Recreation
   Key coursework: Park & Recreation Design; Field Ecology; Tourism Planning; Video/Film Production; Entrepreneurship in Recreation; Resort Marketing & Management; Ski Area Management

Study Abroad, **University of Waikato,** New Zealand
February to June 2004

Paid Internship, **Spirit Skate Park,** South Burlington, VT
February to June 2003

- Worked in tandem with owner, providing sales, customer service, and maintenance support.
- Only employee first year of operation.
- Assisted in variety of day-to-day operations, park monitoring, retail shop sales, merchandising, and promotion.
- Created a demand for a unique skateboarding video; sold 50 copies on first run; currently creating additional copies for retail sale.

technology savvy

- PC & Mac; spreadsheets, word processing, Internet
- Canon GL-1 video camera; Final Cut Pro software

summer employment

Conestoga Country Club, Harrisburg, PA—Waiter	2002
Hoffman Auto Supply, Burlington, VT—Delivery Clerk	2001

Degree: BA, Business Management.
Job Target: Sales and marketing position.
Strategy: Made the most of academic projects and limited extracurricular activities to demonstrate teamwork and initiative.

JOHN MEADOWS
534 Cherry Lane • Haymarket, VA 22036
H: 703-222-2222 • C: 703-222-2222 • Email: meadows@email.com

CAREER FOCUS & VALUE TO EMPLOYER

SALES & MARKETING

- Business major with a keen interest in a sales and marketing career. Committed to continued learning and the improvement of business-related skills.
- Communication, interaction, and relationship-building skills acquired through work experience, volunteer activities, team sports, and academic projects.
- Computer experience includes MS Office (Word, Excel). Created and managed Excel databases. Completed courses in Web page creation and electronic information exchange. Confident in learning and using new business applications.

EDUCATION & COLLEGE ACTIVITIES

B.A. in Business Management
UNIVERSITY OF VIRGINIA, Charlottesville, VA—Graduation: Summer 2005
- Maintained required GPA to receive Bright Futures Scholarship all 4 years in college.

Associate of Arts with focus on **Business Management**
NORTHERN VIRGINIA COMMUNITY COLLEGE, Fairfax, VA—Graduated 2003
- Academic Dean's List (2002)
- Bright Futures Scholarship recipient

Academic projects, college activities, and volunteer work:
- Completed several group projects for business classes. Two examples: Built a database for a virtual business (Information Management Systems) and completed a study on the effect of repetitive advertising on consumers (Consumer Behavior).
- Member of Pi Kappa Alpha Fraternity, ranked as UVA's top academic fraternity (2002) and fraternity of the year (2002 and 2003) for grades and philanthropic/community activities.
- Participated in Pi Kappa Alpha charity fund-raisers for *Children's Miracle Network, Christmas for the Kids,* and *Habitat for Humanity*. Member of *Habitat for Humanity* team that built three houses during spring break.
- Participated in intramural sports. Former top seed on Haymarket High School's tennis team.

Relevant business courses:

Organizational Behavior	Cross-cultural Management	Strategic Management & Business Policies
Principles of Purchasing	Contemporary Leadership	Multinational Business Operations
Managerial Accounting	Introduction to MIS	Electronic Information Exchange
Competitive Dynamics	Business & Society	Managing Service Organizations
Consumer Behavior	Web Page Creation	Microsoft Business Applications
Professional Selling	HR Management	Financial Management of Firms

COLLEGE WORK EXPERIENCE

MEADOWS CONSULTING SERVICE, Haymarket, VA—2003
Database Manager—Hired to build Excel database and input data from various sources for an impact evaluation of a state grant to Fairfax County Schools.

HAYMARKET HEALTH AND FITNESS, Haymarket, VA—Summer 2002
Assistant Manager—Interacted with customers to sell memberships, diplomatically resolve customer service problems, and answer questions. Also performed finance and accounting duties.

Letters of recommendation available upon request.

Degree: BS, Biology.
Job Target: Medical/pharmaceutical sales position.
Strategy: Pulled together biology education and science-related work experience plus a variety of part-time sales jobs to position this individual for a new career in sales—after a short stint in a laboratory convinced him to change careers.

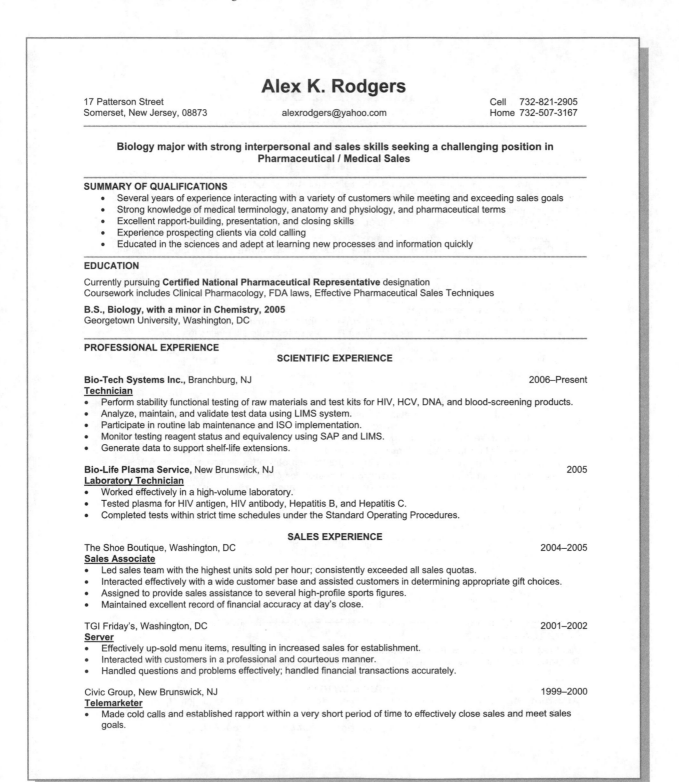

Alex K. Rodgers

17 Patterson Street
Somerset, New Jersey, 08873

alexrodgers@yahoo.com

Cell   732-821-2905
Home 732-507-3167

Biology major with strong interpersonal and sales skills seeking a challenging position in Pharmaceutical / Medical Sales

SUMMARY OF QUALIFICATIONS

- Several years of experience interacting with a variety of customers while meeting and exceeding sales goals
- Strong knowledge of medical terminology, anatomy and physiology, and pharmaceutical terms
- Excellent rapport-building, presentation, and closing skills
- Experience prospecting clients via cold calling
- Educated in the sciences and adept at learning new processes and information quickly

EDUCATION

Currently pursuing **Certified National Pharmaceutical Representative** designation
Coursework includes Clinical Pharmacology, FDA laws, Effective Pharmaceutical Sales Techniques

B.S., Biology, with a minor in Chemistry, 2005
Georgetown University, Washington, DC

PROFESSIONAL EXPERIENCE

SCIENTIFIC EXPERIENCE

Bio-Tech Systems Inc., Branchburg, NJ   2006–Present
<u>Technician</u>

- Perform stability functional testing of raw materials and test kits for HIV, HCV, DNA, and blood-screening products.
- Analyze, maintain, and validate test data using LIMS system.
- Participate in routine lab maintenance and ISO implementation.
- Monitor testing reagent status and equivalency using SAP and LIMS.
- Generate data to support shelf-life extensions.

Bio-Life Plasma Service, New Brunswick, NJ   2005
<u>Laboratory Technician</u>

- Worked effectively in a high-volume laboratory.
- Tested plasma for HIV antigen, HIV antibody, Hepatitis B, and Hepatitis C.
- Completed tests within strict time schedules under the Standard Operating Procedures.

SALES EXPERIENCE

The Shoe Boutique, Washington, DC   2004–2005
<u>Sales Associate</u>

- Led sales team with the highest units sold per hour; consistently exceeded all sales quotas.
- Interacted effectively with a wide customer base and assisted customers in determining appropriate gift choices.
- Assigned to provide sales assistance to several high-profile sports figures.
- Maintained excellent record of financial accuracy at day's close.

TGI Friday's, Washington, DC   2001–2002
<u>Server</u>

- Effectively up-sold menu items, resulting in increased sales for establishment.
- Interacted with customers in a professional and courteous manner.
- Handled questions and problems effectively; handled financial transactions accurately.

Civic Group, New Brunswick, NJ   1999–2000
<u>Telemarketer</u>

- Made cold calls and established rapport within a very short period of time to effectively close sales and meet sales goals.

Degree: BS, Marketing.
Job Target: Marketing/advertising position.
Strategy: Devoted most of the space on the resume to part-time work experience and one relevant internship.

NITA K. SHANE

11 Stanton Avenue • Corning, CA 95973 • 530-824-8259 • Cell: 530-789-1568 • nita@hotmail.com

MARKETING/ADVERTISING PROFILE

Motivated, talented professional offering a bachelor's degree in marketing, diverse experience, and a solid understanding of marketing and advertising strategies. Experience in conceptualizing, planning, promoting, and executing multifaceted projects. Customer-focused communicator with proven ability to understand customer needs and a commitment to satisfaction and prompt service. Top producer, willing to go the extra mile to meet deadlines and achieve company goals. Expertise includes

• Conceptual Planning	• Web-Based Marketing	• Advertising Campaigns
• Strategy Development	• Marketing Penetration	• Media/Client Relations
• Project Management	• Competitive Analysis	• Ad Copy Creation

EDUCATION AND TRAINING

B.S. Marketing with Minor in Communication, California State University, Sacramento—2004

Certificate of Completion, Media School, Grey Advertising, San Francisco, CA—2005
Won award for best innovation and creativity for media project. Developed marketing campaign for new product by focusing on the wants/needs of our target audience and by creating product awareness through proper placement.

Foreign Languages: Fluent in Punjabi and have an understanding of Hindi.

EXPERIENCE

GREY ADVERTISING, SAN RAFAEL, CA—2005
Media Coordinator

Contributed to research, analysis, and recommendations designed to guide clients in the selection of effective marketing strategies. Responded to project-specific and general client questions and requests on a daily basis.
  • Increased visibility by continually monitoring online campaigns to ensure proper placement and accessibility.
  • Communicated among all departments to ensure smooth, on-time delivery of marketing campaign.
  • Planned and organized buying for interactive media.

TALYOR MOTORS INTERNSHIP, SACRAMENTO, CA—2004
Advertising Associate Intern

Developed and implemented an informative event at CSUS campus. Guided development of advertising campaign and theme development. Coordinated talent search and auditions for product commercials. Contacted community sponsors and local radio stations for advertising and entertainment.
  • Targeted more than 200,000 impressions—developed public service announcements, press releases, flyers, banners, and bulletins to promote event participation.
  • Met all deadlines and created an outstanding event with attendance exceeding 3,000 students.

STATE OF CALIFORNIA, DEPARTMENT OF HEALTH SERVICES, SACRAMENTO—2001 to 2002
Student Assistant/Analyst

Maintained and updated provider database for Med-Cal applications. Acted as contact for direct-mail marketing. Provided customer qualification screening and satisfactory resolution of case issues.

AFFILIATIONS

Member of American Marketing Association (Advertising Director 2004), California State University Chapter

---

Degree: BA, Political Science.

Job Target: International business development.

Strategy: Used an eye-catching format to call attention to class projects, internship and work experience, and educational qualifications.

FRED MOSBACH

3592 Bogart Avenue, Apartment 1J • Columbus, Ohio 43201

E-Mail: FredJD@homespun.com • Home: 614-766-7784 • Cellular: 614-306-6636

FOCUS: International Business Development

- **Classically educated team player;** significant travel to Europe, Asia, and the Middle East.
- **Strong crisis management skills;** able to steer and support operations through volatile situations.
- **Dedicated to global affairs;** recognized for willingness to learn with ability to succeed in diverse arenas.
- **Proven record of effectively managing multiple tasks** without compromise to quality; employ innovation, creativity, and enthusiasm when approaching projects.
- **Proficient with Microsoft Word and Excel.**

EDUCATION

THE OHIO STATE UNIVERSITY ... Columbus, Ohio

Bachelor of Arts in Political Science, 2005

Treasurer ... Delta Chi Fraternity (March 2004 to February 2005)

REPRESENTATIVE PROJECTS

Labor & Business: Contributed to group project requiring business decisions/conclusions made for Barrier Toys' handling of unions and employment in Germany and Sweden; strategies included methods of communicating with media and advertising to improve image of company, use of lobbyists to communicate with international governing bodies, and comprehensive action plans to improve workplace image for employees.

International Affairs: Produced several major documents defining methods to improve democratic process in Italy; documents focused heavily on theories based on active political parties, historical settings, and nature of Italian political state.

WORK HISTORY

STATE OF OHIO SENATE—Senate Page: Displayed professionalism, workflow management skills, and motivation while participating in sessions and committee meetings with responsibility for allocating bills, generating documents, and assisting senators and reporters with special projects; simultaneously assisted senators with delivery of packages to governor's office, Ohio House of Representatives, and Ohio Department of Education. Columbus, Ohio (September 2004–December 2004)

COVER TO COVER—Sales Associate: Enhanced business development and maximized profit potential with dedicated customer service, visual merchandising, shipment processing, overstock/damaged inventory returns, inventory sourcing, and store re-stock and clean-up. Performed managerial duties including store opening/closing, cash/credit handling, bank deposits, post office runs, data management, and store closings. Within months of hire, assumed increased responsibility for managerial activities. Columbus, Ohio (January 2002–August 2004)

Additional operations and business development assignments at **FedEx** (June 2001–September 2001); **Victoria's Secret** (November 2000–January 2001), **Gap, Inc., Warehouse** (June 2000–September 2000); **Gap** (August 1999–November 1999), **Kroger** (September 1998–August 1999), and **Young's Nursery** (June 1998–August 1998).

Degree: BS, Finance.

Job Target: Financial services sales.

Strategy: Emphasized an on-campus investment club that provided a good source of relevant experience, even though his involvement was only part-time.

DAVID MARTIN

29224 Jones Avenue NE ◆ East Lansing, MI 48824 ◆ 517-461-9706 ◆ davidmartin@david.com

FINANCIAL SERVICES CANDIDATE

Driven, intelligent, hardworking professional pursuing entry-level opportunities in the **Financial Services** industry. Demonstrated success utilizing sound customer-service techniques, solid relationship-building talents, and proficient communication skills. Recognized for being a team player who is eager, enthusiastic, and focused. **Core strengths and abilities include**

◆ Financial Analysis	◆ Securities Research	◆ Market / Sector Knowledge
◆ Presentation Creation	◆ Performance Analysis	◆ Stock Trading / Investing
◆ Customer Service	◆ Business Development	◆ Leadership / Team Building

EDUCATION

Bachelor of Science in Finance—Michigan State University; East Lansing, MI　　　　**Graduated 2005**
Minor in International Business—Copenhagen Business School; Denmark

Key Coursework: Portfolio Theory and Investment; Corporate Finance; Cost and Managerial Accounting; Strategic Management and Company Analysis; Financial Institution Analysis (Brokerage Houses, The Stock Exchange, Banks, Corporate Mergers); International Marketing; International Investment

FINANCIAL SERVICES EXPERIENCE

JAGUAR INVESTMENT FUND; Michigan State University　　*Technology Sector Analyst*　　**2004–2005**
- Assisted with managing and selecting technology-sector investment opportunities to grow $1M+ investment fund 6% in 2004.
- Conducted securities and sector research; created and delivered financial and investment presentations.

ADDITIONAL WORK HISTORY

SEARS; East Lansing, MI　　**2003–Present**
Sales Associate
- Achieved top sales position in Men's Sportswear Department as well as fourth place in storewide sales competition.

USA FITNESS; East Lansing, MI　　**2002–2003**
Personal Trainer
Recruited to provide one-on-one fitness training to clients after creating a customized weight and diet plan.
- Recipient of "Outstanding Customer Service Award."
- Achieved recognition as top trainer in nutritional supplement sales.

JOHNSON, BLACK, DRAKE, EDWARDS; East Lansing, MI　　**2001–2002**
Office Assistant
Provided assistance to attorneys, performing research projects and organizing the file room.

MOORE-JACKSON MARTIAL ARTS; East Lansing, MI　　**1999–2001**
Assistant Instructor
Instructed students ranging in age from 10 to 55 years old and assisted with daily operation efforts, including accounting, student retention, and recruitment activities.

TECHNOLOGY SKILLS INVENTORY

Word • Excel • PowerPoint • Outlook • HTML • Java

105

Degree: BA, Architectural Studies.

Job Target: Architectural resource library manager.

Strategy: Pulled together a very diverse educational background to show strong qualifications for the target position.

JUSTIN RHODES

721 W. 26th Street ♦ Oklahoma City, OK 54923 ♦ 250-481-3862
justindrhodes@hotmail.com

ARCHITECTURAL RESOURCE LIBRARY MANAGER

Strong organizational and problem-solving skills useful for managing complex and diverse systems of information. Ability to communicate effectively at all levels of organization, achieving thorough comprehension of issues and requests. Talent for utilizing databases and research information with positive end results. Service orientation.

Industry knowledge a plus, possessing a Bachelor of Arts in Architectural Studies.

EDUCATION

University of Oklahoma School of Architecture   2005
Bachelor of Arts: Architectural Studies; Emphasis: Music

Architecture: Programs include construction techniques and materials, freehand drawing, architectural acoustics, design theory, computers, history of the city, and historical study from ancient to modern. Experience with presentation boards, project finish books, and furniture specifications.
Design Project: 200-seat multipurpose concert hall with calculations for reverberation times.

Music: Research and historical study of music with emphasis on Latin American, Masterworks, Jazz, and Rock. Worked independently on piano study and was a member of chorale, men's glee, and Collegium Musicum choirs.
Paper: "The Buena Vista Social Club"

Liberal Arts: Avant-garde coursework including *The Geography of Wine*, which explored architecture through a geographical eye and its pertinence to wine.
Paper: "Architecture of the Vineyard"

University of Maryland–Peabody Conservatory of Music   Fall 2004
Semester class focus: *Breaking Musical Barriers*. Final project culminated in original composition for solo piano.
Composition: E-Flat Smoothie

TECHNICAL SKILLS

Hardware: Apple and Personal Computer
Software: MS Office Suite: Word, Excel, PowerPoint, Outlook; AutoCAD 2000; Adobe Illustrator, Photoshop

WORK EXPERIENCE

Golf Discount of Oklahoma City, Oklahoma City, OK   1999–Present
Customer Service, Inventory, Sales
▷   Perform daily customer relations and telephone service, meeting the needs of 100+ clients weekly.
▷   Receive and record inventory, anticipating client requests and providing in-demand merchandise.
▷   As direct vendor contact, build knowledge of product quality, dependability, instruction, and cost, ultimately strengthening and securing sound professional relationship.

Law Offices of R. Andrew Williams and Ray Wholfe, Oklahoma City, OK   Summer 2004
Legal Assistant
▷   Designed, created, and executed interior decorating project; completed under assigned budget.
▷   Performed video documentation validating unsatisfactory workmanship of refurbished building.
▷   Wrote and edited client chronologies and brochures for pending lawsuits.

INTERESTS/HOBBIES

Avid musician with 19 years of piano, 5 years of guitar, and a self-produced and performed album, *Fairy Tales Aside*. Interest in and support of photography and painting continue to sharpen and fine-tune creative skills.

106

Degree: BS, Human Resource Management.

Job Target: Clerk/administrator position.

Strategy: Included comments from supervisors and make the most of this very "average" student's work-study experience.

ALICE LONGACRE

210 Elm Street ▪ Hartford, Connecticut 06106 ▪ 860.292.2422 ▪ longacre@qty.com

PROFILE

- Organizational abilities; derive great satisfaction from creating order from chaos.
- Solid record-keeping skills.
- Problem-solving talents; enjoy solving sticky challenges.
- Welcoming, friendly attitude.
- Good sense of humor; able to appreciate even the most difficult situations.

EDUCATION

Central Connecticut State University, New Britain, CT
Bachelor of Science, **Human Resource Management**   2005

EXPERIENCE

Central Connecticut State University, New Britain, CT
Student Intern, Human Resources Department   Academic Year 2004–2005
- Assisted with screening of secretarial candidates: administered keyboarding and Excel tests, collected documentation, and organized files.
- Coordinated mailings to employees regarding health insurance options.

Work-Study Student, Registrar's Office   Academic Year 2003–2004
- Helped facilitate student registrations and course add-drops.

Work-Study Student, Athletic Department   Academic Year 2002–2003
- Developed system for keeping track of athletic equipment, using simple sign-out/sign-in procedure.

Hartford Hospital, Hartford, CT
Summer Assistant, Volunteer Services   June–August 2004
- Assembled packets for new volunteers.
- Arranged for volunteers to be photographed for name badges.

McDonald's, New Britain, CT
Counterperson/Cashier   2000–2003
- Took customer orders accurately and cheerfully.
- Dealt with difficult customers appropriately.

Comments from Supervisors

"Alice did a great job helping with the hiring of several secretaries. She kept track of documentation, organized files, and put candidates at ease while they were being tested."
—Mary Smith, Director of Human Resources

"We were losing a lot of equipment before Alice developed a simple system of keeping track. She's extremely organized and a joy to work with."
Joseph Jones, Football Coach

"Alice was a great help in organizing our packets for new volunteers. We were sad to see her go."
—Oscar Burns, Volunteer Coordinator

107

Degree: BS, Recreation, Parks, and Tourism.
Job Target: Hospitality management position.
Strategy: Showcased the significant impact this student had on the small bed-and-breakfast where he completed a short but meaningful internship.

George Major

913 NW 7 Court
Miami, Florida 33181

305-555-0912
georgemaj@yahoo.com

Hospitality Management Professional

Highly professional new college graduate with a reputation for improving quality, efficiency, and guest satisfaction during a three-month full-time internship. Strengths:

- **RAPID RAPPORT BUILDING**
- **ATTENTION TO DETAIL**
- **EMPLOYEE SUPERVISION**

- **MARKETING & PROMOTIONS**
- **RELATIONSHIP DEVELOPMENT**
- **EFFECTIVE PRESENTATIONS**

Microsoft Word, Excel, PowerPoint; Guest All

"Prior to George joining us as an intern in May, we felt obliged to always be on the premises. For the first time in 19 years we do not have to be there at all times. George cares for the inn, our staff, the property, and, most of all, our guests just as we would."
—Catalina & Jose Perez, Owners of the Palm House Inn

Education

University of Florida, Gainesville, Florida
Bachelor of Science in Recreation, Parks and Tourism, August 2005
Concentration: **Hospitality Management and Commercial Recreation**
Completed courses in event planning, resort development, evaluation of leisure services, risk management, hospitality management, and operations.

Experience

Palm House Inn   Gainesville, Florida   May–August 2004
A 54-room historic bed-and-breakfast on a two-acre in-town property with eight one- to three-bedroom cottages and a restaurant.
OPERATIONS MANAGEMENT INTERN
Assisted the owners in managing catering, food preparation, room service, laundry, housekeeping, the restaurant, front desk, purchasing, inventory, accounting, and grounds maintenance.

- Expanded the restaurant menu and introduced cook-to-order selections. Developed standards for attractive food presentation. Trained employees. The inn received excellent feedback from guests on the improvement.
- Created the first detailed checklist for housekeeping staff, resulting in a dramatic increase in room and cottage appearance.
- Developed relationships with local wedding planners and churches, resulting in a significant increase in room reservations by family and friends of wedding parties.
- Reduced checkout time by five minutes by preparing bills in advance.

Page 1 of 2

107 *(continued)*

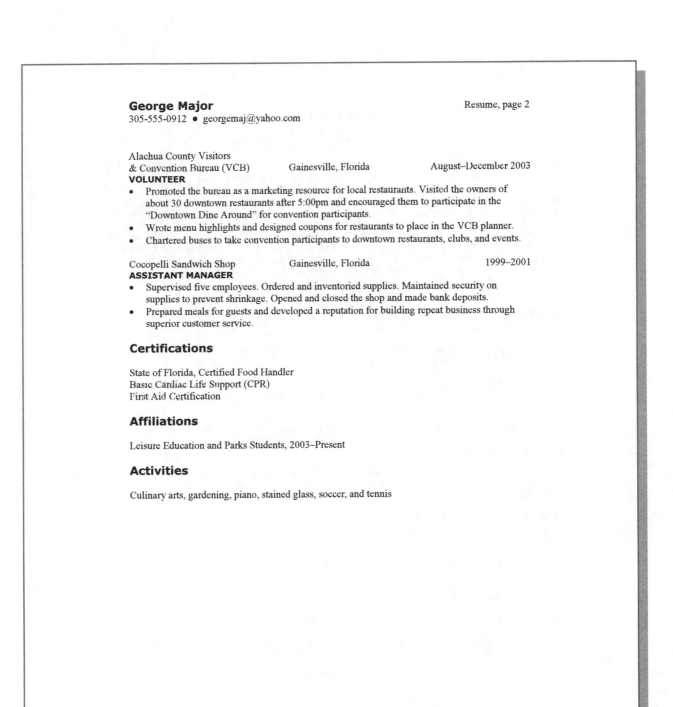

George Major   Resume, page 2
305-555-0912 ● georgemaj@yahoo.com

Alachua County Visitors
& Convention Bureau (VCB)   Gainesville, Florida   August–December 2003
VOLUNTEER
- Promoted the bureau as a marketing resource for local restaurants. Visited the owners of about 30 downtown restaurants after 5:00pm and encouraged them to participate in the "Downtown Dine Around" for convention participants.
- Wrote menu highlights and designed coupons for restaurants to place in the VCB planner.
- Chartered buses to take convention participants to downtown restaurants, clubs, and events.

Cocopelli Sandwich Shop   Gainesville, Florida   1999–2001
ASSISTANT MANAGER
- Supervised five employees. Ordered and inventoried supplies. Maintained security on supplies to prevent shrinkage. Opened and closed the shop and made bank deposits.
- Prepared meals for guests and developed a reputation for building repeat business through superior customer service.

Certifications

State of Florida, Certified Food Handler
Basic Cardiac Life Support (CPR)
First Aid Certification

Affiliations

Leisure Education and Parks Students, 2003–Present

Activities

Culinary arts, gardening, piano, stained glass, soccer, and tennis

108

Degree: BA, Radio and Television.
Job Target: Television, film, or radio production position.
Strategy: Emphasized extensive hands-on involvement with two college radio stations.

Macey M. Ash
1991 Manchester Ave., Appling, GA 30802
Home: (706) 541-9991 | mm_ash@jitaweb.com

DJ / ASSISTANT PRODUCER OF SHORT DOCUMENTARIES / PRODUCTION MANAGER
with a skill set applicable to television, film, and radio positions

---

Professional with production-management and on-air experience that flows into audio and digital editing, operations management, staff training and coaching, and copywriting and editing. Wrote and narrated documentaries, commercials, and news stories in coordination with topical and timely world events. Researched and verified information for stories to ensure factual newscasts and other on-air details. Authored, produced, and voiced commercial/promotional copy. Collaborated with managers and subordinates to provide creative guidance and discuss production changes. Participated in the entire production process, from concept and planning to quality assurance and airing.

PROFESSIONAL EXPERIENCE

ASSISTANT PRODUCTION MANAGER, FALL/SPRING, 2003–2004
College Radio Station, University of South Carolina, Columbia, SC

- Oversaw the production of music programs, news, interviews, and infotainment talk shows created by the production department; assessed for quality and accuracy.

- Assisted with hiring, directing, and supervising production personnel, which also involved selecting, training, and coaching new hires who possessed little or no experience creating high-quality radio programs.

- Met with managers and subordinates to collaborate on operations, production improvements, and delegation of duties. Troubleshot production quality (station IDs, show promos, underwriting, PSAs, and sound effects).

- Applied a hands-on supervisory style with students and recommended new software and hardware upgrades that enhanced sound quality; received recognition from the campus newsletter.

ASSISTANT PRODUCER, 2001–2002
Georgia University & State University, Georgia Media Productions, Milledgeville, GA

- Assembled and shot storyboards; selected graphics, props, and backdrops for visual appeal; and rotated audio/visual requirements in relation to footage and specs.

- Supported the production department with directing and producing several short documentaries: "Campus Living," "Classes to Addiction," and "Making Decisions."

- Researched and interviewed individuals and experts; wrote and edited content.

- "Campus Living," a 12-minute documentary, is currently used as an informational and educational video within the college recruitment department.

EDUCATION

B.A., Radio and Television, 2005
University of South Carolina, Columbia, SC

HARDWARE & SOFTWARE

Mac/PC; Cool Edit Pro, Nuendo, Avid Xpress, Logic, Final Cut Pro

---

Degree: AS, Recording Arts.
Job Target: Audio production position.
Strategy: Detailed class projects and provided an extensive list of equipment knowledge. Provided a summary of work experience that emphasizes many of the traits employers value.

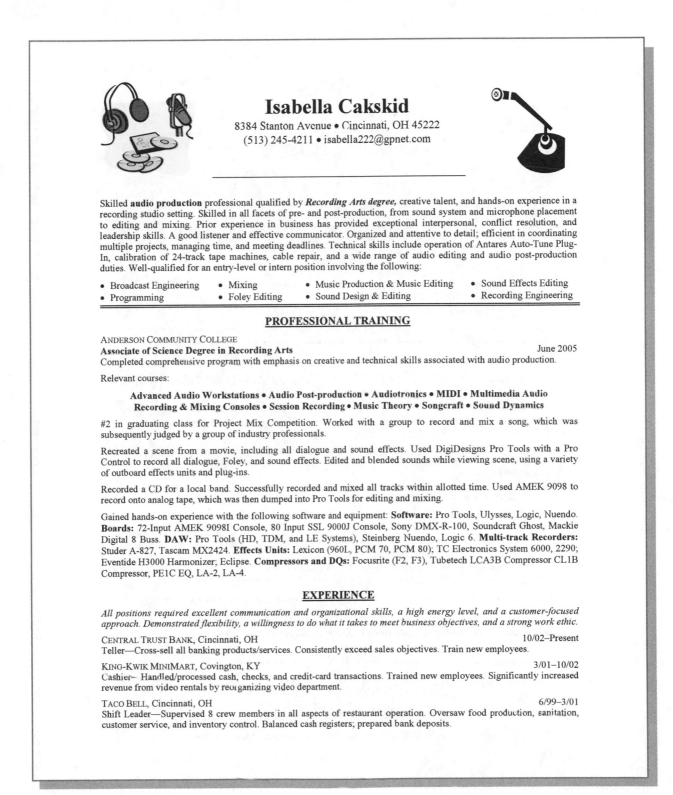

Isabella Cakskid

8384 Stanton Avenue • Cincinnati, OH 45222
(513) 245-4211 • isabella222@gpnet.com

Skilled **audio production** professional qualified by *Recording Arts degree,* creative talent, and hands-on experience in a recording studio setting. Skilled in all facets of pre- and post-production, from sound system and microphone placement to editing and mixing. Prior experience in business has provided exceptional interpersonal, conflict resolution, and leadership skills. A good listener and effective communicator. Organized and attentive to detail; efficient in coordinating multiple projects, managing time, and meeting deadlines. Technical skills include operation of Antares Auto-Tune Plug-In, calibration of 24-track tape machines, cable repair, and a wide range of audio editing and audio post-production duties. Well-qualified for an entry-level or intern position involving the following:

- Broadcast Engineering
- Programming
- Mixing
- Foley Editing
- Music Production & Music Editing
- Sound Design & Editing
- Sound Effects Editing
- Recording Engineering

PROFESSIONAL TRAINING

ANDERSON COMMUNITY COLLEGE
Associate of Science Degree in Recording Arts   June 2005
Completed comprehensive program with emphasis on creative and technical skills associated with audio production.

Relevant courses:

**Advanced Audio Workstations • Audio Post-production • Audiotronics • MIDI • Multimedia Audio
Recording & Mixing Consoles • Session Recording • Music Theory • Songcraft • Sound Dynamics**

#2 in graduating class for Project Mix Competition. Worked with a group to record and mix a song, which was subsequently judged by a group of industry professionals.

Recreated a scene from a movie, including all dialogue and sound effects. Used DigiDesigns Pro Tools with a Pro Control to record all dialogue, Foley, and sound effects. Edited and blended sounds while viewing scene, using a variety of outboard effects units and plug-ins.

Recorded a CD for a local band. Successfully recorded and mixed all tracks within allotted time. Used AMEK 9098 to record onto analog tape, which was then dumped into Pro Tools for editing and mixing.

Gained hands-on experience with the following software and equipment: **Software:** Pro Tools, Ulysses, Logic, Nuendo. **Boards:** 72-Input AMEK 9098I Console, 80 Input SSL 9000J Console, Sony DMX-R-100, Soundcraft Ghost, Mackie Digital 8 Buss. **DAW:** Pro Tools (HD, TDM, and LE Systems), Steinberg Nuendo, Logic 6. **Multi-track Recorders:** Studer A-827, Tascam MX2424. **Effects Units:** Lexicon (960L, PCM 70, PCM 80); TC Electronics System 6000, 2290; Eventide H3000 Harmonizer; Eclipse. **Compressors and DQs:** Focusrite (F2, F3), Tubetech LCA3B Compressor CL1B Compressor, PE1C EQ, LA-2, LA-4.

EXPERIENCE

All positions required excellent communication and organizational skills, a high energy level, and a customer-focused approach. Demonstrated flexibility, a willingness to do what it takes to meet business objectives, and a strong work ethic.

CENTRAL TRUST BANK, Cincinnati, OH   10/02–Present
Teller—Cross-sell all banking products/services. Consistently exceed sales objectives. Train new employees.

KING-KWIK MINIMART, Covington, KY   3/01–10/02
Cashier— Handled/processed cash, checks, and credit-card transactions. Trained new employees. Significantly increased revenue from video rentals by reorganizing video department.

TACO BELL, Cincinnati, OH   6/99–3/01
Shift Leader—Supervised 8 crew members in all aspects of restaurant operation. Oversaw food production, sanitation, customer service, and inventory control. Balanced cash registers; prepared bank deposits.

Degree: BS, Biological Sciences.
Job Target: Laboratory technician.
Strategy: To overcome the fact that this student had no relevant work experience or college extracurricular activities, summarized classroom learning under specific areas of knowledge that are relevant in lab positions.

Brenda Cox

939 South Gramercy Place, Indianapolis, IN 46239
Residence: (317) 787-4885 ● e-mail: brenda.cox@sbcglobal.net

LABORATORY TECHNICIAN

Recent college graduate seeks to apply formal training in Biological Sciences to begin career in a Medical Laboratory performing analyses and critical tests.

EDUCATION

Bachelor of Science in Biological Sciences (BS)
UNIVERSITY OF INDIANAPOLIS, Indianapolis, IN 2005

QUALIFICATIONS

- Project Management
- Customer Service
- Vertebrate Histology
- Laboratory Equipment
- Research / Analysis / Problem Solving
- Teamwork
- Tissue Slides
- Southern Transfer & Gene Detection

RELEVANT TRAINING / COURSEWORK

- **Microbiology:** Morphology, cultivation, and biochemical activities of microorganisms. Survey of viruses, bacteria, blue-green algae, fungi, and their diversity in natural environments.
- **Genetics:** Nature and function of genetic material with emphasis on transmission and population genetics. Exceptions to and extensions of Mendelian analysis, gene mapping, quantitative genetics, and the change of gene frequencies with time.
- **Human Parasitology:** Aspects of parasitology, including epidemiology, diagnosis, and identification of parasites in three major categories: protozoology, helminthology, and anthropodology.
- **Submicroscopic and Macroscopic Chemistry:** Structure and properties of atoms and molecules and physical and chemical behavior of large collections of atoms and molecules.
- **Organic Chemistry:** Principles, theories, and applications of the chemistry of carbon compounds.
- **Quantitative Analysis:** Chemical methods of analysis covering traditional as well as modern techniques and equipment; emphasis on calculations and interpretation of analytical data.
- **Laboratory Medical Microbiology and Immunology:** Identification of etiological agents of disease; bacteria, fungi, and viruses using cultural and immunological methods.

WORK EXPERIENCE

Team Member, **Lockwood's Tropical Fish, Inc.,** Greenwood, IN, 2004–Present
- Package wholesale orders.
- Maintain healthy environment for tropical fish.

Cook / Customer Service, **KFC,** Broad Ripple, IN, 1999–2004
- Filled customer orders and prepared food.

Degree: BS, Biology.
Job Target: Zookeeper.
Strategy: Blended class experiences, an internship, and extracurricular activities to paint a picture of someone with consistently strong interest in animals and the outdoors.

JEREMY POPLAR

2958 Elm Avenue, Apartment C • Olympia, Washington 98501
Home: (360) 222-1313 • jeremypoplar624@yahoo.com • Local: (816) 444-1616

CAREER OBJECTIVE
Zookeeper

Self-motivated college graduate offering **science-based education** with experience and hands-on skills in supervision and customer service. Strong work ethic evident in focused perseverance to finish projects and accomplish objectives. Team player.

EDUCATION

Bachelor of Science, Park University, Kansas City, Missouri, 2005
- Major: Biology with Emphasis in Zoology / Minor: Chemistry
  - Courses: Herpetology, Invertebrate Zoology, Ecology, Computer Applications
- **Internship:** Biology Seminar Lab Assistant, Fall 2003
  - Taught "Photosynthesis" and "Dissection of the Pig"; graded student papers.
- Celebration 2004—An Interdisciplinary Undergraduate / Graduate Symposium
  - **Presentation:** "Road-Kill Effect on the Wild Mammals of Western Missouri," based on research paper detailing two-month automobile-trip class project comparing type and number of animals killed on highways vs. country roads.
- Extracurricular activity: River Wildlife Club, member for two years

EXPERIENCE

Shift Manager, Buster's Big Boy, Kansas City, Missouri   9/03 to 12/04
- Supervised and trained two to three wait staff at any one time. Investigated and resolved customer complaints. Cooked and served food.

Kitchen Assistant, Applejack Restaurant, Kansas City, Missouri   6/03 to 9/03
- Delivered food orders to diners' tables. Cleaned kitchen.

Dishwasher, Shasta Restaurant, Kansas City, Missouri   3/03 to 6/03
- Assisted with food preparation. Sanitized dishes.

Cook, Burgers-to-Go, Kansas City, Missouri   9/02 to 6/03
- Prepared fast-food orders, working effectively in fast-paced environment.

Groundskeeper Assistant, Park University, Kansas City, Missouri   9/01 to 9/02
- Maintained college campus grounds utilizing commercial lawn care equipment.

ADDITIONAL INFORMATION

- Partially financed college expenses with part-time employment while studying.
- Proficient with Microsoft Word, PowerPoint, and Excel.
- Hobbies include hiking, fishing, and reading.

112

Degree: AS, Network Administration.
Job Target: Help desk position.
Strategy: Matched deep-seated interest in problem-solving, mechanics, and mysteries to current goal of working at a technical help desk.

JOE DETONEZ

1234 25th Street, Edmonds, WA 98117
(206) 592-2022 • joed@earthlink.net

CAREER TARGET: HELP DESK POSITION

SUMMARY OF QUALIFICATIONS

Intuitive 2006 graduate in networking administration. Strong diagnostic, logic, observation, and analytical skills: innate ability to discern irregularities in a situation. Broad interest in computer hardware, security, and forensics. Proven ability to handle multiple projects and address customer needs. Adept at reading and interpreting technical documentation and manuals, demonstrated by ability to maintain high-end automobiles. Learn new technologies quickly.

Proficiencies include the following:

Business Skills	**Technical Skills & Training**
• Customer Service	• Network Admin: LAN/WAN
• Problem Solving	• A+, Installs, Upgrades, Assembly
• Inside Sales	• Linux, UNIX, Windows XP
• General Office	• Computer Forensics
• Training	• Exchange Server 2000/Outlook

EDUCATION

South Seattle Community College
A.S., Network Administration, 2005
Coursework: Computer Forensics, Exchange Server, Linux/UNIX, A+ core certification classes, Windows XP Professional: Active Directory, Server, TCP/IP, Network Plus, technical writing

Graduate, Tyee High School, Federal Way, WA. Tech-Prep Program.

WORK EXPERIENCE

Porter, Bellevue Motors, September 2002–present
Detailer, Shtronz Airport Detailing, April 2001–February 2002
Lot Attendant, Jaguar of Kirkland, December 1999–April 2001
Customer Service Associate, Hollywood Video, June 1999–November 1999
Valet, At Your Service Valets, March–June 1999 and November–December 1999
Customer Service Representative, Hollywood Video, June 1998–February 1999
Customer Service Representative, Taco Bell, July 1996–August 1997
Office Assistant/Copy and Print Room Helper, Lane Powell Bryant, August–November 1996

COMMUNITY SERVICE

Participated in a wide variety of fund-raising and community activities, including
• Lakeside High School / Southend Food Bank / Friends of the Library Book Sale

INTERESTS

Avid interest in mysteries, criminal psychology, and police work.

Degree: BS, Business Administration.
Job Target: Position in marketing or economics.
Strategy: Combined job activities with key class projects in a meaty Experience section.

BARBARA GIBSON

1234 North Shore ▪ Parkville, Missouri 64152
816.522.1256 ▪ gibsonbarbara@kc.rr.com

QUALIFICATIONS SUMMARY

- Educated and experienced in **Marketing, Business, and Economics.**
- Motivated worker contributing to a winning outcome using project-management skills.
- Personable and team-focused with a consultative approach.
- Computer skills: MS Word, Excel, PowerPoint, Publisher; familiar with Access.

EDUCATION

Bachelor of Science in Business Administration—Marketing Concentration, 5/05
Park University, Parkville, Missouri

Economics Coursework:
Macroeconomics, Microeconomics, Managerial Economics, Intermediate Economics

---

PROFESSIONAL / EDUCATIONAL EXPERIENCE

PRINTING EXCELLENCE, Kansas City, Missouri, Summer/Winter 2004
EXECUTIVE SUPPORT ANALYST
- Day-to-day initiatives involved highly consultative interface with key decision-makers.
- Challenged with initial design of an MS Publisher brochure for a Printing Excellence account; customized brochure for five additional accounts with company-wide distribution.
- Pinpointed and turned around accounts-receivable problem, analyzing addresses and serial numbers of 350 machines to reduce monthly billing errors to zero.
- Instrumental during Sprint Corporation's "Move Booths," performing instructional services to 500+ employees over 5-day period.

NORTH SHORE GOLF CLUB, Parkville, Missouri, Summer 2001
GOLF COURSE MAINTENANCE ASSISTANT ▪ ASSISTANT GOLF CART ATTENDANT
- Promoted to Golf Course Maintenance Assistant tasked with upkeep of company's first impression to customers—visual grooming of professional course, a #1 priority.
- As Assistant Golf Cart Attendant, assumed front-line customer-service role preparing golf carts for play and greeting/serving golfers to ensure repeat business.

PARK UNIVERSITY, Kansas City, Missouri, 2000 to 2004
MANAGEMENT INFORMATION SYSTEMS PROJECT
- Member of project team tasked with research of target company's information systems.
- Interfaced with COO to gain understanding of company processes and objectives.
- Presented findings—company needed to update hardware/software—to a receptive COO.

PERSONAL SELLING PROJECT (This project impacted 45% of class grade.)
- Originated sales proposal and presented to classmate and professor; earned an "A" grade.

FORECASTING PROJECT
- Tracked / reported on 2 years of company's (Apple Computers) regression and trendlines.
- Analyzed 4 years of statistics/regression for company's (Printing Excellence's) revenues.

Degree: BA, Business Management.
Job Target: Management trainee.
Strategy: Capitalized on a strong and relevant internship plus college projects to show capabilities and potential. Performance review quotes, at the end, provide a strong endorsement of his innate qualities and work ethic.

REES DONOVAN TYLER

5555 Lexington Avenue, Apt. C • Maryville, Minnesota 55113
612-501-5555 • reesd9@hotmail.com

BUSINESS GRADUATE

Career Goal: Management trainee position used as first professional opportunity to launch career in business administration.

Strong interpersonal skills and experience gained from education, internship, and positions as part of academic and customer service–oriented teams. Hands-on group experience examining marketing practices of a local business, developing an entrepreneurial business plan, and designing strategic promotion plan.

Computer Skills: Proficient: Microsoft Word, Excel, PowerPoint, and Internet Explorer ~ User Skills: Microsoft Access

EDUCATION

BACHELOR OF ARTS, BUSINESS MANAGEMENT, Luther College, Decorah, Iowa 2004

Relevant Coursework:
❏ Financial Management • Financial Accounting • Marketing/Guerrilla Marketing • Sales, Promotion, and Advertising Management Information Systems • Human Resource Management • International Management • Investments

Team Projects:
❏ Developed and presented an entrepreneurial business plan (including mission statement, distribution of ownership, competitive analysis, financial plan, marketing plan, and more).
❏ Examined marketing practices of two-year-old business, gaining "real-life" experience as part of Guerrilla Marketing team. Suggestions offered to owner (many adopted): develop concrete marketing plan and tracking tool, create customer database, conduct competitive analysis, and improve professionalism.
❏ Repositioned American Express Blue card by creating copy platform outlining advertising objectives, target audience, major selling points, creative strategy, and promotion plan.

International Experience: "Entrepreneurship in a Tourist-Based Economy," Canary Islands, Spain (1/03)

INTERNSHIP EXPERIENCE

JOHN ANDERSON FINANCIAL GROUP, Minneapolis, Minnesota   (Summers) 2003 to 2005
Financial Advisor Intern—Shadowed financial advisor during meetings, learning customer-service skills and nuances of financial services business. Researched market funds, prepared paperwork, and entered data into computer.
❏ Created a new marketing campaign, organizing binders for each client.

WORK EXPERIENCE

MY GARDENER, Burnsville, Minnesota   April 2005 to Present
Gardener / Landscape Assistant—Work directly with company owner on a 4-person team to maintain or improve landscapes for an affluent client base.
❏ Building on professionalism, gained respect of owner, offered opinions, and accepted additional responsibilities.

WINTER PARK RESORT, Winter Park, Colorado   October 2004 to April 2005
Lift Operator—Supervised use of ski-lift equipment, ensuring skiers got on and off lift safely. Monitored equipment for mechanical problems. As a resort ambassador, greeted guests, anticipated needs, and provided information about facilities and services (including snow conditions, trails, weather conditions, and hours of operation).
❏ Performance review quotes: "… Rees's work is accomplished ahead of time and needs no correction… record of attendance is excellent… we can count on Rees… makes an effort to see that customers are satisfied. Thank you for being flexible under changing conditions… Excellent professional appearance… works well with others…"

115

Degree: BS, Regional Development.
Job Target: Internship or entry-level position in commercial real-estate development.
Strategy: Built a strong qualifications section and traits/skills summary to offset lack of relevant experience or stellar academic record.

Fred E. Smith, Jr.
520-998-4134
fsmith1990@hotmail.com

6521 E. Drachman
Tucson, AZ 85719

OBJECTIVE

To begin a career and gain experience as an intern in commercial development and real estate investment.

TRAITS AND SKILLS

Customer-driven and people-oriented. Effective communicator with excellent verbal and interpersonal skills. Honest and hard worker. Quick learner with demonstrated ability to work well with the public under stressful conditions and smoothly resolve any conflicts that may arise. Excellent at multitasking and completing projects on target. Have the ability to train others.

QUALIFICATIONS

- Able to maintain a daily schedule.
- Enjoy heavy customer contact and handling.
- Strong communication skills with peers and team members.
- Readily comprehend instructions, rules, and regulations whether written or verbal.
- Able to provide leadership in varying situations.
- Good organization and time-management skills.
- Function well in cooperative team situations.
- Maintain professional demeanor under stress.
- Experienced traveler.

UPPER-DIVISION COURSES

Economic Geography	Computer Cartography	Introduction to Planning
Advanced Applications— Remote Sensing	Principles and Practices in Regional Development	Population Geography

TECHNICAL AND COMPUTER PROFICIENCIES

Excel	PowerPoint	IDRISI-32
Arc-Map 9	Word	Collaboratus

EDUCATION

University of Arizona—B.S., Regional Development, 2005

High School—The Kent School, Kent, CT, 2000

WORK HISTORY

A variety of part-time jobs while supporting my college experience:

PCZ Enterprises—Tucson, AZ	Rebuilding Historic Homes	2003 to present
Famous Sam's—Tucson, AZ	Door Security	2003
Starpass Golf Resort—Tucson, AZ	Waiter	2002
Blackjack Pizza—Tucson, AZ	Delivery Agent	2002
Wendy's—Phoenix, AZ	Customer Service Rep.	2001
Circle-K—Phoenix, AZ	Customer Service Rep	2001
Prime Masonry—Phoenix, AZ	Commercial Construction	1997

CHAPTER 10

Resumes and Strategies for Nontraditional Students

How do resume writing and job search strategies differ for nontraditional students, those who finish their college educations later in life? Whether you've earned your educational credentials to enter a new profession or to advance your career in your present field, you offer a wealth of experience that traditional new grads do not. So it might seem that your resume would be very different from those presented thus far in this book.

But in reality, all good resumes are based on the same principle of presenting your strongest qualifications and value to employers as these relate to your career goal. As a nontraditional student, you do have more years and more experiences to draw from than most new grads. Your resume might look a bit different and will probably include a heftier section for your work experience. Yet the exercises, activities, strategies, and ideas presented throughout this book will work just as well for you as they will for a younger, less experienced graduate.

When preparing your resume, start with a clear understanding of your job target and the required skills and qualifications. Then evaluate all of your past experiences—your jobs, recent college education, extracurricular activities, volunteer and leadership roles in the community, hobbies, and other activities of your life. Look for specific examples that demonstrate the skills you want to use, and include these in your resume.

Don't overlook the fact that a strong work history can give you a definite edge in your job search. Even if your experience is unrelated to your current goals, you can use your work history to show your work ethic, reliability, and other skills that are always in demand, no matter what type of work you do: leadership and initiative; communication skills; interpersonal skills; organization, time management, planning, and follow-through skills; and problem-solving abilities.

When evaluating your work history, look for small assignments and special projects that allowed you to engage in activities related to your current goals. Use these examples as evidence of your skills, even if they were short-term or not really "part of your job." And be sure not to overload your resume with details of your job activities that will position you squarely as what you "used" to be, not what you have become or how you want to be perceived.

Review the resumes in this chapter, taking careful note of the strategies the resume writers used to position newly qualified graduates for their new careers. Some of the resumes feature strong and detailed experience sections, while others use functional headings to call out skills that were gained through a variety of experiences. Remember that there are no rules for where and how you must present your background, and you don't have to include everything. Picture yourself in your next job and make sure your resume qualifies you for that job, no matter how or in how much detail your prior experience is presented.

Resume Number	Degree	Job Target
116	BA, Psychology	Medical or pharmaceutical sales
117	BS, Business Administration	Retail management
118	BA, English	College public relations—entry-level
119	BLS (Bachelor of Liberal Studies) in Business, emphasis in Human Resource Management	Entry-level position in human resource management
120	Certificate in Human Resources (recent); BSW (prior)	Human resources position
121	BSW (most recent) along with two associate degrees and GPN/LPN training	Administrative support position in social work/social services while he pursues his MSW
122	BS, Business Administration	A position in banking, investment, or finance
123	AS, Computer Science	Help desk/computer support technician
124	BS, Business Administration	MIS position

Degree: BA, Psychology
Job Target: Medical or pharmaceutical sales.
Strategy: Emphasized the three areas of strength she brings to her goal: medical knowledge (from experience as a medical assistant), business knowledge (from bartender experience), and interpersonal skills (from customer-service positions that also included some sales-type activities).

ELLYN C. MUDRA

14 Callea Road, Apt. 45 • Chicago, IL 60604 • (312) 223-9841 • ellynmudra@hotmail.com

JOB TARGET: PHARMACEUTICAL SALES

PROFILE

- Enthusiastic, motivated medical professional with excellent rapport-building skills.
- Wide variety of clinical experiences: Family Practice, Obstetrics & Gynecology, Asthma, Allergies, and Neonatal.
- Positive business relationships with 40+ medical practices in the Chicago area.
- Proven ability to identify problems and implement solutions.
- Strong communication and negotiation skills.
- Member of the American Psychological Association.

EDUCATION & TRAINING

Bachelor of Arts in Psychology—Pre-Med concentration (expected Dec. 2005)   University of Illinois, Chicago, IL
- Courses include anatomy & physiology, chemistry, organic chemistry, and microbiology.

Emergency Medical Technician Training (1996)   Jacksonville, NC

Hospital Corpsman Training (1995)   U.S. Naval School of Health Sciences, San Diego, CA

PROFESSIONAL EXPERIENCE

Medical Assistant (2000–present)   Allergy Relief Center, Chicago, IL
- Contribute to the high level of patient compliance and patient satisfaction in this clinic.
- Conduct patient education. Utilize patient education and persuasive ability in explaining the benefits of immunotherapy to patients who are afraid of shots.
- Administer allergy injections. Determine appropriate dosages within guidelines provided by physicians.
- Train new medical assistants and front-office staff.
- Organize patient records and ensure accurate documentation of injections given by other staff members.

Bartender (1999–2003)   The Fun Place, Chicago, IL / Woody's, Chicago, IL
- Developed and maintained a loyal customer base through rapport-building and excellent service.
- Was able to deal tactfully and appropriately with demanding customers.
- Worked within a decreased liquor budget. Sold customers on specific products, depending on what ingredients were available.
- Trained new employees.

Hospital Corpsman (1993–1997)   U.S. Naval Hospital, Camp Lejeune, NC
- Provided patient care, including administering medications and intravenous therapy, performing venipuncture, assisting with minor surgeries, and assisting with Cesarean sections.
- Developed an admission checklist for infants that decreased staff errors and increased efficiency.
- Conducted patient education, including neonatal care.
- Volunteered for position of Forms Control Supervisor. Ensured availability of more than 400 forms that were used throughout the hospital. Managed a budget of $30,000. Developed a database to efficiently keep track of forms.
- Trained nurses and other corpsmen. Taught co-workers to use monitoring equipment.

Emergency Medical Technician (1996–1998)   Onslow County Rescue Squad, Jacksonville, NC

AWARDS

- Chosen as Honor Recruit out of a Basic Training class of 85 members. This award recognizes superior commitment, integrity, and teamwork (1995).
- U.S. Army Reserve Scholar/Athlete Award (1994).

Degree: BS, Business Administration.
Job Target: Retail management.
Strategy: Created a functional section highlighting relevant skills; supported retail industry target with a "relevant employment highlight" section.

Steven Toner
1547 London St., Fredericton, NB J0A-2E4
(741) 894-1234 ♦ toner@hotmail.com

RETAIL BUSINESS MANAGER
Hands-on experience in sales and customer service.

Broad-based knowledge of all aspects of business and store management encompassing ability to develop ongoing client relationships with individual attention to detail. Superior communication and bookkeeping proficiencies. Positive attitude and adaptability to adapt to fast-paced environments. *Relevant capabilities:*

Operations Management	Merchandising / Store Setup	Customer Relations
Selling Techniques	Conflict / Time Management	Cash Management
Promotions / Advertising	Supervision / Training	Opening / Closing Routines

---

HIGHLIGHTS OF SKILLS & QUALIFICATIONS

MANAGEMENT SKILLS
- ✓ Instrumental as leader and motivator of team achieving "Most Improved Section" award for two consecutive years.
- ✓ Acted as complaint resolution point, solving even the most complex of difficulties quickly and efficiently to the satisfaction of all involved.
- ✓ Participated in strategic corporate planning, including organizational direction, staff hiring & scheduling, and purchasing of stock.

FINANCIAL & BOOKKEEPING KNOWLEDGE
- ✓ Directed all bookkeeping and payroll functions, including weekly and monthly financial reporting to directors' level.
- ✓ Strong academic preparation within degree program.

CUSTOMER SERVICE EXPERTISE
- ✓ Recognized as "Best Employee of the Week" while working as a front-line representative of Pet Value, a national retail chain.
- ✓ Acknowledged for superior customer retention in a highly competitive retail arena.
- ✓ Demonstrated attention to clientele needs through launching of customer-driven delivery system.

RELEVANT EMPLOYMENT HIGHLIGHT

Senior Salesperson—Value Store, Moncton, NB   2000–present

Operationally responsible for entire franchise store, covering more than 2,000 square feet of retail space. Main product included high-end hair-care supplies servicing salons throughout the area. Given full authorizing responsibility in the absence of the owner. Demonstrated extensive knowledge in retail management, including maintenance, security, purchasing, merchandising, administration, bookkeeping, warehousing, and distribution. *Highlights of accomplishments:*
- ➤ Assisted in increasing store revenues to $487K, achieving regular bonuses based on improving year's monthly projections by +10%.
- ➤ Led staff in major year-end inventory, assuring quality monitoring and recording over all corporate stock.
- ➤ Assumed responsibility for hiring and training new staff members, as well as the daily supervision of up to 5 customer-service representatives.

EDUCATION

Bachelor of Business Administration, *St. Thomas University,* Fredericton, NB, 2005

"Putting customers first is a lost art in retail today...but not in my store!"
Work philosophy from Steven Toner — 2005

118

Degree: BA, English.
Job Target: College public relations—entry-level.
Strategy: For this new graduate who will be in her early 50s when she finishes her degree, used a functional approach to eliminate dates; downplay prior unrelated experience; and draw from her mix of professional, volunteer, and college projects.

CHRISTINA MORAN

18 Apple Street, Nyack, NY 10568
(845) 359-4532
chris_moran@email.com

OBJECTIVE

Key member of a **college public relations** team contributing my 14 years of professional experience, passion for academia, and proven writing and organizational skills.

EDUCATION

Bachelor of Arts, English, May 2005
Saint Thomas Aquinas College, Spring Valley, NY
Alpha Sigma Lambda Honor Society

RELATED SKILLS AND ACHIEVEMENTS

Writing & Editing	• Created advertising copy for the *Friends of the Branch Library* newsletter to help generate funds for building a new library.
	• Wrote a weekly report on the status of international shipments for the president of ABC Baby Toys.
	• Wrote an A-grade, 20-page thesis on "William Butler Yeats: The Impact of His Passion for Mysticism and Maude Gonne on His Poetry."
Coordinating & Communicating	• Tracked international shipments of infant and construction products and reported status to management. Followed through to ensure orders were delivered on time.
	• Researched orders held in customs and facilitated clearance by maintaining daily contact with the New York Port import broker.
	• Communicated materials delays to contractors and negotiated acceptance of partial shipments to job sites.
	• Coordinated visitors to Nyack Hospital while working as a volunteer.
Computer Applications	• Proficient with Microsoft Office, Internet navigation, and e-mail.
	• Used a proprietary software program to track shipments.

CAREER HISTORY

Volunteer, Friends of the Branch Library & Piermont Thrift Shop, Piermont, NY

Import Control Specialist, ABC Baby Toys, Orange, NJ

Assistant to General Import Manager, Building Supplies, Inc., New York, NY

Budget Control Specialist, New York University Geological Observatory, Spring Valley, NY

Degree: BLS (Bachelor of Liberal Studies) in Business, emphasis in Human Resource Management.
Job Target: Entry-level position in human resource management.
Strategy: Featured degree and coursework applicable to the position; downplayed prior unrelated work history.

Jalice Thompson

3310 Farnsworth Avenue
Hartford, Connecticut 06120
Home: (203) 811-5432
Email: jalicet@hotmail.com

FOCUS   Entry-level position in Human Resource Management where academic foundation, along with business background and strengths in customer service, will be of value.

EDUCATION   Wesleyan University, Middletown, Connecticut.
Bachelor of Liberal Studies in Business with emphasis in Human Resource Management
(will be received June 2006; studies completed December 2005)

Coursework included recruiting, classification, human resource policy, compensation, benefits, performance appraisal, employee relations training, and planning.

Quinnipiac College, New Haven, Connecticut.
Undergraduate coursework in Business
Dean's List

PROFILE
- ☒ College graduate with an emphasis in Human Resource Management.
- ☒ High confidence in professional abilities.
- ☒ High interest in organizing human resource programs and projects that will attract and retain employees.
- ☒ Skilled user of MS Word, Excel, and PowerPoint.
- ☒ Life-long learner, constantly updating skills.
- ☒ Known for high work ethic…work at a project until it is completed satisfactorily.

EMPLOYMENT HISTORY

2000–2001, **Claims Specialist I,** Aetna Insurance, Hartford, Connecticut.

Demonstrated customer service skills. Cited for high work productivity. Specialized in setting up systems to organize projects, including back-up plans.

1998–1999, **Family care and undergraduate studies.**

1997–1999, **Owner/operator,** Licensed Family Day Care Service, Middletown, Connecticut.

Developed and delivered programs to help young children learn basic skills. Managed all aspects of a small business, from planning to accounting.

120

Degree: Certificate in Human Resources (recent); BSW (prior).

Job Target: Human resources position.

Strategy: Used the profile to highlight aspects of HR that relate to her background as well as her recent HR certification.

Jane L. Morrissey

22 Mattabessett Road • Woodstock, VT 05411 • 802.885.9654 • Janelmor@aol.com

Summary

- **Accomplished and Dedicated Human Services Professional** qualified for opportunity demanding experience in recruiting, interviewing, hiring, training, mediating, and evaluating; key skill development in designing and facilitating training programs addressing wide range of requirements. Expert editorial and Microsoft Word/Excel/PowerPoint abilities.

- Very effective communication and interpersonal skills; irreproachable professional ethics.

- **Human Resources Certificate** (90 classroom hours ... Springfield Community College, Springfield, VT — 2005) ... successfully completed coursework in **Compensation, Benefits, Labor Law, Recruiting, Interviewing, Hiring, Training and Development,** and **Documentation.**

Professional Experience

1992–Present
BREWSTER CHILDREN'S SERVICES • South Woodstock, VT
Foster Parent Developer, Resources Dept. (1998–Present); **Foster Care Worker** (1992–1998)
Responsible for identifying, recruiting, screening, and evaluating participant families. Use effective case-management skills, serving as agency liaison among key stakeholders and support personnel as well as through representation at court hearings and intervention during emergencies.
- Provide ongoing development to participants, including orientation and pre-service training.
- Negotiate effectively with social welfare organizations and professionals to procure services; maintain confidential assessment records, detailed case notes, and psychosocial summaries.
- Utilize highly effective motivational strategies working with challenging and occasionally unmotivated audiences. Credited with creating increased professionalism and commitment to program objectives among participant foster families. Draw on excellent interpersonal skills in cultivating and maintaining relationships among all parties.
- Positively managed responsibilities throughout merger with another agency that doubled households of foster parents served (from 200 to 400).

Distinctions ...
- Recognized for significantly decreasing turnover and improving morale among foster parents through design and implementation of innovative development programs; selected/purchased relevant materials to complement hands-on program. Number of attendees participating increased substantially while turnover rates stabilized.
- Planned, implemented, and directed such successful specialty programs as recruitment events and holiday parties; continued to coordinate and monitor ongoing recognition dinners on regular basis.
- Initiated, wrote, and launched quarterly publication of newsletter; authored articles for agency-wide newsletter.
- Developed and implemented caseload-management applicant-processing and tracking system.

Complementary Career Background includes freelance and newspaper writing/editing as well as administrative skills. Developed, investigated, and authored many feature articles for local newspaper; edited textbooks for medical publishing house.

Education
TUFTS UNIVERSITY • Boston, MA
- **Bachelor of Social Work (B.S.W.),** Summa Cum Laude Graduate (1992)

121

Degree: BSW (most recent) along with two associate degrees and GPN/LPN training.
Job Target: Administrative support position in social work/social services while he pursues his MSW.
Strategy: Positioned for job target by emphasizing blend of health-care experience (10 years) and administrative support for a government agency (although 10+ years ago) plus the recent BSW degree. Focused primarily on "value offered" skills and education while putting less emphasis on actual nursing experience by using a modified functional approach.

MATTHEW DORRIS

1321 Paxton Circle
Whites Creek, TN 37080
Home (615) 746-3941

Email: mattdorris@hotmail.com

Goal – Administrative position with a social services agency.

Recent B.S.W. graduate with ten years of experience providing hands-on health care to a diverse patient population plus three years of experience in accounting and administrative support for a state agency. Recognized for leadership qualities and abilities—given responsibility for training and supervising others. Possess strong analytical and organizational skills that complement interpersonal abilities.

VALUE OFFERED:

➢ **Project Management / Supervisory Skills:** Able to set priorities—efficiently manage progress of work and competing demands. Effectively direct people to high levels of performance.

➢ **Strong Communication Skills:** Articulate in both written and spoken communications—effectively convey ideas and information to professionals at all levels.

➢ **Computer Abilities:** Experienced with word processing (MS Word) and spreadsheet (Lotus 1-2-3) applications. Confident in learning and using new technology.

Education

BACHELOR OF SOCIAL WORK—3.6 GPA—Member, Pinnacle Honor Society Vanderbilt University—Nashville, TN	May 2005
ASSOCIATE OF SCIENCE IN NURSING—3.5 GPA Tennessee State University—Nashville, TN	1998
GRADUATE PRACTICAL NURSE (GPN)—3.9 GPA—Class Valedictorian Nashville Memorial Hospital School of Nursing—Nashville, TN	1995
ASSOCIATE OF APPLIED BUSINESS MANAGEMENT—3.7 GPA Member, Phi Theta Kappa Honor Society University of Kentucky—Lexington, KY	1990

Career Highlights

HEALTH CARE EXPERIENCE:
Provide high-tech nursing services for hospital, rehabilitation, geriatric, psychiatric, and nursing home patients. Administer prescribed medications and treatments. Experienced in medical and post-surgical care, upper airway and tracheotomy care; IV therapy; and care of feeding tubes, catheters, and dressings. Supervise and manage work assignments of five to six technicians. Educate patients and family members on medications and diet.

Charge Nurse RN, VILLAGE GREEN CONVALESCENT CENTER, Madison, TN	2003–Present
Staff Nurse RN, SUMNER REGIONAL MEDICAL CENTER, Gallatin, TN	2001–2003
Staff Nurse / Pool Nurse RN, NASHVILLE MEMORIAL HOSPITAL, Nashville, TN	1998–2001
Staff Nurse LPN, VANDERBILT UNIVERSITY MEDICAL CENTER, Nashville, TN	1996–1998
Pool Nurse LPN, BAPTIST HOSPITAL, Nashville, TN	1995–1996

ADMINISTRATIVE SUPPORT EXPERIENCE:

Account Clerk, KENTUCKY BOARD OF PAROLES, Lexington, KY	1991–1994

➢ Maintained accurate records of payments collected from parolees; audited travel claims; coordinated meetings for parole officers; and created financial reports, graphs, and spreadsheets.

➢ Trained and supervised new account clerks. Reported to Accounting Manager.

122

Degree: BS, Business Administration.

Job Target: A position in banking, investment, or finance.

Strategy: Capitalized on seven years of grocery/management experience, specifically the ability to offer leadership, build relationships, and provide customer satisfaction. Demonstrated productivity, the ability to meet objectives, and a progression from courtesy clerk to grocery manager.

ERIC H. KATAYAMA

92-9876 Kukui Street • Mililani, Hawaii 96789
E-mail: ekatayama@onlinealoha.com
Tel: (808) 245-1234

Seeking Mid-Entry-Level Position in...

BANKING / INVESTMENT / FINANCE
Relationship Building, Customer Service Excellence, and Leadership

Enhancing Organizational Success Through Customer Satisfaction

---

Recent college graduate offering academic credentials in Finance and Business Administration—worked full-time while pursuing education. Seven years of practical experience satisfying customer needs and developing productive working relationships. Verifiable record of sound management skills.

> *"Eric has a strong desire to succeed and pays close attention to details. He has excellent interpersonal skills and will be an asset to any organization."* Store Manager, Foodmart

EDUCATION & TRAINING

Finance Major—B.S., Business Administration, 3.1 GPA
University of Hawaii, Honolulu, Hawaii, 2005

Zenger Miller Frontline Leadership
Management Training, 2003

EXPERIENCE

Foodmart, Inc., Kailua, Hawaii — 1997 to Present

Grocery Manager (May 2000 to Present)
Oversee store operations on nightly basis, personally supervising up to 40 employees. Handle grocery department orders totaling 40% of store sales. Train new employees and develop managers in training.

- Consistently lead store to profit-sharing goals, regularly finishing in top 15% of Western Division for customer-service benchmarks.
- Sustained department productivity levels despite staff reductions of 30+%.
- Set all-time store sales record for 2003.
- Promoted from...

Stock Clerk / Cashier (July 1998 to May 2000)

- Consistently received above-average evaluations from supervisors.
- Charged with entire store when no managers available.
- Selected to handle grocery-department ordering.
- First in two years to be promoted from **Courtesy Clerk** (June 1997 to July 1998).

COMMUNITY INVOLVEMENT

Treasurer, Mililani Leeward Community Board
Participant, Foodmart Employee Fundraiser Cookouts
Coordinator, Kailua Foodmart Softball Team

TECHNICAL SKILLS

Microsoft Office
Microsoft Money
10-key calculator

References Furnished on Request

Degree: AS, Computer Science.
Job Target: Help desk/computer support technician.
Strategy: Emphasized course work and used employment and personal activities to showcase intangible qualities such as leadership, customer service, and training abilities.

Dwayne Prescott
1226 Rambling Way, Columbia, MD 21044
410-997-7555 Home ▪ dpres18@yahoo.com

OBJECTIVE

Help Desk / Computer Support Technician position

PROFILE

✓ Recent computer-degree graduate with proven organizational abilities.
✓ Demonstrated track record of achieving goals in a team environment.
✓ Highly motivated and dependable—able to take responsibility for projects.
✓ Proven skills in problem solving and customer service.

EDUCATION

Columbia Community College, Columbia, MD   2004–2005
A.S., Computer Science
Computer courses completed in

✓ Networking Essentials	✓ Beginning Windows NT
✓ A+ Certification	✓ Administering Windows NT
✓ Intermediate Word XP	✓ Windows NT Core Technologies
✓ Beginning Word XP	✓ Windows NT Support By Enterprise
✓ Beginning Access XP	✓ Beginning Business on the Internet
✓ TCP / IP protocol	✓ Beginning FrontPage XP

University of Maryland, College Park, MD   2003–2004
General first-year coursework in Bachelor's Degree program.

EMPLOYMENT

The Cutting Edge, Laurel, MD   2003–2005
Receptionist/Cashier

▪ Successfully handled front desk and 3 incoming telephone lines for busy, upscale hair salon with 15 stylists. Greeted and logged in steady stream of customers, coordinating appointments with hairdresser availability.

▪ Developed cooperative, team-oriented working relationships with owners and co-workers in this 18-station salon.

▪ Managed customer problems and complaints with tact and attention to prompt customer service. Commended by owners for resourcefulness.

▪ Gained experience in opening and closing procedures, cash register receipts, counter sales, light bookkeeping, and telephone follow-up.

Columbia Aces Soccer Camp, Columbia, MD   2002, 2003 Summers
Trainer / Coach

▪ Assisted Women's Soccer Coach in 200-participant practice-intensive soccer camp. Worked with individuals, as well as teams, to improve their attitude and resulting soccer performance.

ACTIVITIES & AWARDS

Maryland Mavericks Soccer Semi-Pro Team—Center Half   2000–2004
✓ Team consistently ranked in top 10 semi-pro teams in the nation.

Wilde Lake High School Soccer Team   2000–2003
✓ Co-captain of team that won the State Soccer Title in 2002.
✓ Recognized as one of the top three mid-fielders in the state in 2003.

Degree: BS, Business Administration.
Job Target: MIS position.
Strategy: Created a strong, comprehensive summary of education, computer skills, and other professional abilities. Used work experience to provide supportive evidence of diversity of skills.

GEORGE A. PORTER

1555 Nottingham
Mt. Pleasant, MI 48888

577.727.7749
georgeaport23@aol.com

PROFESSIONAL QUALIFICATIONS

A dedicated and resourceful young **MIS Professional** offering a unique combination of knowledge and skills in a variety of areas. Creative and enthusiastic, with proven success in building and managing relationships with peers, coworkers, customers, and the general public. Excellent attendance with employers and school. Confident, decisive, and committed to professional growth and opportunity. Dependable, self-motivated, hardworking, and a quick learner. Experience includes

Analytical & Problem-Solving Skills • Oral & Written Communication • Customer Service • Team Participation
Community Outreach • Leadership • Computer Troubleshooting • Project Planning & Coordination • Reporting

EDUCATION

BACHELOR OF SCIENCE IN BUSINESS ADMINISTRATION
CENTRAL MICHIGAN UNIVERSITY, Mt. Pleasant, MI, 2005
• Major: *Management Information Systems*

COMPUTER SKILLS

Systems & Languages	MS Windows NT Visual Basic 6.0	MS Windows 2000 & XP ASP/HTML	CDS Systems Visual IFPS-Plus	COBOL Oracle PL/SQL
Software	MS Office	MS Project	Lotus 1-2-3	Networking TCP/IP

RELEVANT EXPERIENCE

GREEKTOWN CASINO / SOARING EAGLE CASINO & RESORT, Detroit & Mt. Pleasant, MI   2004–2005
COMPUTER TECHNICIAN
Duties included updating customer accounts, tracking customer comp points, and producing customer gambling activity reports. Also provided system maintenance and troubleshooting, as needed.

OTHER EXPERIENCE

B & D CONSTRUCTION, Bloomington, IN   2001–Present
INSTALLER
Work effectively with teams to install pool liners in commercial pool systems.

GREEKTOWN CASINO / SOARING EAGLE CASINO AND RESORT, Detroit & Mt. Pleasant, MI   1999–Present
DEALER
Oversee various casino games played by the public. Responsibilities include setting up and paying of complicated wagers, game protection, customer relations, and the handling of large currency transactions.

SOLID CONCRETE, INC., Howell, MI   1994–1999
CONCRETE CUTTER/CORE DRILLER
In charge of specialty equipment and company vehicles. Serviced clients in a professional and efficient manner, consistent with company values.

Resume Development Worksheet

Use chapter 2 to guide you through each step of completing this worksheet and then drafting and polishing a great resume. Even when your resume is completed, keep these worksheets; they'll come in handy every time you update your resume or adapt it for a different job target.

Resume Development Worksheet

Header/Contact Information

Name _____

Home address _____

_____

_____

Home telephone _____

School address (if applicable) _____

_____

_____

School telephone (if applicable) _____

E-mail address (permanent and professional sounding)

_____

Pager (if necessary) _____

Fax (if necessary) _____

Objective, Goal, or Target Statement

_____

_____

Skills Summary (Evidence of Core Qualifications)

_____

_____

_____

_____

_____

_____

(continued)

Education

Graduate Degree

Name of school, city, state _____

_____

_____

Degree, year earned _____

Major _____

GPA (if 3.0 or higher) _____

Major coursework (if needed to describe unusual major or flesh out resume) _____

_____

_____

_____

Academic honors _____

_____

_____

_____

Thesis or other special projects _____

_____

_____

Scholarships/fellowships _____

_____

_____

_____

Extras _____

_____

_____

Undergraduate Degree

Name of school, city, state _____

_____

_____

Degree, year earned _____

Major _____

Minor (if relevant to your career target) _____

GPA (if 3.0 or higher) _____

GPA in major (if significantly higher than overall GPA) _____

Major coursework (if needed to describe unusual major or flesh out resume)_____

_____

_____

_____

Academic honors_____

_____

_____

_____

Scholarships_____

_____

_____

Co-op or internship experience (may appear here or in "Experience" section)_____

_____

_____

_____

Special projects, team projects, thesis_____

_____

_____

_____

Extracurricular activities/leadership activities_____

_____

_____

_____

_____

Volunteer activities_____

_____

_____

_____

International study_____

_____

Extras_____

_____

_____

_____

_____

_____

(continued)

Additional Training/Certification

High school experience (if notable and relevant) _____

_____

_____

_____

_____

Experience (Employment and/or Co-op or Internship)

Company name, city, state _____

_____

_____

Job title, dates of employment _____

_____

_____

Summary of job duties _____

_____

_____

_____

_____

_____

Accomplishments/highlights/contributions _____

_____

_____

_____

_____

_____

Company name, city, state _____

_____

_____

Job title, dates of employment _____

_____

_____

Summary of job duties _____

_____

_____

_____

_____

Accomplishments/highlights/contributions _____

_____

_____

_____

_____

_____

Company name, city, state _____

_____

_____

Job title, dates of employment _____

_____

_____

Summary of job duties _____

_____

_____

_____

_____

_____

Accomplishments/highlights/contributions _____

_____

_____

_____

_____

_____

Additional Information (important things about you that don't fit the other categories)

_____

_____

_____

_____

_____

_____

_____

_____

_____

_____

_____

Find a Professional Resume Writer

This book could not have been written without the excellent contributions of professional resume writers from around the world—all of them members of the Career Masters Institute, the premier careers-industry organization that represents practitioners from all careers practices.

If you need professional assistance with your resume or with any aspect of your job search, contact one of these experts!

Sheila Adjahoe
Principal, The Adjahoe Group
Upper Marlboro, MD 20774
Phone: (301) 350-5137
Fax: (301) 324-7736
E-mail: sheilaadjahoe@yahoo.com
Resume: 119

Lynn P. Andenoro, CPRW, JCTC
President, My Career Resource
1214 Fenway
Salt Lake City, UT 84102
Phone: (801) 883-2011
Fax: (801) 582-8862
E-mail:
Lynn@MyCareerResource.com
www.MyCareerResource.com
Resumes: 77, 79, 87, 95

Jennifer Nell Ayres
President, Nell Personal
Advancement Resources
Pacific Palisades, CA 90272
Phone: (310) 909-3240
E-mail: info@nellresources.com
www.nellresources.com
Resume: 53

Ann Baehr, CPRW
Best Resumes of New York
Long Island, NY
Phone: (631) 435-1879
E-mail: resumesbest@earthlink.net
Resume: 33

Carla Barrett, CCM, CEC
Career Designs
6855 Irving Rd.
Redding, CA 96001
Phone: (530) 241-8570
Fax: (530) 248-3351
E-mail: carlab@careerdesigns.com
www.careerdesigns.com
Resume: 102

Jacqui D. Barrett, MRW, CPRW, CEIP
Career Trend
11613 W 113th St.
Overland Park, KS 66210
Phone: (913) 451-1313
Fax: (801) 382-5842
E-mail: Jacqui@careertrend.net
www.careertrend.net
Resume: 113

Beverly Baskin, Ed.S., LPC, NCCC, CPRW
Mitchell Baskin, MMS, PE
BBCS Counseling Services
6 Alberta Dr.
Marlboro, NJ 07746
Also in Iselin and Freehold, NJ
Toll-free phone: (800) 300-4079
Fax: (732) 972-8846
E-mail: info@bbcscounseling.com
www.baskincareer.com
Resume: 93

Janet L. Beckstrom, CPRW
Owner, Word Crafter
1717 Montclair Ave.
Flint, MI 48503
Toll-free phone: (800) 351-9818
Fax: (810) 232-9257
E-mail: wordcrafter@voyager.net
Resumes: 4, 6, 7

Rima Bogardus
Garner, NC
Resumes: 88, 96, 116

Arnold G. Boldt, CPRW, JCTC
Arnold-Smith Associates
625 Panorama Trail, Building One, Ste. 120C
Rochester, NY 14625
Phone: (585) 383-0350
Fax: (585) 387-0516
E-mail: Arnie@ResumeSOS.com
www.ResumeSOS.com
Resumes: 16, 71, 82

Carolyn Braden
Hendersonville, TN
Resumes: 40, 55, 121

Martin Buckland, MRW, CPRW, CJST, CEIP, JCTC
President, Elite Resumes
1428 Stationmaster Ln.
Oakville, Ontario, L6M 3A7
Phone: (905) 825-0490
Fax: (905) 825-2966
E-mail: martin@AnEliteResume.com
www.AnEliteResume.com
Resume: 85

Diane Burns, CPRW, CCM, IJCTC, FJST, CCMC, CEIP
Career Marketing Techniques
E-mail: diane@polishedresumes.com
www.polishedresumes.com
Resumes: 56, 92

Camille Carboneau, CPRW, CEIP
Owner/Operator, CC Computer
Services & Training
P.O. Box 50655
Idaho Falls, ID 83405
Phone: (208) 522-4455
E-mail: camille@ccComputer.com
www.SuperiorResumes.com and
www.ccComputer.com
Resumes: 44, 46

Lisa Chapman
Chapman Services Group, LLC
3130 S. 11th St.
Niles, MI 49120
Toll-free phone: (866) 687-9700
Fax: (309) 401-3390
E-mail: lisa@chapmanservices.com
www.chapmanservices.com
Resume: 104

Freddie Cheek, M.S.Ed., CCM, CPRW, CRW, CWDP
Cheek & Cristantello Career Connections
406 Maynard Dr.
Amherst, NY 14226
Phone: (716) 553-6945
E-mail: fscheek@adelphia.net
www.CheekandCristantello.com
Resumes: 9, 64, 72, 73

Fred E. Coon, LEA, JCTC, CRW
Stewart, Cooper & Coon
2111 E. Highland Ave.
Phoenix, AZ 85016
E-mail:
fcoon@stewartcoopercoon.com
www.stewartcoopercoon.com
Resume: 115

Norine T. Dagliano, CPRW
Principal, ekm Inspirations
616 Highland Way
Hagerstown, MD 21740
Phone: (301) 766-2032
Fax: (301) 745-5700
E-mail:
norine@ekminspirations.com
Resumes: 35, 41, 99

Dian R. Davis, NCC, LPC, MCC
Career-Dreams
P.O. Box 1994
Laramie, WY 82073
Phone: (307) 778-1130
Fax: (307) 778-4312
E-mail: ddavis@career-dreams.com
www.career-dreams.com
Resume: 8

Michael Davis, GCDF, NCDA
member, MBTI Qualified
940 Ashcreek Dr.
Centerville, OH 45458-3333
Phone: (937) 438-5037
E-mail: msdavis49@hotmail.com
Resume: 110

Kirsten Dixson, JCTC, CPRW, CEIP
Principal, New Leaf Career Solutions
Exeter, NH (Greater Boston)
Toll-free phone: (866) NEW LEAF (639-5323)
Toll-free fax: (888) 887-7166
E-mail: info@newleafcareer.com
www.newleafcareer.com
Resumes: 18, 118

Nina K. Ebert, CPRW/CC
A Word's Worth
New Egypt/Jackson, NJ
Phone: (732) 349-2225
Phone and Fax: (609) 758-7799
E-mail:
keytosuccessresumes@comcast.net
www.keytosuccessresumes
Resumes: 13, 36, 67

Cory Edwards, CERW, CCMC, CECC
Partnering For Success, LLC
P.O. Box 650042
Sterling, VA 20165-0042
Phone: (703) 444-7835
Toll-free phone: (800) 611-3234
Fax: (703) 444-2005
E-mail: resumewriter@aol.com
Resume: 75

Debbie Ellis, MRW, CPRW
Phoenix Career Group
Toll-free phone: (800) 876-5506
Fax: (859) 236-3900
E-mail: debbie@
phoenixcareergroup.com
www.phoenixcareergroup.com
Resumes: 2, 42, 48

Michelle M. Fleig-Palmer, MBA, CCM
Doctoral Student, University of Nebraska-Lincoln
College of Business Administration
Lincoln, NE 68588
Phone: (308) 865-8574
Fax: (308) 865-8917
E-mail: fleigpalmerm@unk.edu
Resume: 49

Joyce Fortier, MBA, CCM, CCMC, CPRW, JCTC
Create Your Career
23871 Lebost
Novi, MI 48375
Phone: (248) 478-5662
Fax: (248) 426-9974
E-mail: careerist@aol.com
www.careerist.com
Resume: 124

Louise Garver, JCTC, MCDP, CPRW, CEIP, CMP
Career Directions, LLC
115 Elm St., Ste. 203
Enfield, CT 06082
Phone: (860) 623-9476
Fax: (860) 623-9473
E-mail: TheCareerPro@aol.com
www.resumeimpact.com
Resumes: 23, 70, 80, 83

Rosemarie Ginsberg, CPRW, CEIP
Career Planning Solutions
P.O. Box 162564
Altamonte Springs, FL 32716-2564
E-mail: info@
careerplanningsolutions.com
www.careerplanningsolutions.com
Resume: 47

Sharon Graham, CRS, CPRW, CEIP
Graham Management Group
5327, 4th Line
Milton, Ontario L9T 2X8
Phone: (905) 878-8768
Fax: (905) 876-2058
E-mail:
info@grahammanagement.com
www.grahammanagement.com
Resume: 97

Susan Guarneri, MS, NCC, NCCC, MCC, LPC, CCMC, CPRW, CEIP, JCTC, CWPP
President, Guarneri Associates/CareerMagicCoach
6670 Crystal Lake Rd.
Three Lakes, WI 54562
Toll-free phone: (866) 881-4055
Fax: (715) 546-8039
E-mail: Resumagic@aol.com
www.resume-magic.com and
www.careermagiccoach.com
Resumes: 24, 39, 62, 123

Alice Hanson, CPRW
Aim Resumes
P.O. Box 75054
Seattle, WA 98175
Phone: (206) 527-3100
Fax: (206) 527-3101
E-mail: success@aimresumes.com
Resume: 112

Erika C. Harrigan
Success Partners
P.O. Box 212
Franklin Park, NJ 08823
Phone: (732) 501-0375
Fax: (732) 821-5037
E-mail: eharrigan@
successpartnerservices.com
Resume: 101

Peter Hill, CPRW
President, Distinctive Resume Service
Honolulu, HI 96826
Phone: (808) 384-9461
E-mail:
distinctiveresumes@yahoo.com
Resume: 122

Gay Anne Himebaugh
Seaview Resume Solutions
2855 E. Coast Hwy., Ste. 102
Corona del Mar, CA 92625
Phone: (949) 673-2400
Fax: (949) 673-2428
E-mail:
gayanne@seaviewsecretarial.com
Resume: 3

Lee Hogaboom, CPRW
Power Punch Resume
222 Pinevale Way
Sour Lake, TX 77659
Toll-free phone: (866) 441-6012
E-mail:
powerpunchresume@aol.com
Resume: 105

Andrea J. Howard, MS Ed
Employment Counselor, Career
Central
New York State Department
of Labor
175 Central Ave.
Albany, NY 12205
Phone: (518) 462-7600, ext. 124
E-mail: usaah3@labor.state.ny.us
www.labor.state.ny.us
Resume: 52

Gayle Howard, CERW, CCM,
CPRW, CRW
Top Margin Resumes Online
P.O. Box 74
Chirnside Park 3116
Melbourne, VIC, Australia
Phone: 61 3 9726 6694
Fax: 61 3 9726 5316
E-mail:
getinterviews@topmargin.com
www.topmargin.com
Resumes: 66, 69, 84

Lynn Hughes, MA
Lubbock, TX
Resumes: 22, 29, 30

Deborah S. James, CPRW, CCMC
President, Leading Edge Resume
& Career Services
1010 Schreier Rd.
Toledo, OH 43460
Phone: (419) 666-4518
Toll-free phone: (800) 815-8780
Fax: (419) 791-3567
E-mail: djames@
leadingedgeresumes.com
www.leadingedgeresumes.com
Resume: 58

Marcy Johnson, NCRW, CPRW,
CEIP, CWPP
President, First Impression
Resume & Job Readiness
11805 U.S. Hwy. 69
Story City, IA 50248
Phone: (515) 733-4998
Fax: (515) 733-4681
E-mail: success@resume-job-
readiness.com
www.resume-job-readiness.com
Resumes: 14, 59, 114

Shanna Kemp, M.Ed.
Round Rock, TX 78664
Resume: 19

Bill Kinser, MRW, CPRW, CCM,
CEIP, JCTC
To The Point Resumes
P.O. Box 135
Fairfax, VA 22038-0135
Phone: (703) 352-8969
Toll-free phone: (866) RESUME-1
Fax: (703) 991-2372
E-mail: bkinser@
tothepointresumes.com
www.tothepointresumes.com
Resumes: 1, 17

Cindy Kraft, CCMC, CPRW, JCTC,
CCM
President, Executive Essentials
P.O. Box 336
Valrico, FL 33595
Phone: (813) 655-0658
Fax: (813) 354-3483
E-mail: cindy@career-management-
coach.com
www.career-management-
coach.com
Resume: 31

Louise Kursmark, CPRW, JCTC,
CCM, CEIP, MRW
President, Best Impression Career
Services, Inc.
9847 Catalpa Woods Ct.
Cincinnati, OH 45242
Phone: (513) 792-0030
Fax: (513) 792-0961
E-mail:
LK@yourbestimpression.com
www.yourbestimpression.com
Resumes: 5, 11, 27, 28, 78, 79

Rolande LeCompte LaPointe,
CPC, CIPC, CPRW, IJCTC, CCM,
CSS, CRW
President, RO-LAN Associates, Inc.
725 Sabattus St.
Lewiston, ME 04240
Phone: (207) 784-1010
Fax: (207) 782-3446
E-mail: RLapointe@aol.com
Resume: 68

Lorie Lebert, CPRW, IJCTC, CCMC
President, The Loriel Group
P.O. Box 91
Brighton, MI 48116
Phone: (810) 229-6811
Toll-free phone: (800) 870-9059
Fax: (810) 222-0101
E-mail: Lorie@DoMyResume.com
www.CoachingROI.com and
www.ResumeROI.com
Resumes: 12, 63

Kathleen McInerney, BS, JCTC,
CEIP
Career Edge, Inc.
1701 NE 115 St., #21-A
Miami, FL 33181
Phone: (305) 891-4554
Fax: (305) 891-4774
E-mail: mcin3753@bellsouth.net
Resume: 107

Jan Melnik, CPRW, CCM, MRW
President, Absolute Advantage
P.O. Box 718
Durham, CT 06422
Phone: (860) 349-0256
Fax: (860) 349-1343
E-mail: CompSPJan@aol.com
www.janmelnik.com
Resume: 120

Nicole Miller, CCM, CRW, IJCTC,
CECC
Mil-Roy Consultants
Ottawa/Petawawa, ON, Canada
Phone: (613) 687-2708
E-mail: resumes@
milroyconsultants.com
www.milroyconsultants.com
Resume: 117

Meg Montford, MCCC, CCM, CMF
Abilities Enhanced
P.O. Box 9667
Kansas City, MO 64134
Phone: (816) 767-1196
E-mail: meg@abilitiesenhanced.com
www.abilitiesenhanced.com
Resume: 111

Doug Morrison, CPRW, MRW
President, Career Power
2915 Providence Rd., Ste. 300
Charlotte, NC 28211
Phone: (704) 365-0773
Fax: (704) 365-3411
E-mail:
doug@careerpowerresume.com or
dmpwresume@aol.com
www.careerpowerresume.com
Resumes: 38, 43

Ellen Mulqueen, CRW
The Institute of Living
200 Retreat Ave.
Hartford, CT 06106
Phone: (860) 545-7202
Fax: (860) 545-7140
E-mail: emulque@harthosp.org
http://instituteofliving.org/
Programs/rehab.htm
Resume: 106

William G. Murdock, CPRW
President, The Employment
Coach
7770 Meadow Rd., Ste. 109
Dallas, TX 75230
Phone: (214) 750-4781
Fax: (214) 750-4781
E-mail: bmurdock@swbell.net
www.resumesinaction.com
Resume: 89

Helen Oliff, CPRW, CFRWC, CEC
Turning Point
2307 Freetown Ct. #12C
Reston, VA 20191
Phone: (703) 716-0077
E-mail:
helen@turningpointnow.com
www.turningpointnow.com
Resumes: 50, 51

Don Orlando, MBA, CPRW, JCTC,
CCM, CCMC
The McLean Group
640 S. McDonough St.
Montgomery, AL 36104
Phone: (334) 264-2020
Fax: (334) 264-9227
E-mail: yourcareercoach@aol.com
Resumes: 61, 90, 91

Teresa L. Pearson, CPRW, JCTC,
CFJST, Master in Human Relations
President, Pearson's Resume
Output
Meriden, KS 66512
E-mail:
pearsonresume@earthlink.net
Resume: 25

Sharon Pierce-Williams, M.Ed.,
CPRW
President, TheResume.Doc
609 Lincolnshire Ln.
Findlay, OH 45840
Phone: (419) 422-0228
Fax: (419) 425-1185
E-mail:
Sharon@TheResumeDoc.com
www.theresumedoc.com
Resumes: 26, 45, 65

Michelle Mastruserio Reitz, CPRW
Printed Pages
3985 Race Rd., Ste. 14
Cincinnati, OH 45211
Phone: (513) 598-9100
Fax: (513) 598-9220
E-mail: michelle@printedpages.com
www.printedpages.com
Resume: 109

Barbara Robertson
Rensselaer, IN
Resumes: 15, 20, 34, 74

Teena L. Rose, CPRW, CEIP, CCM
Resume to Referral
1824 Rebert Pike
Springfield, OH 45506
Phone: (937) 325-2149
E-mail:
admin@resumetoreferral.com
www.resumebycprw.com
Resume: 108

Janice Shepherd, CPRW, JCTC,
CEIP
Write On Career Keys
2628 E. Crestline Dr.
Bellingham, WA 98226
Phone: (360) 738-7958
Fax: (360) 738-1189
E-mail:
Janice@writeoncareerkeys.com
www.writeoncareerkeys.com
Resumes: 21, 32, 94

Karen M. Silins, CMRS, CCMC,
CRW, CECC, CEIP, CTAC, CCA
President, A+ Career & Resume,
LLC
Kansas City, MO
Phone: (816) 942-3019
Fax: (816) 942-1505
E-mail:
karen@careerandresume.com
www.careerandresume.com
Resume: 57

Billie Ruth Sucher, MS, CTMS,
CTSB
President, Billie Sucher &
Associates
7177 Hickman Rd., Ste. 10
Urbandale, IA 50322
Phone: (515) 276-0061
Fax: (515) 334-8076
E-mail: betwnjobs@aol.com
Resumes: 76, 98

Karen Swann, CPRW
President, TypeRight
313 Wild Cherry Lane
Clemson, SC 29631
Phone: (864) 653-3351
Fax: (864) 653-7701
E-mail: k_swann@bellsouth.net
Resumes: 54, 81

Roleta Fowler Vasquez, CPRW,
CEIP
President, Wordbusters Resume &
Writing Services
433 Quail Ct.
Fillmore, CA 93015-1137
Phone: (805) 524-3493
E-mail: resumes@wbresumes.com
www.wbresumes.com
Resumes: 10, 86

James Walker, MS
Counselor, ACAP Center
Bldg. 210, Rm. 006, Custer Ave.
Fort Riley, KS 66442
Phone: (785) 239-2278
Fax: (785) 239-2251
E-mail: jwalker8199@yahoo.com
Resume: 60

Jean West, CPRW, JCTC
College-Resumes.com
413 Walnut St., #5206
Green Cove Springs, FL 32043
Toll-free phone: (888) 590-2534
Fax: (815) 550-8753
E-mail: jean@college-resumes.com
Resume: 100

Janice Worthington, MA, CPRW,
JCTC, CEIP
Worthington Career Services
6636 Belleshire St.
Columbus, OH 43229
Toll-free phone: (877) 973-7863
Fax: (614) 523-3400
E-mail: janice@
worthingtonresumes.com
www.worthingtonresumes.com
Resume: 103

Linda Wunner, CPRW, IJCTC,
CEIP, CCMC
President, A+ Career & Resume
Design
E-mail:
linda@successfulresumes.com
www.successfulresumes.com
Resume: 37

Index